Fostering entrepreneurship

ORGANISATION FOR ECONOMIC CO-OPERATION AND DEVELOPMENT

BML 2648-9/3

ORGANISATION FOR ECONOMIC CO-OPERATION AND DEVELOPMENT

Pursuant to Article 1 of the Convention signed in Paris on 14th December 1960, and which came into force on 30th September 1961, the Organisation for Economic Co-operation and Development (OECD) shall promote policies designed:

- to achieve the highest sustainable economic growth and employment and a rising standard of living in Member countries, while maintaining financial stability, and thus to contribute to the development of the world economy;
- to contribute to sound economic expansion in Member as well as non-member countries in the process of economic development; and
- to contribute to the expansion of world trade on a multilateral, non-discriminatory basis in accordance with international obligations.

The original Member countries of the OECD are Austria, Belgium, Canada, Denmark, France, Germany, Greece, Iceland, Ireland, Italy, Luxembourg, the Netherlands, Norway, Portugal, Spain, Sweden, Switzerland, Turkey, the United Kingdom and the United States. The following countries became Members subsequently through accession at the dates indicated hereafter: Japan (28th April 1964), Finland (28th January 1969), Australia (7th June 1971), New Zealand (29th May 1973), Mexico (18th May 1994), the Czech Republic (21st December 1995), Hungary (7th May 1996), Poland (22nd November 1996) and Korea (12th December 1996). The Commission of the European Communities takes part in the work of the OECD (Article 13 of the OECD Convention).

Publié en français sous le titre :
Stimuler l'esprit d'entreprise

Foreword

When I first arrived at the OECD, I emphasised that the balance between economic growth, social cohesion and political stability was at the heart of our mission. This priority should also be applied to effectively fighting unemployment. Given the growing pressures on Member countries to come up with innovative solutions to the problem, stimulating entrepreneurship is one of the most promising ways of increasing job creation and boosting the economy, without distorting market forces.

Fostering entrepreneurship involves both removing the impediments that too often persist and arranging the conditions that enable entrepreneurs to flourish. New priorities have been adopted to enable entrepreneurs to take advantage of creative market forces. The days when governments sought to pick winners through direct and indirect subsidies are largely behind us. Rather policymakers are seeking to leverage the dynamic nature of entrepreneurship, to devise programmes that support market mechanisms which may not be well adapted to entrepreneurship, e.g., venture capital and regulatory burden, and promote entrepreneurship among the population at large. Results suggest that such policies are even more effective when they contain a large local component, enabling them to respond more closely to the reality on the ground.

Entrepreneurship is unevenly developed between countries. This book therefore compares national experiences that provide valuable lessons for better understanding the factors that affect entrepreneurship in general, while highlighting conditions specific to each country. Another important contribution of this study is that it addresses all the facets of entrepreneurship, moving further afield into the non-profit sector and entrepreneurship in the transition economies.

I am convinced that essential lessons can be learned from the wide range of national and local experience analysed in this study, which is an integral part of *The OECD Jobs Strategy*. Developing entrepreneurship is essential both to boost economic growth and to optimise employment policies. It is a major contributor to the sustainable development of our societies.

Donald J. Johnston
Secretary-General of the OECD

Table of contents

Tables

Figures

Boxes

Introduction

The bases of entrepreneurship

A dynamic wealth-creating process of identifying economic opportunities and acting upon them

Entrepreneurship is central to the functioning of market economies. Entrepreneurs are agents of change and growth in a market economy and they can act to accelerate the generation, dissemination and application of innovative ideas. In doing so, they not only ensure that efficient use is made of resources, but also expand the boundaries of economic activity. Entrepreneurs not only seek out and identify potentially profitable economic opportunities but are also willing to take risks to see if their hunches are right. While not all entrepreneurs succeed, a country with a lot of entrepreneurial activity is likely to be constantly generating new or improved products and services. It is also likely to be highly adaptable, so that opportunities are seized upon as soon as they emerge. As the United States and Italy have demonstrated with such examples as Wal-Mart, Starbucks, and Benneton, entrepreneurial activities are not confined to new, high-tech industries, but are spread across a wide range of activities and involve innovative approaches to all major business functions, including marketing, organisation and distribution. And in the former centrally-planned economies entrepreneurs also play a fundamental role in advancing the transition process.

A complex concept

While it is hard to precisely measure how much entrepreneurship is going on...

Measuring the amount of entrepreneurship taking place in a country is difficult to do, in part because there is no consensus about what would be a reliable and practical set of indicators. Some emphasise the number of new firms starting up, while others consider turnover in the number of firms to be more important. Some would focus on small and medium sized enterprises (SMEs) where the owner(s) and manager(s) are the same. But others concentrate on the performance of fast-growing firms, whether new or well-established. And some associate entrepreneurship with the development of "high-tech" industries. None of these approaches is able to provide a complete picture of the state of entrepreneurship: each one takes only one aspect of it. Nonetheless, while many large and well-established firms can be very entrepreneurial, measures of small and especially new firm development are more often used as indicators of entrepreneurial activity. But even for these firms, it is difficult to find reliable international comparisons, despite a number of efforts.

... entrepreneurship In a number of ways, the United States manifests a high
is clearly degree of entrepreneurship. It is characterised not only
more developed by many successful well-established firms producing a
in some countries constant stream of new, innovative products and services,
than others but also by the dynamic process of many new firms starting up while unsuccessful firms restructure or close.
The five country case studies presented here all pointed to aspects of entrepreneurship which, in comparison with other countries, could be improved: Australians have not been very successful in bringing their inventions to their home market and instead have seen them being developed in other countries. The Netherlands has a well developed enterprise culture and commercial orientation, and many of its best performers are long-established medium and large companies. However, the Netherlands authorities have sought to increase the amount of venture capital going to start-ups. Similarly, in Sweden, some large and well established firms are extremely entrepreneurial, but small firms seem to be unable to grow beyond medium size, and self employment rates remain very low. Spain, which is still undergoing a major economic transformation form a strong corporatist tradition and the heavy regulation of the past, is also seeking to identify barriers hindering the growth of its small firms. And entrepreneurs in the US felt that an excessively complex tax system was hampering entrepreneurial activity.

Three key factors

Framework Entrepreneurship is the result of three dimensions work-
conditions, ing together: conducive framework conditions, well-
government designed government programmes and supportive cul-
programmes tural attitudes. Achieving proper framework conditions
and culture – the institutional arrangements within which economic
are crucial activity takes place – should be the foundation of policy:

there is little sense and much scope for waste in working against poorly functioning markets. Well-designed and well-targeted government programmes can also complement framework conditions. Such programmes can be especially important in areas not directly influenced by framework conditions. For example, *inter alia*, they can encourage and maximise the benefits of collaborative behaviour, augment the flow of information for financing entrepreneurship and provide a flexible response to location-specific factors affecting entrepreneurship. Supportive cultural attitudes also complement framework conditions. For instance, other things being equal, an environment in which entrepreneurship is esteemed, and in which stigma does not attach to business failure resulting from reasonable risk-taking, will almost certainly be conducive to entrepreneurship. Indeed, efforts to improve framework conditions so as to bring about a closer relationship between risk and return, or between individual effort and reward, may be slow to show results unless cultural attitudes support risk-taking and individual reward.

Cultural factors affect the way business is conducted...
Although cultural attitudes are formed through complex processes that are not clearly understood, it is a commonly accepted view among practitioners and analysts dealing with entrepreneurship that cultural factors affect the way in which business is conducted. Such factors affect, for instance, the willingness to co-operate with others. Similarly, community structures and relationships that reinforce trust and personal reputation can reduce the costs of transacting business. And the quality of public policy may be superior in localities with a strong civic tradition and a high degree of political participation. Conversely, an environment characterised by mistrust may oblige entrepreneurs to spend time and money to protect against the potentially opportunistic behaviour of those they work with. This may deter some forms of entrepreneurial initiative. However, "culture" is a broad and diffuse concept and there has been little systematic assessment of its impact on entrepreneurship or its policy ramifications, although several statistical analyses have recently appeared that demonstrate a positive impact of "trust" on economic development. These studies, based on surveys of values, point a way to new avenues of research and, possibly, new emphases in policy. For example, the role of education in creating positive attitudes towards entrepreneurship merits further attention.

... and help to shape the institutional framework
Cultural attitudes will also play a role in shaping a country's institutional framework. Here it is clear that certain features of the institutional framework can act to discourage entrepreneurship (or divert it into less

economically beneficial activities, such as rent-seeking or even illegal behaviour). Improving the institutional framework is an essential ingredient in fostering entrepreneurship. In turn, the institutional framework, which is clearly amenable to policy, is likely to affect cultural norms, especially over prolonged periods of time. The transition to a market-based economic framework in Central and Eastern European countries and the Newly Independent States provides a striking illustration of the importance of the interrelationship between framework conditions and culture. The establishment of well-defined property rights and other basic market legislation unleashed a pent-up entrepreneurial drive which led to a rapid increase in the registration of private sector enterprises, even in countries where entrepreneurship had been absent for many decades. Unfortunately, in some cases, the absence of other important framework conditions, such as an efficient banking sector or comprehensive bankruptcy legislation, is hindering further enterprise development. Also, the high level of informal activity in these economies suggests that corruption and heavy taxation weigh particularly heavily on entrepreneurs and discourage them from participating in the formal economy.

Ensuring well-functioning markets

A stable macroeconomic environment encourages the growth of entrepreneurship... OECD work has repeatedly emphasised the important interaction between sound macroeconomic policies and structural policies designed to improve the functioning of markets. While sound macroeconomic performance on its own is insufficient to foster entrepreneurship, it can certainly help. Entrepreneurial activity is significantly easier to carry out in a stable macroeconomic environment with low inflation: this allows entrepreneurs to clearly interpret signals about demand and prices and makes it possible for them to develop sensible business plans and strategies based on the fundamental strengths of their projects. Sound government budget positions also help by minimising the need for government borrowing, thereby ensuring that real interest rates are set by private savings and investment, and are not unduly influenced by the government's need for funds.

... providing sound structural policies are in place Sound structural policies are also essential to produce well-functioning markets for goods and services as well as for capital and labour. Moreover, the interaction between these markets means that impediments in one market may prevent the benefits of reforms in others from being realised. Product and factor markets are generally more flexible in the United States than in other

countries, where further efforts are required to put in place the structural policies necessary to produce well-functioning markets. However, if sound structural policies have not been implemented, entrepreneurial activity will not be completely suppressed. Instead, some would-be entrepreneurs are likely to be diverted into various rent-seeking activities rather than productive economic activities.

Competitive product markets

Competition is vital to respond to demand from consumers   Competition allows consumers to indicate clearly what they want and ensures that the entrepreneur receives clear feedback on how well he or she is performing. It spurs entrepreneurs to try harder and take risks. Competition can be enhanced in a number of ways. Import liberalisation has provided significant increases in competition within all OECD countries in recent years. The development of the *European Single Market* has also led to increased competition within Europe. In addition, increased access to foreign markets has enabled domestic producers to compete more actively and seek the rewards of a more entrepreneurial approach.

Deregulation of monopoly sectors and strengthening of competition laws have helped   Introduction of competition in sectors previously thought to be inherently monopolistic has also been important in providing scope for entrepreneurship. The United States has tended to deregulate these sectors earlier than in some other countries, although some of these sectors are only now being fully deregulated. Spain is putting in place a competitive framework for a number of sectors where inefficient public monopolies have existed in the past. In Australia, telecommunications have only very recently been fully opened to competition and the shipping industry remains subject to a number of restrictive practices. In some other sectors, some licensing restrictions still apply in the Netherlands and Spain, and limit the opportunities for entrepreneurs although the Netherlands has significantly simplified its requirements in recent years. In Sweden, competition laws were tightened several years ago, but market structures have proved difficult to change, particularly in industries such as public utilities, telecommunications, railways and air transport, which tend to have oligopolistic features due to high sunk costs. The market for professional services also remains strongly regulated. More progress has been achieved in the Netherlands, where competition law was recently reformed. In any case, it may take some time before the improvements made in the framework governing product markets are fully exploited by entrepreneurs.

More competition
in public services
would also
stimulate more
entrepreneurial
activity

Public services are another area where significant scope exists for enhancing competition. In the United States, fewer services are provided by the public sector and there is widespread use of sub-contracting for those services that are publicly funded. In contrast, the public sector in Sweden provides a wide range of services leaving little scope for private competition to develop. To a lesser extent, competition in the provision of public services is also limited in the Netherlands and Spain. The benefits of such competition are two-way: not only does it provide more opportunity for entrepreneurial activity, but it also results in more efficient and more innovative public services being developed.

Effective protection
of intellectual
property
encourages
the emergence
of new products
and processes

Development and diffusion of new products and new ways of producing and distributing existing ones, are stimulated by competition. Effective protection of intellectual property reinforces this process. It is difficult to get an accurate assessment of the overall effectiveness of patent protection although in one survey in the Netherlands innovating firms judged patent protection as significantly less effective at protecting them against imitations than a time lead on competitors, keeping qualified people in the firm, and secrecy. Protection of intellectual property may play a more important role for research in academic institutions. Some institutions operate deliberate policies to encourage commercialisation of research. For example, the *Australian Commonwealth Scientific and Industrial Research Organisation* (CSIRO) actively encourages the spin-off of new companies and negotiates arrangements to bring intellectual property generated from publicly funded research into newly started companies. And some institutions encourage the use of research results by allowing individual researchers to receive a significant share of any future commercial rewards. The income that the institutions themselves receive from commercialisation of this research in turn adds to their funds for future research work.

Efficient capital markets

Efficient capital
markets channel
finance to the most
promising projects

All firms need finance, and a well-functioning capital market is essential to ensure that a good supply of finance is available and that it is allocated to the most appropriate projects. Financial liberalisation has been a major feature of all OECD economies and this undoubtedly explains why the availability of finance to most businesses seems to have become less of a concern over recent years. In many OECD countries, however, start-ups are likely to face some extra difficulties in finding finance since by definition they have no track record and around half of them are likely to close again within the first five years. However, the typical start-up does not involve much finance, often using own savings, borrowing from family and friends or drawing on other sources of personal finance.

Venture capital is particularly important for financing high risk high return projects...

Although venture capital provides funding for a very small proportion of the business sector, and even a small proportion of start-ups, this equity finance is extremely important for financing larger projects with prospects of rapid growth. The US entrepreneurship case study shows that a number of factors seem to have helped the development of venture capital. A ready supply of capital is available, especially after the removal of restrictions on investment by pension funds in non-listed equity in the early 1970s. These pension fund investments are exempt from capital gains tax. Successful venture capital investments can easily be realised by making an *Initial Public Offering*. The venture capital market in the United States has also benefited from being able to develop innovative forms of contract arrangements and deal-making within a permissive legal framework.

... but venture capital markets are unevenly developed from one country to another

Venture capital markets elsewhere are less developed and generally involve less risky projects and generate lower returns. Restrictions on institutional investors' holdings of unlisted equity are one explanation. Another explanation has been the difficulty of exit for venture capital. However, the successful listing of a number of foreign firms on NASDAQ (*National Association of Securities Dealers Automated Quotation system*), together with initiatives by local stock exchanges and EASDAQ (*European Association of Securities Dealers Automated Quotation system*), indicates that exit is no longer a major constraint. Nevertheless, EASDAQ and local second tier markets remain hampered by variations in the rules applying to public listing in different European countries. Other possible explanations include the suggestion that European entrepreneurs may be particularly reluctant to accept the loss of control that goes along with venture funding. Another suggested explanation is that there may be insufficient projects coming forward in European countries to warrant the development of the specialised skills and expertise required to manage venture capital investments. Neither of these effects can be quantified, although anecdotal evidence from the United States suggests that venture capitalists benefit from being close to their investments and each other and benefit from being able to specialise in a particular type of firm or technology.

"Angel" investors
provide finance
and active
management
involvement
in the projects

An important source of informal equity capital is so-called angel investment. Angel investors not only take a significant financial stake in the company but also contribute specific skills or general management advice to the company. By its nature the angel investor market is difficult to quantify or analyse, but studies in Australia and the Netherlands suggest that this investment may be at least as large as the formal venture capital market and in the United States it is significantly larger. Many angel investors are successful entrepreneurs, bringing the lessons of their own experience to the new business. Services to help angels and would-be entrepreneurs to find each other have been established in the Netherlands and in the United States. Angel investors can be discouraged by the tax treatment of their investments and constraints on their capacity to exit from their investment. Nevertheless, survey evidence suggests that the biggest constraint on the expansion of angel investment is the quality of the proposals coming to them.

The impact of loan
guarantee schemes
needs to be more
carefully evaluated

Theory suggests that credit may be rationed because lenders have incomplete information about the projects proposed by borrowers. This rationing may hit small entrepreneurial firms particularly hard, since they are perceived to be more risky and often do not have collateral to cover loans. One way in which Governments have sought to mitigate the debt financing problems faced by small businesses has been by introducing loan guarantee schemes. Evidence suggests that these programmes have increased the supply of credit for small firms, but that in some cases these firms have grown at the expense of others, or that they would have been established even without the scheme. Thus, in implementing such programmes, care should be taken to avoid unduly distorting market decisions by evaluating the programmes' costs and benefits, both for those who receive the guarantees and in terms of economic and entrepreneurial activity more widely.

Flexible labour markets

Firms need to be
able to quickly
and easily expand
and contract
their work-force
when their
development
decisions change

Flexible labour markets are important to entrepreneurship insofar as they enable firms to respond quickly and easily to changes in circumstances. Firms' willingness to take risks and expand their work-force is likely to be affected by the ease with which they can lay workers off again if their decision to expand turns out to be wrong. Restructuring to obtain a more dynamic and entrepreneurial approach within well-established firms will also be hampered if it is excessively costly to manage the restructuring. Employment protection legislation makes it difficult and costly for employers to shed staff in the Netherlands, Spain and Sweden, despite modifications that have been made in recent years in order to reduce this cost. Temporary contracts and other measures have been developed to make it easier for firms to expand their work-force, but these measures have only gone part of the way to ease the burden on firms, and have produced undesirable insider-outsider consequences for the labour market as a whole. In Spain, in particular, the employment protection legislation is probably a significant factor discouraging entrepreneurship and it may explain in part the high number of one-person businesses. While Australian employment protection legislation has generally been less strict than that of many OECD countries, unfair dismissal legislation still acts to discourage hiring of workers by small companies, despite simplifications introduced in 1997. In the United States, too, there is some evidence that the costs associated with wrongful dismissal suits have discouraged employment.

Labour markets need worker mobility and flexible employment packages In contrast, the United States offers much less protection to its workers but workers can and do move more easily from one position to another. To some extent this reflects the currently more buoyant labour market conditions, but it also reflects the greater flexibility within the US labour market. This flexibility has also helped to foster entrepreneurship by allowing the development of more flexible and innovative working arrangements. The United States has also led the way in developing more flexible remuneration packages: these have been particularly useful in helping starting companies to reduce their immediate costs and sharing the risks while encouraging loyalty and extra work effort through the use of stock options and performance-linked pay.

More flexible wage setting arrangements are encouraging entrepreneurship Wage setting arrangements are becoming more flexible, which tends to encourage entrepreneurial developments, although more changes may need to be made. Australia implemented legislation in 1997 that could produce a major shift from a central awards system to enterprise bargaining. It also provides for individual contracts and reduces the monopoly power of unions in the bargaining process. Spain also passed legislation in 1997 that aimed to simplify and improve the collective bargaining process, which is extremely complex and involves negotiations at various levels. Earlier reforms allowed the inclusion of a broader variety of work-related terms in the bargaining process and have resulted in improved functional and geographical mobility, but little use has been made of the option of providing an opt-out clause in the case of a firm's financial distress. In the Netherlands, wage rigidities are still reinforced by the current administrative extension of sectoral wage agreements, and only limited use has been made of new bottom wage scales and "opt-out" clauses. In Sweden, the institutional framework for wage bargaining will be basically unchanged when the social partners enter the 1998 wage-bargaining round despite clear evidence of rigid real wages and strong wage-wage links throughout the 1990s.

Reducing the burden of government

Government actions should avoid discouraging entrepreneurship Choosing structural policies so that markets function well is an essential element not only for entrepreneurship but also for achieving sustained economic performance in general. A useful starting point for a strategy aimed more directly at fostering entrepreneurship would be the Hippocratic principle of *"do no harm"*. Many government policies and actions can discourage entrepreneurship and need to be re-examined.

Reducing the administrative burden and compliance costs

The paperwork and costs involved in setting up a new business should be reduced to a minimum... Starting a business is more complex and time consuming in some countries than others. In the United Kingdom, the paperwork involved in setting up a company is about one week, and in Australia, Japan and Sweden too, it is a straightforward matter. However in the Netherlands it is still a complicated process to set up a new company, despite the 1996 liberalisation of the *Establishment Law.* And in Italy and Spain, the administrative requirements can take around half a year to comply with and involve several different agencies. Setting up an incorporated company in European countries and Japan also requires a minimum amount of capital which must be maintained.

... and the ongoing cost of complying with government imposed requirements should be lowered Ongoing costs of complying with government administrative, regulatory and reporting requirements may also be quite high and discouraging to entrepreneurial activity. However, identifying and measuring the compliance burden turns out to be quite difficult, in part because some of the costs would be incurred by the business anyway, even in the absence of government requirements. A common framework that would allow for a comparison of compliance costs across countries is not yet established. Nevertheless individual country estimates indi-

cate that compliance costs can be significant, especially for smaller firms and newer firms. This is because there are some economies of scale in complying with government requirements (providing employee data or VAT returns for example) and newer firms in particular have to invest time and effort in establishing what their obligations are (for example, what records they have to keep, what environmental regulations apply, etc.). However, for a number of reasons, surveys of perceived burden felt by business may not be a reliable guide to the actual burden that these businesses face and more objective assessments are required.

Streamlining administrative requirements and better co-ordination between public agencies would reduce the burden   The recent focus on compliance costs has led to a number of efforts to reduce the compliance burden through better co-ordination between different parts of the administration and sharing of data as well as making the interfaces between the administration and businesses more user-friendly. For example, in France, entrepreneurs may deposit all the required documents at one office, a *Centre de Formalités d'Entreprises*, which then transmits them to the appropriate authorities. In the Netherlands, a single collection point has been established for all employee-related data. And the Australian government intends to establish a single registration process for the *Taxation office, Securities Commission, Bureau of Statistics* and the *Insurance and Superannuation Commission*, to reduce duplication. More broadly, governments are reviewing the existing regulatory requirements to see where requirements can be streamlined or even abolished. The Netherlands programme *"Towards Lower Administrative Costs"* has already led to the simplification of a number of regulations affecting business. They have also adopted a "business effects test" that assesses the impact on business of draft legislation.

Simplifying corporate taxation

Tax compliance needs to be simplified and made more transparent   The administrative costs and compliance burden of the tax system are a particular problem in some countries. For example, American entrepreneurs point to the tax system's ambiguity, frequent changes, expiration clauses and layers of national and regional taxation as among the main sources of the high compliance burden. Many OECD countries are undertaking to reduce the complexity of their tax systems. The UK government has acknowledged that the "language of tax" is itself a hurdle and has undertaken to rewrite tax legislation in simple, understandable language. Countries are also increasingly using information technology as a means of reducing the compliance burden. Electronic filing is now possible in a number of countries, such as Canada, the Netherlands and the United States.

Excessively complex More generally, taxes play a particularly complex role in
tax systems may the climate for entrepreneurship. Ideally taxes should
result in significant have a minimal effect on the decisions that entrepreneurs
distortions to make, but in practice there are many distortions within tax
decision-making systems that do influence the decisions they make. The
tax regimes in Australia, the Netherlands, Spain, Sweden and the United States are complex, and it is difficult to estimate marginal effective tax rates, let alone what effect they have on decision-making. Nevertheless there are some features that may be particularly relevant to entrepreneurship. First is the double taxation of dividends that occurs in the Netherlands and Sweden. This encourages firms to rely more on retained earnings to finance expansion, than if dividends were taxed on the same basis as other investment income. This bias towards retained earnings may inhibit the flow of capital into firms which have more promising projects. The capital tax levied on new equity in the Netherlands and in Spain provides additional discouragement to equity finance. The tax treatment in the Netherlands and the United States also favours investment in owner occupied housing rather than productive activities. Second is the treatment of operational losses. In the Netherlands and the United States, losses can be carried forward for 15 or more years, whereas in Spain they can be carried forward only for up to five years. This is particularly hard for new companies which often take several years to reach a profitable position.

Excessive payroll A further effect of the tax system which discourages entre-
taxes have adverse preneurship comes through high payroll taxes which
effects on makes it more difficult to hire labour at a price commen-
entrepreneurial surate with the value of the employee to the entrepre-
activity neur. This is particularly an issue in the Netherlands,
Spain and Sweden. In the Netherlands, the government has taken steps to reduce non-wage labour costs, especially for low-skilled workers. In Sweden, the high total tax wedge on labour should be seen as a major impediment to the development of the personal services sector. In contrast, this sector has been a significant source of growth in other countries, especially in the United States.

Reducing the cost of firm closure and bankruptcy

Firm closure, The closure of unsuccessful firms is a necessary, if unwel-
where necessary, come, part of the entrepreneurial process which allows

should not be obstructed... resources to move to more productive uses. Only a small proportion of closing firms are bankrupt, and most firm closures do not involve losses to creditors. Nevertheless, policies that restrict the scope for enterprises to restructure or close down completely diminish the ability of an economy to adjust quickly and discourage entrepreneurs from starting up. For example, France's and Spain's bankruptcy legislation placed strong emphasis on maintaining employment in loss-making firms and those firms that eventually closed generally incurred more losses than if they had been allowed to close at an earlier stage. Recent legislation intends to restore creditors' rights and may alleviate these costs.

... and where the costs and social stigma of bankruptcy are unduly high, they should be reduced For the individual entrepreneur, too, bankruptcy legislation differs significantly. In the United States, an individual can declare bankruptcy, settle the outstanding debts as far as possible from his existing assets and immediately start over with a clean slate. In the United Kingdom, obtaining a general discharge from previous debts may take up to two years and new legislation in Germany will introduce a discharge clause which will free the debtor of the remainder of his debt in seven years. However, in the Netherlands, Spain and Sweden, the consequences of personal bankruptcy are much more severe: with minor variations, persons who go bankrupt are required to settle their debts in full, from future earnings if necessary. An appropriate balance needs to be found between the rights and obligations of owners and creditors of a firm. Excessive personal bankruptcy costs will discourage potential entrepreneurs, but costs that are too low do not encourage entrepreneurs to be financially disciplined, undermining the protection of creditors and thus limiting the supply of funds to entrepreneurs. The discouragement to risk taking is often reinforced by social attitudes: in the United States, business failure is generally seen as a reasonable outcome of a "good try" whereas in European countries it seems to be viewed more as a personal failure with social stigma attached.

Making it easier for potential entrepreneurs to take the plunge

Loss of social insurance and the risk of unemployment may discourage would-be entrepreneurs from leaving secure jobs Some features of the labour market and social insurance provisions combine to discourage people from launching an entrepreneurial venture. Studies of entrepreneurs in the Netherlands and the United States show that the typical new entrepreneur is someone in their mid-thirties to mid-forties who has worked for two or three well-established enterprises and then decides to establish a business, often drawing directly on the skills and experience acquired in previous employment. In the United States, there is a steady flow of people back and forth between self-employment and salaried employment: if a business venture fails, they can reasonably easily get another job. This is much less the case in the Netherlands, Spain and Sweden because of higher unemployment or, possibly, some bias against employing older workers or the availability of early retirement. Furthermore, a move from salaried employment to self-employment not only increases the probability of a future period of unemployment (since around half of all starting businesses fail within the first five years) but may also involve surrendering some or all acquired rights to permanent contracts, severance payments, unemployment insurance and in some cases, pensions. As a result, the risks faced by someone starting a business in those countries are much higher than in the United States. In Spain high youth unemployment also tends to reduce the pool of potential entrepreneurs, because they are less likely to have acquired the necessary skills and experience due to fewer years in active employment and once secure employment is finally obtained, they may be less likely to risk leaving it for self-employment.

Optimising programmes and policies to foster entrepreneurship

Programmes designed to assist businesses are widespread

Programmes and policies aimed at fostering entrepreneurship cannot substitute for well-functioning markets and proper framework conditions. However, government programmes, if well designed, can complement and support appropriate framework conditions. Many OECD countries have a wide range of programmes designed to assist business, although not all of these have the fostering of entrepreneurship as their primary objective. In some cases programmes are targeted on different types of businesses, for example, small businesses, high-tech enterprises, start-ups and so forth. Other programmes are targeted on specific aspects of business such as finance, innovation, development of business skills, and so on. These programmes have generally evolved in a patchwork fashion over the years, although many countries, such as Australia, the Netherlands and Spain have made recent efforts to try and develop a more coherent strategy for the promotion of business. Spending on such programmes can be high. In the United States, for instance, the annual figure of US$65 billion has been quoted as the total cost of all federal business support programmes.

Entrepreneurship can often be fostered at little

In complementing framework conditions, well-designed programmes to foster entrepreneurship can, for example, encourage and maximise the benefits of collaborative

*cost by well-
designed
programmes*
behaviour; increase the flow of information for financing entrepreneurship; encourage awareness of entrepreneurship and improve skills formation; and, as discussed in the next section, add flexibility to policy when factors affecting entrepreneurship are location-specific. Such programmes can be inexpensive, as is the case, for example, with information dissemination on procedures for establishing a business; publicly commending entrepreneurial efforts through awards such as "most successful business of the year", which make role models more visible; and government support for programmes such as business competitions in schools and universities which can help students to get useful practical experience and give encouragement. Programmes of this sort have the added virtue of not interfering with market incentives.

*The evaluation of
programmes and
policies is essential*
Too frequently there is a lack of systematic evaluation of programmes supporting entrepreneurship. It is incumbent on public authorities supporting such programmes to encourage a culture of evaluation and bench-marking and to adjust programmes or alter the policy mix where findings suggest that this is required. The need for proper evaluation is highlighted by the scale of resources expended on various forms of business support. Structured design, monitoring and evaluation must be built into support programs from the outset, and where possible should include cost-benefit analysis to determine the social return to the programmes concerned. Evaluation should be one part of a logical framework involving, *inter alia*, clear initial specification of objectives, outputs and expected impact. Evaluation is not without technical difficulties, and sometimes encounters institutional resistance. It must be emphasised therefore that evaluation, if appropriately structured, can also provide a powerful programme management tool. Evaluations may also be costly. Indeed, economies of scale and scope may apply, which underlines the importance of co-operation with central levels of government.

*Policies to support
self-employment
have often been
cost-effective*
Many OECD countries offer active employment policies such as self-employment programmes for the unemployed to encourage them to create their own jobs. Rather than being offered income support, the unemployed are encouraged to formulate a business idea and receive financial assistance and counselling in order to create an enterprise. Although not a panacea for unemployment (less than 5 per cent of the unemployed will chose to become self-employed), these programmes have proven to be a cost-effective alternative to income support, even accounting for those unemployed who would have created an enterprise anyway in the absence of the programme. Also, the programmes show that a higher percentage of programme

participants than non-participants succeed in finding long-term employment, even if their businesses fail.

Addressing the regional and local dimensions

There are
pronounced local
variations in levels
of entrepreneurial
activity

Entrepreneurship has various territorial dimensions relevant for policy. First, the nature of entrepreneurial activity often varies markedly across sub-national regions owing to differences in demography, wealth, education, occupation profiles, infrastructure endowment and other factors. Within the same country some regions have enterprise birth rates up to six times higher than others. The transition economies offer a striking contrast between large urban areas showing signs of dynamic entrepreneurial activity and most rural areas lagging behind. Indeed, the spatial concentration of business activity can be extremely significant from a national standpoint: according to one estimate some 380 clusters of firms in the US together produce 61 per cent of the country's output. "Hot spots" of entrepreneurship exist in such places as Silicon Valley in the United States, Gladstone in Australia and the Valencia region in Spain. Concentrations of firms often provide an environment conducive to entrepreneurial activity. They can also give rise to economies of agglomeration which can confer important competitive advantages. Clearly, then, entrepreneurship is often strongly affected by local and regional economic, social and institutional conditions. Indeed, given the variety of location-specific factors which affect entrepreneurship and the opportunities for encouraging entrepreneurship through local measures, policies which fail to take account of regional and local differences are less likely to be successful.

Local authorities
are well equiped
to foster
entrepreneurship...

At the same time, many important programmes to support entrepreneurship are best designed and implemented by local authorities. Business incubators, advisory and information services, business networks, loan-guarantee consortia, information brokerages for informal venture capitalists, training schemes and entrepreneurship awareness programmes are just some of the many relevant local initiatives. Indeed, the diversity and rate of innovation in local policy instruments to support entrepreneurship is considerable. Relative to central initiatives there are particular advantages in encouraging entrepreneurship through local measures: actions can be better tailored to the specific needs of businesses (a consideration central, for instance, to the UK's *Training and Enterprise Councils*), and the involvement of a wider range of actors can bring a richer mix of competencies to the issue. Furthermore, a number of acute social problems – such as distressed urban areas, and unemployment among minorities – are highly concentrated geographically and would greatly benefit from a local response to stimulate entrepreneurship: in such areas the social benefits of promoting entrepreneurship may be particularly high. Furthermore, it is at the local level where the need for policy co-ordination is perhaps greatest.

... particularly to assist inter-firm collaboration Most clusters of firms, especially large or region-wide agglomerations, have occurred spontaneously rather than as an outcome of public policy. It is probably unwise for policy-makers to attempt to create entirely new clusters. The clustering of firms has complex determinants, and there are numerous possible sources of inefficiency in such a course of action. Indeed, policies aimed at creating clusters of high-tech firms (*e.g.*, techno-poles, science parks) have had mixed results. However, policy can consolidate some of the benefits of existing or embryonic clusters by ensuring suitable institutional conditions. For example, amongst other actions, promoting the establishment of suppliers' associations and learning circles, facilitating contacts among participants in the cluster and ensuring effective extension services can all increase the benefits to firms of belonging to a cluster. Initiatives to facilitate inter-firm collaboration can also support attitudinal changes helpful to business activity in general.

Integrating entrepreneurship and social objectives

Non-profit organisations can achieve social objectives through entrepreneurial means... Non-profit organisations provide a wide range of services, such as in health and care, educational support, skills development, cultural programmes, environmental protection, scientific or social research, community support networks and so forth. These non-profit organisations are distinguished from the market sector by their desire to provide these services in order to achieve social objectives rather than to maximise profits. Even so, the experience of some countries has shown that this sector can also benefit from a more dynamic and entrepreneurial approach. Such an approach can facilitate the achievement of social objectives rather than conflict with them. By being highly responsive to client demand, willing to take risks and innovative, while adopting effective and productive methods of service delivery, this sector can deliver better social and economic results.

... and this helps governments Many non-profit organisations are oriented towards creating new high-quality services for people who would be

to better respond   unable to pay market-based prices and in this way they
to social concerns   often complement the activities of government agencies.
Indeed most of these organisations receive direct or indirect funding from government, and contracting out public social services to the private non-profit sector may be an effective means of delivering such services. At the same time, careful attention to the conditions attached to government grants to these organisations may encourage them to develop more entrepreneurial approaches. Some of these organisations also place particular emphasis on harnessing hitherto unused or under-used resources, and thereby play an important role in assisting the re-insertion of the most disadvantaged people into the work-force. Many of these organisations play a significant role in active labour market programmes by providing valuable basic work-skills training. Other organisations are oriented towards community development through networking, and the pooling of information, skills and financial resources to find appropriate solutions to pressing social and economic issues. All in all, a responsive and dynamic non-profit sector can play an important role in supporting entrepreneurial activity in the economy at large, while making it easier to address the most important social concerns.

Policy guidelines

As more countries move towards fostering entrepreneurship, the evidence is mounting that, implemented comprehensively, entrepreneurship policies represent an effective response for countries wanting to strengthen their adaptability and improve their economy's ability to create jobs. Concrete policy recommendations have been tailored to the five different countries examined in depth (and are presented in the individual chapters in Part II). For other OECD countries, specific and concrete policy conclusions can only be drawn after in-depth examination. Nevertheless, some broad policy guidelines can be drawn and these are summarised below. Each country would need to examine how these could best be applied within its own situation.

Broad policy guidelines

Examine the overall institutional framework within which economic activity takes place to establish whether it provides maximum scope for entrepreneurship to flourish. In particular:

– Identify and dismantle remaining barriers to competition which limit the incentive on enterprises to innovate and perform more dynamically. Promote competition in all sectors of the economy, including the provision of public services. Provide effective protection of intellectual property.

– Examine whether current regulations governing financial institutions and/or financial markets inhibit or facilitate the availability and optimal allocation of finance for entrepreneurial activities.

– Allow scope for flexible employment contracts to be negotiated, with remuneration arrangements and working conditions that are well adapted to the needs of dynamic enterprises. Relax employment protection measures that inhibit restructuring or discourage entrepreneurs from taking on new workers.

– Examine the costs of complying with government imposed administrative or regulatory requirements and identify where reductions could be made, either by removing the requirement to comply or by reducing the administrative burden involved (including through better co-ordination between different government agencies).

– Examine the overall effects of the tax system on entrepreneurship, and identify any particular features which act to discourage entrepreneurs or the financing of entrepreneurial activity. Ensure that the tax system is transparent and that compliance is straightforward.

– Review and simplify the registration procedures required to create a business. Ensure that firms are able to close quickly should they wish to do so.

– Ensure that personal bankruptcy legislation provides an appropriate balance between encouraging risk-taking and protecting creditors.

– Re-examine the effects that social insurance provisions may have on encouraging or discouraging would-be entrepreneurs.

Ensure that specific programmes designed to foster entrepreneurship operate as part of an integrated and coherent strategy that complements the framework conditions. In particular:

– Avoid policies that stem from a too-narrow definition of entrepreneurship (e.g., that entrepreneurship is only about start-ups or only about high-technology) and which may divert attention from getting the broader economic policy settings right.

– Widen the target population for entrepreneurship programmes, where possible, to attract the participation of women, the young and minorities.

– Undertake regular and comprehensive evaluation of programmes, and ensure that evaluation findings are acted on.

Improve the effectiveness of entrepreneurship programmes by drawing on the knowledge of sub-national levels of government. In particular:

– Ensure that resources for programmes to foster entrepreneurship are decentralised where appropriate in order to bettor tailor programmes to the specific needs of an area and its businesses.

– Provide regular opportunities to exchange information at a national level on the experiences of local authorities in designing and implementing entrepreneurship programmes.

Seek to identify and implement low-cost and effective programmes with minimal distortionary effects on market incentives. For example:

- Promote public awareness of entrepreneurship and examine the role the education system could play in developing entrepreneurial skills and attitudes.
- Increase opportunities for the unemployed to create their own jobs through self-employment schemes.
- Facilitate networking among firms in order to foster a culture of mutual co-operation and risk-taking.
- Promote the entrepreneurial non-profit sector by contracting-out where possible the delivery of public services which meet pressing demands in economic and social development.

Part I

DEVELOPING NEW POLICIES
FOR ENTREPRENEURSHIP

Chapter I

Why Entrepreneurship Matters

The basic policy message of the OECD *Jobs Study* (OECD, 1994*a*) is clear: high unemployment should be addressed by seeking to improve countries' capacity to adapt to change. The OECD *Jobs Study* reviewed the labour-market experiences of OECD Member countries during the past quarter-century and found that while some countries enjoyed relatively good records on employment many others, notably in continental Europe, saw rising unemployment. The study resulted in a statement of policy recommendations to raise employment.

Fostering Entrepreneurship is the follow-up study pertaining to one of the recommendations of the Jobs Strategy: to increase economic dynamism by improving the environment for entrepreneurial activity. The study seeks to identify areas in which there is a role for government in promoting entrepreneurship and, in turn, job creation. As entrepreneurship is affected by a very broad range of economic and institutional factors, a policy (or set of policies) for entrepreneurship should concern policymakers from a number of ministries and levels of government. The study seeks to consider the issues of relevance to this potentially diverse readership.

This work has benefited from inputs from several OECD Directorates and, in particular, from a study of entrepreneurship in five countries (Australia, the Netherlands, Spain, Sweden and the United States) which was undertaken in conjunction with the Economic Development Review Committee (EDRC) process. This latter exercise has allowed the study's conclusions to be based on country-specific experiences.

A central topic of policy debate

It has long been recognised that entrepreneurship plays a central role in economic development and that entrepreneurs are essential agents of change in a market economy. In recent years however there has been increased interest in entrepreneurship. This growth in interest has occurred among governments,

---

Box 1.1. **The OECD Jobs Strategy**

1. Set macroeconomic policy to both encourage growth and, in conjunction with good structural policies, make it sustainable.
2. Enhance the creation and diffusion of technological know-how by improving frameworks for its development.
3. Increase flexibility of working-time (both short-term and lifetime) voluntarily sought by workers and employees.
4. Nurture an entrepreneurial climate by eliminating impediments to, and restrictions on, the creation and expansion of enterprises.
5. Make wage and labour costs more flexible by removing restrictions that prevent wages from reflecting local conditions and individual skill levels, in particular of younger workers.
6. Reform employment security provisions that inhibit the expansion of employment in the private sector.
7. Strengthen the emphasis on active labour market policies and reinforce their effectiveness.
8. Improve labour force skills and competencies through wide-ranging changes in education and training systems.
9. Reform unemployment and related benefit systems – and their interactions with the tax system – such that societies' fundamental equity goals are achieved in ways that impinge far less on the efficient functioning of labour markets.
10. Enhance product market competition so as to reduce monopolistic tendencies and weaken insider-outsider mechanisms while also contributing to a more innovative and dynamic economy.

Source: OECD, 1997*b*.

---

broad segments of the general population and established firms. An important indication of the significance now accorded to entrepreneurship is the *Council Resolution* by the European Commission to prepare by October 1998 draft guidelines on developing entrepreneurship for Member States.

Government interest in promoting entrepreneurship has various motivations. While seen as a means of combating unemployment and poverty, the promotion of entrepreneurship is perceived to yield additional benefits such as raising the degree of competition in a given market, fuelling the drive for new economic opportunities, and helping to meet the challenges of rapid change in a globalising economy. A reliance on private initiative as a source of employment creation is also clearly attractive in a context both of restricted public expenditures and a preference among many policymakers for supply-side solutions to unemployment. Promoting entrepreneurship is thus viewed as part of a formula that will reconcile economic success with social cohesion. In addition, European governments see that the private sector in the United States has for some time played a much greater role in employment creation than in Europe. Policymakers are therefore interested in whether differences in the employment record are attributable to different levels of entrepreneurial activity.

Throughout the OECD new opportunities for entrepreneurship have been created by technological change, evolving business practices and the reform of regulatory environments. Simultaneously, established firms in many fast-changing markets increasingly view "intrapreneurship" (entrepreneurial behaviour within an existing company) as essential to competitive success. And in many sectors, the break-up of large business units into smaller ones has been considered essential for achieving flexibility, with new business formats often placing a premium on entrepreneurial aptitude.

Current understanding

Entrepreneurship takes innumerable forms and appears in small and large firms, in start-ups and established enterprises, in the formal and informal economy, in legal and illegal activities, in innovative and traditional concerns, in high- and low-risk undertakings, and in all economic subsectors. Despite the central importance of entrepreneurship in the market economy some aspects of the subject are under-researched. Indeed, a number of the issues in which current understanding is incomplete have potentially important policy implications. For example, the effects of education on entrepreneurship have not been fully examined. Whether and how national *curricula* might be modified, which age groups should be targeted and how widespread might be the impact of educational initiatives are all issues in need of greater assessment. Similarly, a generalised deficiency in many programs of public support to business start-ups and small business is the scarcity of systematic evaluation. This shortcoming can seriously hinder the choice of efficient and effective policy and, more broadly, represents an unnecessary weakness in the comprehension of entrepreneurship.

The multifaceted nature of any new policy

A variety of macroeconomic, microeconomic, institutional and social factors affect the scope of entrepreneurial endeavour. For example, a stable and propitious macroeconomic environment is essential for investment and growth and will affect the return on investment projects and thus the number of prospective ventures which are attempted. At the microeconomic level, a properly designed and enforced competition policy will be important in avoiding entry barriers for new or diversifying firms. At the institutional level, without organisations to provide a range of essential services the level of business activity may be less than optimal. And a commercial environment characterised by mistrust may require that entrepreneurs invest in mechanisms to defend against the potentially opportunistic behaviour of counterparts, with these added transaction costs possibly deterring some forms of entrepreneurial initiative.

The varied considerations outlined above mean that policy must work at different levels, and may involve considerable complexity. They also imply that an entrepreneurship policy will vary in content from one country and region to another according to the specific institutional arrangements and economic policies already in place. For example, a policy to foster entrepreneurship in a distressed urban area will clearly have a different content from one concerned with furthering entrepreneurship in an existing area of high-technology enterprise.

Much has been done over the years to improve and develop the wide range of policies and programs which affect entrepreneurship. However, in some countries there is still a need to ensure the overall coherence of policy: one facet of policy should not militate against another. Policy trade-offs are also inevitable. For instance, the drive for simplification of tax regimes, sought by many firms, diminishes the scope for using fiscal policy in pursuit of selective economic and social objectives. Assessing the appropriate balance in policy trade-offs is a subject which merits further attention.

Possibly the most innovative areas of policy action relate to an enhancement of entrepreneurship issues in education and attempts to create support for entrepreneurship among the public.

Fostering entrepreneurship shows that the establishment of conducive framework conditions is central to promoting entrepreneurship (Chapters 2 to 5). Other means of fostering entrepreneurship such as subsidies should not be used to correct for inappropriate framework conditions. However, a focus on specific programs and policies is necessary when market or systemic failures occur. As the study points out, one area in which the need for selective initiatives is particularly evident relates to the spatial distribution of entrepreneurial activity. Different regions and localities in the same country can exhibit marked variations in the extent and success of entrepreneurship. An entrepreneurship policy which fails to account for such variations is likely to be suboptimal. In broad terms, local initiatives have such advantages as being able to better tailor activities to needs, concentrate resources where most required and mobilise a wide range of actors relevant to entrepreneurship. Proper co-ordination between local and national authorities is also important, for example in establishing common standards of service provision, disseminating information on best practices, and ensuring that actions are not undertaken locally which may be wasteful from a national perspective. With various forms of decentralisation and the growth of local initiatives ongoing in many countries, optimal co-ordination between local and national levels is an issue requiring further consideration.

As with other areas of economic life, information problems affect the framing of policy. Information problems are compounded by the breadth of factors impinging on entrepreneurship, and by the previously referred to dearth of evaluations of many support programs. Indeed, a challenge for policymakers is the quantitative assessment of cost benefit ratios in various entrepreneurship support programs. Policymakers must also be attentive to the magnitude of possible displacement and dead-weight effects stemming from policy. Displacement effects occur when some companies loose business as a result of support given to other firms. Dead-weight problems arise when resources are used to encourage behaviour (such as lending) which would have occurred anyway. These effects of policy can be difficult to predict and measure, although every effort must be made to avoid the waste they involve.

The remainder of this study, divided in two parts, will examine the conditions that influence enterprise formation, growth, innovation and risk-taking, and will further investigate how OECD country-experience can be used to improve policies. This first part, "Policies for entrepreneurship", continues with Chapter 2 which will consider the concept of entrepreneurship, as well as issues of enterprise size and job creation. Chapter 3 will examine differences in taxes and administrative burdens as well as touching upon the role of regulation in facilitating market access. Chapter 4 considers the legislation and regulations which facilitate efficient systems of finance, and Chapter 5 reviews issues in human resources. Chapter 6 examines the critical role of local authorities and institutions in advancing entrepreneurship. Entrepreneurship policy, like the rest of the Jobs Strategy, has important ramifications for social stability and cohesion. The role of entrepreneurship in satisfying otherwise unmet social needs is taken up in Chapter 7. Part II, "Learning from other Countries", contains the five country studies of entrepreneurship in Chapters 8 through 12. Entrepreneurship is also of great interest to transitional economies engaged in fundamental economic and social change. Chapter 13 therefore reviews the experience of countries with economies in transition in developing entrepreneurship.

While various national surveys have already been undertaken, this study represents one of the first attempts to synthesise the international experience of entrepreneurship. *Fostering Entrepreneurship* makes clear that the subject is multifaceted and that framing policy is complex. However, the potential rewards of a proper attention to the many issues which affect entrepreneurship are significant.

Chapter II
Entrepreneurship: Helping Job Creation

One of the keys to a buoyant economy capable of adjusting to economic developments and structural change is entrepreneurship. Entrepreneurs are essential agents of change in a market economy, and entrepreneurship fuels the drive for new economic and technological opportunities and efficient resource use. The efficiency of an economy is enhanced when alert entrepreneurs act to facilitate trade between parties with different preferences and resource endowments. Growth is promoted when entrepreneurs accelerate the generation, dissemination and application of innovative ideas, be these technological or organisational. Not only do entrepreneurs seek to exploit business opportunities by better allocating resources, they also seek entirely new possibilities for resource use and thereby redraw the boundaries of economic activity.

Entrepreneurship has a number of social benefits. As a means of combating unemployment and poverty, the demonstration effect of entrepreneurship and of an active approach generally may help address issues of dependency and passivity often cited in debates over traditional forms of welfare. Entrepreneurship can also offer solutions to those whose efforts in the mainstream economy have been frustrated. For example, the number of women entrepreneurs is increasing, in part due to the "glass ceiling" experienced in working for others. Also, many immigrants failing to find employment seek alternative opportunities through self-employment. The opportunity for workers to start their own business also provides a specific incentive to play the role of problem-solver in the work place, rather than simple executor of pre-defined tasks. Finally, many acute social problems – such as unemployment among minorities, and distressed urban areas – require, among others, a local response involving the stimulation of entrepreneurship. The encouragement of entrepreneurship in an area in decline, or in an area that is underdeveloped, may also have advantages over some long - standing programmes of subsidy to ailing subsectors: entrepreneurship may create new jobs and provide examples for diversification, while the costs to the state of supporting an industry in decline may be incurred indefinitely.

From a policy standpoint it is important to note that the private and social returns to job creation can diverge. This divergence can arise as a consequence of existing policy, such as on taxes and benefits. It may also reflect the environment in which entrepreneurship seeks to establish itself: for instance, new business in a distressed urban area can confer significant benefits to the community. A more general observation, based on "knowledge externalities" – the information-related benefits stemming from the actions of others – has also been made: when an entrepreneur establishes a business valuable information is provided to the market. Other actual and potential entrepreneurs can get to learn what products sell, what marketing strategies work, what general business practices are effective, and so on. Even if the new business should fail, information is passed to the market about what does not work. However, the entrepreneur is not rewarded for supplying this information. His or her private benefits are exceeded by the benefits to society. There may thus be a tendency for the unassisted market to undersupply entrepreneurial activity. There is little if any documentation of this form of market failure. However, empirical work has established the importance of so-called "knowledge externalities" in a number of industries, while the imitative character of entrepreneurship is commonly observed.

For a number of reasons, drawing a statistical link between entrepreneurship and employment is exceedingly difficult. To start with, the extent of entrepreneurial activity in an economy cannot be measured directly. This difficulty has a number of sources. Much entrepreneurship, particularly intrapreneurship (entrepreneurial behaviour within established organisations), can be hard to distinguish from non-entrepreneurial forms of managerial activity. And the interpretation of some forms of quantitative data is far from straightforward. Self-employment, for example, is a frequently used indicator of entrepreneurship, although many self-employed do not consider themselves to be entrepreneurs (especially if, for example, they contract exclusively to a single firm). Measurement problems likewise reflect the fact that the number of ways of being entrepreneurial is varied and constantly changing. And the profusion of definitions of entrepreneurship is an additional complication (definitional problems are a symptom of the fact that entrepreneurship involves behaving in ways which are new (Baumol, 1993)).

Even if observers were privileged with a direct measure of entrepreneurship, other problems would remain in establishing the link to employment. For example, the causal connection between entrepreneurship and employment can run in both directions: entrepreneurship creates new products and services which often leads to enterprise start-up and growth with accompanying job creation but also forces less efficient firms out of the market. In addition, analysts face the problem of separating the influence of entrepreneurship from the effects on employment of other variables such as labour market and macroeconomic policies, technological change and agglomeration economies (with the latter operating in many renowned centres of entrepreneurship such as Silicon Valley, parts of northern Italy, etc.). Indeed, the authors of this study found no quantitative empirical literature which had attempted this task.

Finally, the transmission mechanisms by which entrepreneurship affects employment may act in a number of indirect ways and over a considerable period of time. For example, if entrepreneurs exploit profit opportunities by introducing new labour-displacing technologies then employment may suffer in the short-run. But if these technologies facilitate increases in productivity and the growth of real incomes then the associated higher levels of spending will provide a source of employment creation.

What is entrepreneurship?

Despite its importance and overarching presence in market-based econo-mies, entrepreneurship is an elusive concept. At its most general, it is the ability to marshal resources to seize new business opportunities. Entrepreneurship, defined in this broad sense, is central to economic growth.

Richard Cantillon,[1] who first argued in a systematic way on the issue in the early 18th century, pointed to the entrepreneur as a prime agent in economic activity. Specific definitions, however, have been difficult to agree on. In part this is because entrepreneurship often involves behaving in ways which are new (Baumol, 1993). Indeed, mainstream economics has paid scant attention to entre-preneurship, and the decision-making process central to entrepreneurship is not a well-defined feature of economic thought. In fact, there are severe difficulties in reducing the multi-dimensional and shifting strategies of entrepreneurship to the kind of mechanical maximisation algorithms characteristic of enterprise-level decision-making in standard theory.

As described above, the term has been used in a variety of ways and contexts. It has had two principal uses in recent years, firstly as a description of the creation and growth of new and small businesses, and secondly as a descrip-tion of a more general business characteristic, denoting a willingness to take risks, to be innovative and to take initiatives to exploit business opportunities.

The use of the term entrepreneurship to refer to the creation and growth of new and small businesses is perhaps the most obvious and widely used of the two concepts. Indeed, governments have sought to encourage the start-up, growth and survival of small businesses through a wide range of enterprise support measures. The use of the term to describe a particular form of business behaviour has received less attention, but entrepreneurship in this sense is also critical to the maintenance of business efficiency and competitiveness. While new and small businesses are often considered to be particularly enterprising, this should not obscure the fact that it is essential to the economy that enterprising behaviour is also encouraged in larger and longer established businesses.

The character traits which distinguish entrepreneurs are many and varied, and have been the subject of detailed inquiry. These traits include such attributes as foresight, imagination, intelligence, decisiveness, alertness, and an aptitude for organisation. Psychologists also note less attractive features such as the need for control, mistrust of others and a desire for approval. No list of attributes is suitable to all cases and many of the characteristics mentioned are themselves multifaceted. Many of the behaviours associated with entrepreneurship can be taught. Others may be difficult to emulate. The key consideration is that entrepreneurship is scarce. Even if elements of entrepreneurial behaviour can be taught, not everyone will learn with the same proficiency. Nor, as yet, have many societies attempted to encourage entrepreneurship systematically. As with other inputs to economic activity, the scarcity of entrepreneurial ability endows it with value.

Entrepreneurial behaviour is driven by the search for personal achievement. Monetary reward is clearly central to entrepreneurship. However, it is not always the prime motivation. Other considerations often shape entrepreneurial decision-making. These include the desire for independence, self realisation, creative activity and so forth. A recent survey of firms in Sweden found that only 16 per cent of entrepreneurs felt that the principal function of entrepreneurship was to raise their incomes. Indeed, wealthy entrepreneurs – for whom the value of additional units of income is insignificant – sometimes describe their participation in business as akin to a challenging game.

Different authors have emphasised different facets of entrepreneurship. Schumpeter (1942) stressed the concept of innovation in creating and responding to economic discontinuities; Knight (1940) saw the entrepreneur's role as dealing with risk in a context in which entrepreneurship is inseparable from control of the firm; Casson (1982) wrote that *"an entrepreneur is someone who specialises in taking judgmental decisions about the co-ordination of scarce resources"* (this is the definition of an economic actor as such); and more recently Baumol took a broad view of entrepreneurship as "all non-routine activities by those who direct the economic activities of larger or smaller groups or organisations". Finally, several economists including Brusco (1983) and Piore & Sabel (1984) have pointed to a new form of entrepreneurship based on innovative activity connecting local clusters of firms.

Several analytically important characteristics of entrepreneurship have emerged in the light of these ideas. First, entrepreneurship involves a dynamic process in which new firms emerge, existing firms grow and unsuccessful ones die; this can be thought of in terms of the Shumpeterian notion of "creative destruction". The dynamism of this process is difficult to capture empirically,[2] but one aspect is "turbulence"– the rate at which businesses open and close. Data published in the OECD's *Employment Outlook* 1994 show that country experiences vary somewhat: start-ups (relative to the number of establishments in existence) range from 11 to 17 per cent and deaths from 9 to 14 per cent (Table 2.1). However, in general, countries with high rates of start-up also have high failure rates yet most new start-ups are still in business after a year and cohort analysis shows that about half of all new firms survive for five years (Table 2.2). All European Union member countries and Switzerland have higher start-ups rates than Japan, yet all these have lower start-up rates than the United States (ENSR, 1996). Other evidence demonstrates that the linkage between birth and death rates extends to the regional level, with regions characterised by high birth rates also having high death rates (Storey, 1994). Researchers generally attribute this to high formation rates leading to a higher proportion of the stock of firms which are very young and hence most vulnerable to failure. The ability of firms to exit a market quickly and efficiently also heightens an economy's ability to reallocate resources among competing uses. Analysis of US data across states and cities shows that states with lower firm survival rates are among the most prosperous (Birch *et al.*, 1996). High turbulence may suggest that the economy is taking advantage of new opportunities and is shifting resources away from declining activities.

Table 2.1.   **Enterprise[1] evolution**

Per cent

	New establishments[2]	Closing establishments	Continuing establishments	*of which* expanding[3]	Contracting[3]	Unchanged[3]	Net birth (1-2)
Denmark 1984-89	14.2	13.6	86.4	29.3	25.9	31.2	0.5
Finland 1986-91	11.2	9.8	90.2	29.9	60.3		1.4
France 1984-92	14.3	13.2	86.8				1.1
New Zealand 1987-92	13.7	14.5	85.5	19.4	21.9	44.2	−0.8
Sweden 1987-92	16.8	14.6	85.4	24.1	24.7	36.6	2.2
US[4] 1984-91	13.6	9.2	90.8	15.0	10.3	65.6	4.4

1.   In this table: establishments. Sampling months/periods vary across countries, see the source.
2.   Since these establishments are born during the year, they are not included in the number of establishments at the start of the year, and hence their proportion is not included in the total.
3.   With regard to the number of employees.
4.   These data should be treated with caution, see the source.
Source: OECD, 1994b, Table 3.7.

Table 2.2. **Firm survival rates**

Per cent

	After 3 years	After 5 years
Denmark	69	58
Finland	63	55
France	62	48
Germany	70	63
Ireland	70	57
Italy	66	54
Netherlands	74	. .
Norway	68	53
Portugal	56	47
Spain	70	. .
Sweden	70	59
United Kingdom	62	47
United States	60	50

Source: European Observatory, 1995 and Dennis, 1995.

A second characteristic often cited in debates on entrepreneurship is innovation, where new products and services, and more efficient production techniques are introduced by firms that have identified new market opportunities or better ways of meeting existing demands. One measure of innovative activity is the output of patented knowledge. However, innovation is a phenomenon difficult to capture quantitatively. In many countries much innovative activity goes unpatented, while many patents represent only trivial technological advances. Similarly, data on numbers of technicians, engineers and scientists, while important, relate to an input to knowledge creation, as opposed to innovation achieved. Furthermore, innovation often takes the form of changes in so-called "tacit knowledge", that is, informal and often minor modifications in the organisation and practice of work. Indeed, the large majority of firms do not engage in the production of patentable knowledge; their innovations are economic.

A further characteristic of entrepreneurship is that, to the extent that it implies control of the process by the entrepreneur-owner, it tends to be identified with small businesses which are typically headed by owner-managers. One measure of the extent of the combination of entrepreneurship and ownership is the numbers of self-employed. The proportion of self-employed and employers in total employment is particularly high in Turkey, Mexico, Italy, Korea, Portugal and Spain, and by contrast, is relatively low in Denmark, Germany and the United States (Table 2.3). However, because of the fact that the level of self-employment is determined by a variety of factors, some of which may be cyclical, self-employment cannot by itself be used as an indicator of entrepreneurship.

Table 2.3.   **Non-agricultural self-employment**[1]

Per cent of civilian employment

OECD countries	1970	1980	1985	1990	1991	1992	1993	1994	1995
Australia	9.3	12.7	12.6	12.9	12.8	13.8	14.2	13.8	13.4
Austria	12.7	8.8	6.0	6.6	6.5	6.3	6.3	6.6	–
Belgium	12.0	11.3	12.5	12.9	13.1	13.3	–	–	–
Canada	7.0	6.6	7.5	7.5	7.7	8.0	8.6	9.1	–
Czech Republic	–	–	–	–	–	–	8.9	9.9	11.2
Denmark	10.5	–	7.2	7.2	6.9	6.7	7.0	6.8	–
Finland	–	6.0	6.5	8.8	8.9	9.1	9.5	9.9	–
France	12.5	10.5	10.5	9.3	9.2	9.0	8.8	8.7	8.5
Germany	10.3	7.0	7.6	7.7	7.4	7.7	8.0	8.5	–
Greece	–	30.9	27.2	27.4	28.0	28.4	28.2	28.0	–
Hungary	–	–	–	–	–	–	–	–	–
Iceland	10.1	7.1	8.1	10.8	15.2	13.7	13.1	14.5	–
Ireland	10.8	10.2	11.9	13.4	13.0	13.7	13.9	13.6	–
Italy	24.5	19.2	21.3	22.2	22.2	22.5	22.0	22.3	–
Japan	14.2	13.7	12.9	11.5	11.1	10.7	10.3	10.1	–
Korea	–	–	–	21.8	22.3	23.0	23.2	23.1	23.6
Luxembourg	12.3	9.2	8.5	7.1	6.3	6.1	6.0	5.9	5.8
Mexico	16.6	14.3	–	19.9	26.1	25.5	25.1	24.7	–
Netherlands	–	9.1	8.4	7.8	7.7	8.1	8.7	9.4	–
New Zealand	–	9.0	–	14.6	14.9	15.8	15.7	15.8	–
Norway	8.6	6.5	6.5	6.1	6.1	6.1	6.2	6.1	–
Poland	–	–	–	–	–	10.4	11.1	11.7	11.4
Portugal	13.1	14.9	16.6	16.7	17.9	17.5	18.0	18.9	–
Spain	16.1	16.3	18.1	17.1	17.4	18.2	18.6	18.7	–
Sweden	5.6	4.5	4.5	7.3	7.2	7.9	8.7	9.0	–
Switzerland	–	–	–	–	–	–	–	–	–
Turkey	–	–	–	26.6	27.5	27.7	26.6	26.4	–
United Kingdom	6.7	7.1	10.6	12.4	12.0	12.1	12.2	12.5	–
United States	6.9	7.3	7.5	7.6	7.8	7.5	7.7	7.5	–

1.   Includes employers and persons working on own account.
Source: OECD Labour Force Database.

Local or area-based factors are of considerable importance in the development of entrepreneurship. For example: the success of entrepreneurs and local
financial institutions is often interdependent; local networks are often key to
successful entrepreneurial areas such as Cambridgeshire and parts of Ireland
(OECD, 1996e); many support structures for new firm creation, such as business
incubators, require local knowledge for optimal design; entrepreneurship frequently spreads through imitation, which can be spurred through proximity; some
evolving business phenomena, such as the investment behaviour of informal
venture capitalists, have a local character and the culture of enterprise may be
susceptible to promotion at a local level through investment in social capital.
Because the extent and likely success of entrepreneurship is often tied to the

local milieu, creative policymaking and effective and efficient implementation is required at the local level. Increased international economic integration, termed "globalisation", adds urgency to the policy challenge. This is because internationally mobile factors may become less rooted in local communities than in the past, and thus have less incentive to invest in their prosperity (Rodrik, 1997).

Because the nature of entrepreneurship varies, the problems faced by enterprises also differ. For example, the self-employed and micro-enterprises may be greatly absorbed by difficulties in accessing bank finance and dealing with the administrative burden created by government regulation and taxation. Alternatively, hi-tech enterprises may be concerned with legislation governing intellectual property rights and with the difficulties of hiring skilled workers. Yet other problems face gazelles, such as accessing equity markets to finance their growth.[3] The differing intensity and types of enterprise activity across regions also suggests that concerns differ from area to area.

Enterprise size and job creation

The job creation potential of the small business sector has for some time been a source of considerable debate in the academic literature and in policy development. The debate has been fuelled by a range of studies which have concluded that small businesses contribute disproportionately to employment generation. The studies fall into two main groups; those that concentrate on the changing shares of total employment accounted for by small firms and those that calculate net job creation for different size classes of firm. There is general agreement on the results of the first of these approaches, that small businesses have substantially increased their share of total employment in developed economies in recent years. Indeed, the increasing role of the small firm sector has been advanced by some analysts as a fundamental change in economic organisation in developed economies (Piore & Sabel, 1984). The trend appears to have started in the early-1970s and has continued into the 1990s (Loveman & Sengenberger, 1991; OECD, 1994b). There is more controversy, however, over the second approach, which assesses the net job creation of different sizes of enterprise.

Studies using the net job creation methodology have provided some dramatic results. For example, recent work in the United States concludes that small firms, with 100 or fewer workers, were responsible for nearly 85 per cent of all net new jobs between 1992 and 1996 (Birch et al., 1997a). Table 2.4 summarises the evidence for eight OECD countries, showing the contribution to net employment change of establishments classified according to size category at start or end dates for the period 1984-1992. In all the countries covered, small establishments displayed much more rapid net employment growth compared with larger ones.

Table 2.4. **Net employment change by establishment size class**

Average annual rates as a per cent of total employment

			Establishment size			
		Total	1-19	20-99	100-499	500+
Canada[1]	1983-1991	2.6	2.2	0.6	0.1	−0.3
Denmark	1983-1989	2.2	2.3	0.3	−0.4	
Finland	1986-1991	−1.6	0.9	−0.7	−1.1	−0.7
France[2]	1987-1992	0.9	0.4	0.4	0.3	−0.2
Italy[1, 3]	1984-1992	1.3	1.5	−0.2	−0.2	−0.5
New Zealand	1987-1992	−4.1	0.4	−1.9	−1.5	−1.1
Sweden	1985-1991	1.3	2.6	−0.2	−0.5	−0.6
United Kingdom	1987-1991	2.7	1.6	0.4	0.3	0.4

1. Data refer to firms.
2. Data by establishment size class are not available for the period 1984-87.
3. Sum of size categories does not add as firms temporarily operating with 0 employees are not classified according to size for the period 1986-1992.
Source: OECD, 1994*b*.

Small establishments in fact accounted for most of the net employment growth over the period, whilst, according to this data set, the performance of very small establishments is impressive in comparison with all other sizes. However, such findings must be treated with caution since the technique used may overstate the contribution of small firms in generating jobs. A description of the methodological difficulties involved is given in Box 2.1.

Firm conclusions cannot yet be made on whether the small firm sector is indeed responsible for a disproportionate share of net job creation. What is clear, however, is that the bulk of new jobs created are in a small number of fast growth firms. These fast-growth companies can be found both in the large and small firm sectors. In the United States, gazelles, or fast growing firms, account for only 3 per cent of all firms but are responsible for 70 per cent of gross job growth (Birch *et al.*, 1997*b*). The average gazelle is neither young nor small; more than half are over 15 years of age, compared with 12 years for US companies as a whole, and most gazelles have over 100 employees. The larger gazelles are particularly impressive. Although they account for only 3 per cent of gazelles they represent over 60 per cent of growth attributable to all gazelles. In the United Kingdom and Australia, about 5 to 20 per cent of firms are responsible for as much as 70 to 80 per cent of gross job creation (Hall, 1995). In Sweden only 7 per cent of all larger enterprises (more than 200 employees) were fast growing, but these accounted for the largest absolute job creation among the fast-growers (OECD, 1998*b*).

Self-employment represents the smallest enterprise size, with employment of one person. In a number of countries (Belgium, Ireland, Italy, New Zealand,

Box 2.1.   **Small firms and net job creation: the debate**

Net job creation methodologies calculate for each size class of firm the jobs created through births and expansions minus those lost through deaths and contractions in any given period. Firms are usually assigned to a size band at the start or end of the period in question. The first systematic attempt to measure the source of new jobs using this method presented surprising findings (Birch, 1979). It indicated that between 1969 and 1976, 82 per cent of net job gains occurred in firms with less than 100 workers. Further analysis suggested that this estimate varies with the economic cycle, with small firms providing a greater proportion of new jobs in recessions and a share equal to that of large firms during economic expansions (Kirchhoff, 1994). In the case of Sweden, on the other hand, it can be shown that the major part of net job creation came from newly created and small businesses during both the last recession and recovery (OECD, 1998*b*).

However, a variety of statistical and other arguments have been put forward to suggest that the estimates of small firm net job creation may be biased upwards. One of the most important factors is the phenomenon of regression-to-the-mean bias. This arises from transitory deviations of employment from long-term optimum size, where "temporarily" small firms will gain jobs during their path to equilibrium, whilst "temporarily" large firms will lose jobs (Hughes, 1997). In order to compensate for this problem Davis *et al.* (1993) reassessed the evidence for US manufacturing for the period 1972-1988, using estimates based on the average size of enterprises for the period. Calculating in this way they found no systematic relationship between net job creation and firm size. Evidence for the effect of this regression-to-the-mean bias is less compelling in the UK, where the very smallest surviving firms appear to account for a disproportionate share of net job creation, regardless of whether opening size or average size is used (Oulton & Hart, 1996; Hughes, 1997). To throw more light on the issue of the small firm contribution to job creation further research is needed on what is causing the patterns of net job change in different size categories of enterprise.

Portugal and the UK) self-employment expanded faster than overall, non-agricultural employment during the 1980s. The trend has since stabilised in most of these countries but the Netherlands, Portugal and the UK continue to experience growth in self-employment. Such growth has been explained by strong fiscal incentives, lower administrative burdens, strong incentives for the unemployed to create their own jobs, and growth in the demand for new types of personal and business services. Another reason may be related to spin-offs or sub-contracting of functions which were internal to firms in order to reduce labour costs, share risks and increase flexibility (OECD, 1992*a*). The issue of labour market regulation will be revisited in Chapter 5.

However, in some countries, the predominance of self-employment is the result of a relatively restrictive job security legislation and high employers' social security contributions (OECD, 1992*a*) further demonstrating that firm size is not in itself a sufficient indicator of entrepreneurship. It would appear that, if the job security of new employees is high, employers will be more cautious about taking on new staff on a permanent basis, preferring other forms of employment relationships, such as subcontracting work to self-employed people. Therefore, self-employment can introduce an element of flexibility into the operation of the labour market. However, in such a situation there may be costs in terms of poorer working conditions (such as not being covered by pensions) and extremely long hours. But if such impediments are not driving the creation of small enterprises and self-employment, these forms of business organisation may well represent a positive entrepreneurial response to economic change.

Does geography determine entrepreneurship?

Although international comparisons are difficult to make with any accuracy, it would appear that some countries perform well according to some entrepreneurship indicators but not to others. For example, in some countries, high numbers of enterprises enter and exit the market quickly and efficiently, which heightens their economy's ability to reallocate resources among competing uses. Likewise, some countries have much better developed venture capital markets than others. During the EDRC *review* of Australia, the authorities voiced the opinion that their economy could become more entrepreneurial, in that Australians failed to bring their inventions to market and instead have seen them being developed in other countries. During the other four EDRC *reviews* with special chapters on entrepreneurship, the Netherlands, Spain, Sweden and the United States also pointed to aspects of entrepreneurship which, in comparison with other countries, could be improved. The Netherlands authorities sought to increase the amount of venture capital going to start-ups; Spain and Sweden sought to identify barriers hindering the growth of their small firms; and US authorities felt that an excessively complex tax system was hampering entrepreneurial ability.

As described in Chapter 6, the nature of entrepreneurial activity often varies markedly across regions within a country. There are "hot spots" of entrepreneurship even in countries where national statistics suggest a sluggish economy. A well-known example of regional and local dynamism is the Emilia-Romagna in Italy, one of the most successful economic areas in Europe. Reynolds & Storey (1993) found substantial differences in start-up rates across regions in OECD countries. In the United Kingdom, for example, the rate varied from 10.0 to 59.5 start-ups per 10 000 persons per year (see Table 2.5). Birch et al. (1997b) found marked variations in firm start-up and death rates across the United States. Significant differences also exist in the prevalence of nascent entrepreneurs, with higher levels in the West and North East of the United States and lower levels in the North Central region and the South (Reynolds, 1997).[4] Similarly, the incorpora-

Table 2.5. **Firm birth rates and variations within countries at the regional level**[1, 2]

| | Annual firm births at the regional level (per 10 000 persons) Regional variations | | | |
	Average	Lowest	Highest	Highest/Lowest
	All sectors			
France	118	67	264	3.9
Germany	55	41	90	2.2
Italy	144	74	202	2.7
Sweden[3]	88	56	149	2.7
United Kingdom	72	42	107	2.5
United States	33	18	74	4.1
	Manufacturing only			
Germany	6.8	4.5	12.0	2.7
Ireland[4]	22.3	10.7	42.7	4.0
Italy	26.8	12.7	51.0	4.0
Japan	6.7	4.1	12.7	3.1
Sweden	10.3	4.4	28.7	6.5
United Kingdom[4]	27.5	10.0	59.5	6.0
United States[4]	16.8	2.4	114.0	47.5

1.   All birth rates are for the middle to late 1980s.
2.   Differences between countries in the collection of data mean that cross-national comparisons of the average values are not appropriate.
3.   Population (16-64 years of age) used as denominator.
4.   Manufacturing workers used as denominators.
Source: OECD, 1993.

tion of companies in Australia, as a proportion of all firms (1994/95), varies from 3.9 per cent in Tasmania to 11.7 per cent in Victoria (OECD, 1998*a*).

High levels of entrepreneurial activity are often ascribed to cultural attributes. A near unanimous view held by analysts of entrepreneurship is that culture plays a critical role in determining the level of entrepreneurship. It is also a common view among practitioners and analysts dealing with entrepreneurship that cultural factors are important. Other things being the same, an environment in which entrepreneurship is esteemed, and in which stigma does not attach to legitimate business failure, will almost certainly be conducive to entrepreneurship. However, partly because "culture" is a broad and diffuse concept there has been little systematic assessment of this issue and its policy ramifications. Nevertheless, as this study describes, there have recently appeared a small number of econometric analyses examining the impact of "trust" on economic development. These works, which focus on a key dimension of culture, have been based on European and World values surveys and point a way to new avenues of research in entrepreneurship. Anecdotal evidence suggests that cultural attitudes towards business are amenable to policy action. Cultural change is also likely to be a function of the ways in which a society's institutions operate. Along with the encouragement of experimentation, entrepreneurial attitudes should be instilled through education at a young age. Attitudinal changes may be difficult to achieve in later years. The celebration of positive role models can also be beneficial.

Notes

1. An Irish international banker who wrote *Essai sur la nature du commerce en général* (1755).

2. Generally, statistics of firm births are taken from business registers. However, business registers not only include data on the creation of new businesses but also other data which are not true births: the take-over of an existing business by an entrepreneur; and the relocation of an existing business into another area or industry. Enterprise death statistics include similar flaws: deaths due to the sale of the business and relocation. In addition, cross-country variation could reflect differences in cyclical positions, since company creation and destruction are sensitive to the business cycle.

3. Gazelles are often defined as those firms that manage to maintain a compound growth rate of at least 20 per cent for four years from a starting base of at least $ 100 000 in annual revenue.

4. The Reynolds study surveyed households to estimate the number of nascent entrepreneurs, defined as individuals who were identified as taking steps to found a new business but who had not yet succeeded in making the transition to new business ownership.

Chapter III

Overcoming Barriers to Entrepreneurship

Entrepreneurial dynamism can be hampered by regulations which hinder enterprise start-ups and exit. Barriers to entrepreneurship can stifle innovation if incumbent firms are protected from the competitive forces which generate new ideas. Excessive bankruptcy costs can raise the cost of failure and lead potential entrepreneurs to shy away from risk-taking, although entry and exit regulations are important to protect consumers and to reassure investors that companies are financially disciplined. Efforts are underway in many countries to reduce regulation which was useful in the past but has since become a hindrance. Taxation reduces the returns to entrepreneurship, although taxes also pay for public services that benefit entrepreneurs such as infrastructure and Research and Development (R&D). In any event, both compliance costs and high taxes have been cited by entrepreneurs as barriers to start -up and expansion. This section will review these issues and present examples of how the costs of regulation and taxation are being diminished in a way that need not compromise their legitimate goals. Other barriers regarding hostile local and regional environments will be discussed in Chapter 6.

Regulatory barriers

All OECD countries regulate entry into markets, defining registration requirements and how firms are taxed. Generally, each country has several legal forms of enterprise, each of which offers different privileges and registration and reporting requirements and, when creating an enterprise, entrepreneurs must weigh their relative costs and benefits. For example, limited liability is an attractive legal form because it confines the losses that the owners of a company can incur to a maximum of the amount of capital that they have put in. Limited Companies are also an attractive legal form for investors because of the access it gives them to information on company activities and the recognition of their rights as shareholders and creditors. However, these advantages must be weighed against the heavier reporting costs relative to other forms of organisation, such as unlimited liability companies (*e.g.*, sole traders, *artisans, commerçants*). In all OECD countries, the number of unincorporated businesses (unlimited liability) is substantially larger than the number of incorporated businesses (limited liability) (OECD, 1994*c*).

Table 3.1 details the registration requirements and costs for 3 common types of enterprises: sole trader and unlimited liability enterprises, private limited companies and public limited companies. Generally, the procedures for registering as a sole trader and unlimited liability company are relatively simple and the costs are minimal; as a result, this is the form adopted by most smaller firms. The registration costs tend to be higher for private limited liability companies than for unlimited liability companies. In particular, indirect costs, which include payments to lawyers and business experts, are higher. Finally, public limited companies, that is, limited liability companies which issue shares, tend to be the most complex and expensive form of company to create. The registration requirements and subsequent reporting requirements are higher and the average time it takes to complete the registration is the lengthiest.

Creating a company is more complex in some countries than in others. In Germany about 1 day is required to register an unlimited company, whereas in Italy it can take over 20 weeks. In Spain, an entrepreneur must undertake at least 13 steps and the total time required to fulfil these legal requirements is estimated to take between 19 and 28 weeks. In Australia, costs and procedural delays are minimal, in part due to the practice by some accountants and lawyers who specialise in the sale of "shell companies" which enable entrepreneurs to acquire a limited company almost immediately (OECD, 1998*a*). Policies have been introduced in a number of countries to reduce registration complexity. For example, in France, entrepreneurs may deposit all the required documents at one office, a *Centre de Formalités d'Entreprises* (CFE), which then transmits them to the appropriate authority. The move to reduce complexity has taken place as part of the broader recognition of the complexity caused by several layers of government. This has created a trend towards co-ordination of government regulation and policy resulting in "one-stop shops" managed at the local level.

In addition to registration requirements, skill certification may be required in countries when the activity is deemed to be of an artisanal nature. For example, entrepreneurs in activities characterised as artisanal in Germany (which covers a wide range of activities, from bakers and hairdressers to dispensing opticians) are required to be a *Meister* or to employ a *Meister* (Meager, 1993). This means that an apprenticeship has been completed and specific post-apprenticeship experience and training has been acquired. In addition, entrepreneurs in many countries must produce a business plan certified by a business expert which attests to the enterprise's viability.

Table 3.1. **Company registration requirements**

Unlimited liability (ltd), private company and public ltd company

	Legal form[1]	Pre-registration requirements[2]	Registration offices[3]	Post-registration requirements[2]	Time (week)[4]	Min. charter capital (ECU)[5]	Cost (ECU)[6]
Australia	Proprietary	3	1	1-5	1	0	200-480
	Public	4	1	1-5	1	0	200-480
France	Artisan	6	1	4	1-7	0	1 100-2 700
	SARL/EURL	10	1	5	4-8	8 000	1 900-4 600
	SA	14	1	7	7-15	40 000-250 000	2 200-6 100
Germany	KGT	1	1	2	1 day	0	10-25
	GmbH	6	2	2	8-24	25 000	750-2 000
	AG	6	2	2	8-24	50 000	750-2 000
Italy	Artigiana	7	1	4	4-16	0	1 150
	SRL/SuRL	17	5	3	4-16	10 000	2 200
	SPA	18	4	3	22	100 000	7 700
Japan	Commerçant	2	1	5	1-3	0	350-700
	Yugen Kaisha	6	1	5	2-4	20 000	2 100-6 000
	Kabushiki K.	8	1	5	2-4	70 000	4 600-17 000
Netherlands	Eenmanszaak	1	1	5	3-7	0	0
	BV	3	1	5	12	19 000	1 000–
	NV	2	1	5	12	0	0
Spain	EI	0	3	5	1-4	0	0
	SRL	7	5	5	19-28	3	330+
	SA	7	5	5	19-28	62	330+
Sweden	Enskild Firma	0	1	2	0-4	0	90
	AB	3	1	3	2-4	12 000	1 130
	AB (publ.)	3	1	3	2-4	60 000	1 130
UK	Sole Trader	0	0	3	0	0	300
	Private Limited	1	1	3	1	2	420
	Public Limited	1	1	3	1	70 000	900
USA	Sole Proprietor	0	2-6	2-5	1-2	0	200-800+
	LLC	0	2-6	2-5	1-2	0	200-800+
	Corporation	0	2-6	2-5	1-2	0	200-800+

1. Legal form. Three different legal forms have been selected among each country's many different forms: unlimited liability, limited liability and public corporations. The definitions of these forms vary across countries.
2. Registration requirements. The number of procedures which must be completed before and after registering.
3. Registration offices. The number of offices where the business entity must be registered.
4. Time. The number of weeks required before the registration has been processed by the authorities.
5. Minimum charter capital requirements. The value of assets which a business entity must have and maintain.
6. Cost. The direct costs (fees paid to the registering authorities) and indirect costs (fees paid to lawyers, agents and consultants) of registration.

Source: Logotech S.A., 1997 and submissions from the Australian authorities.

Other regulatory barriers exist which are sector specific. For example, tele-communications have until recently been public-sector monopolies because of "natural monopoly" characteristics or public service considerations, and were protected by regulatory barriers. Regulation in the distribution sector is enforced in many countries to protect the environment and contribute to urban planning or

---

Box 3.1. De-regulation of the distribution sector

The distribution sector accounts for between 8 and 18 per cent of GDP across the OECD area and for between 10 and 20 per cent of total employment. The large size of the sector and its role in channelling goods from producers to consumers make its performance important for the economy. Zoning laws and regulations on shop-opening hours affect the competitive situation of the distribution sector. Zoning laws limit the establishment of new outlets to certain areas. Although intended to protect the environment and contribute to urban planning, regulations can contribute to high land cost for retail outlets and thus to high price levels. They may also favour incumbent (small) shops and act as an entry barrier for new shops. Each OECD country typically has regulations in place with regard to zoning and some countries also allow incumbent retailers to influence the decision-making process with regard to zoning laws. In a few countries, notably Belgium, France, Italy and Japan, national legislation has been introduced to slow-down or disallow the creation of large-scale outlets.

Also, shop-opening hours are legally restricted in many countries. In a few countries, including the USA, Ireland, New Zealand and Sweden, no legal restrictions exist, although in some cases local governments may apply certain restrictions. In others, including Italy and, until recent legislative changes, Denmark, Germany and the Netherlands, opening hours were more restricted. Such restrictions were originally intended to provide shopkeepers with a common pause day, while at the same time creating a level playing field for competition. Although limiting consumer choice, these restrictions particularly protected small, owner-operated shops, for whom it is more difficult to expand opening times. Larger stores have more employees and can use part-time workers and flexible working-time arrangements to fill staffing requirements. The general trends towards more flexible working-time arrangements by consumers, employers and employees, as well as the rise in part-time work, have put opening time restrictions under increasing pressure.

De-regulation of the distribution sector has been implemented in many OECD countries. An evaluation of the liberalisation of shop-opening hours in Swedish food retailing suggests that output and employment increased and prices fell somewhat. Regulation on large-scale stores was eased in Japan in 1992 and the evidence also suggests that competition has increased and that prices have fallen. De-regulation in the UK also appears to have had broadly positive effects. Studies for France and the Netherlands suggest that a further liberalisation of shop-opening hours would increase output and employment in the sector and contribute to lower price levels.

Source: OECD, 1995*b*.

protect the position of small artisanal outlets. In a cross-country review of 5 important economic sectors which are often highly regulated, the OECD (1995b) highlighted the role played by various regulations which barred market entry. The
study noted that many regulations could be lowered or removed because
advances in technology had reduced their usefulness. For example, technical
advances in the electricity sector have made it feasible for relatively smaller
enterprises to generate electricity efficiently. The study also noted that some
regulations resulted in a lack of competition which provided little incentive for
incumbent firms to pursue innovations in production or in creating new goods and
services or in adapting to changing consumer demands. Deregulation in the
telecommunications sector has led to the development of new products and
services (e.g., cellular phones). Furthermore, the deregulation of the distribution
sector in some countries (see Box 3.1) has allowed firms to take advantage of
economies of scale which has contributed to economic growth and job creation.
For a comprehensive review of economic and social regulation and its administrative burden and how deregulation can improve the contestability of markets, see
1997 OECD *Report on Regulatory Reform* (1997c).

Competition policy

Regulatory barriers to entry are not the only barriers that need to be reduced
in order to open the economy to greater entrepreneurial dynamism. Private
barriers to entry can be just as stifling. Existing firms might agree to suppress
competition among them in order to raise prices. Such agreements invariably
require some attempt to keep new competitors from offering what the incum-
bents refuse to in the way of either quantity or quality of product. Collective
boycotts could be used for example to deny new competitors supplies of raw
materials, components and access to distribution channels. Happily, most countries have adopted competition laws which prohibit anticompetitive agreements
among competitors and sanction them with heavy fines and, in a few cases, even
imprisonment. They have also, incidentally, blocked firms from doing the same
thing by merging and then suppressing competition directly.

Generally speaking competition laws also contain provisions which make it
difficult for "dominant firms" to unilaterally seek to protect themselves from new
competition. The intent is to restrict firms to maintaining large market shares
solely by greater efficiency rather than artificial barriers to entry. An example of
such an artificial barrier to entry would be the acquisition of a reputation for
predatory pricing, i.e., responding to a new entrant or seeking to "discipline" an
existing firm, by temporarily charging well below cost. Other examples of artificial
barriers to entry have been found in certain tying arrangements which may make
it necessary for new competitors to enter on a much larger scale and in more

activities than would otherwise be the case. Exclusive dealing requirements are also sometimes used, for example, to deny distribution outlets to other firms. All this is not to say that low pricing, tying and exclusive dealing (or other vertical arrangements not mentioned here) are necessarily bad for competition and for consumers. Low prices are clearly good for consumers and are usually evidence of vigorous competition. In addition, most vertical agreements are adopted because they allow firms to more efficiently serve consumer needs. Entrepreneurs can and should look to competition laws to restrict commercial practices and mergers which harm the competitive process. They should not expect competition authorities to strike down practices merely because they tend to reduce the number of competitors in a particular market.

Bankruptcy legislation

Just as legislation exists to regulate entry, bankruptcy legislation regulates exit by imposing financial discipline on firms and ensuring an orderly enforcement of property rights in the event of failure. That firms are able to exit the market quickly and efficiently heightens an economy's ability to reallocate resources among competing activities. Effective bankruptcy legislation allows entrepreneurs and investors to define the cost of failure (i.e., money at risk), and ensures that all parties will receive the most for their investment should the enterprise fail.

An element of bankruptcy legislation which can encourage entrepreneurship is the discharge clause which applies to unlimited liability companies. A number of countries such as Australia, the United States and the United Kingdom offer the bankrupt individual a "clean slate" by way of discharge: the entrepreneur loses assets to creditors but cannot be pursued for any remaining claims which have not been met. While this approach has some disadvantages because it makes bankruptcy more attractive to debtors with negligible assets, it does allow for considerable flexibility and may help to reduce any stigma attached to business failure. In other countries, by contrast, legislation places more emphasis on creditor protection and, in some cases, the absence of discharge clauses means that failed entrepreneurs can be pursued for several years, a situation which is not conducive to risk-taking activity. In Germany, company managers incur civil liability and may also be liable to criminal penalties (Fialski, 1994). Recent reforms to the German law, to come into force in 1999, will introduce a discharge clause which will free the debtor of the remainder of his debt seven years after proceedings have been terminated. Debtors are discharged in the UK after 2 years and after 3 years in Australia. In contrast, there is no discharge clause in Sweden and a further tightening of the bankruptcy rules is under consideration (OECD, 1998b).

Another element of bankruptcy legislation that can affect the entrepreneurial process is the reorganisation option. Generally, most bankruptcies end in liquidation. This procedure has the advantage of being relatively quick. However, there is a risk that early liquidation will force the closure of firms which are only temporarily insolvent but viable in the longer term. As a result, "re-organisation" procedures are available in several countries to protect potentially viable firms: a firm can apply for protection from its creditors while negotiations are carried out to decide the terms on which it can be reorganised if viable, or wound up if not. Enforcement of existing legislation is also important. The lack of efficiency in the judicial system in Spain and the difficulty to obtain legal enforcement of contracts may discourage risk and impinge heavily on smaller firms (OECD, 1998c).

At the same time, studies have shown that adequate creditor protection is important for vibrant capital markets (La Porta et al., 1996 and 1997) particularly in the supply of financing for smaller firms. By contrast, large, well-established companies find it easier to obtain external financing no matter in which country they are based. Gaillot (1995) also provides evidence that protecting insolvent firms at the expense of creditors has done little to protect employment. In France the bankruptcy law was modified in 1985 to give priority to saving the insolvent enterprise in order to save jobs. As a result, it became more difficult for lenders to repossess collateral. In 1994, reforms were introduced to restore creditors' rights, notably the rights of secured creditors.

Tax burdens

In general, high taxes tend to distort economic activity in a number of ways. Leibfritz et al. (1997) analyses several channels, including effects on saving, investment and labour markets. Such distortions lead to a sub-optimal use of resources and a less efficient and dynamic economy. In particular, high tax rates which reduce the returns to entrepreneurship can impede firm creation or expansion. High marginal income and corporate tax rates penalise very successful enterprises – the gazelles, for example. They may also reduce firms' liquidity by cutting into retained earnings. High tax rates provide an incentive for tax avoidance and evasion, tending to expand undeclared economic activity.

The problem of high taxes has been alleviated to some extent by tax reforms during the last decade that have reduced the two taxes which most affect enterprises: personal and corporate income taxes. Generally, small firms are unincorporated firms and are subject to personal income tax, whereas the earnings of corporations are subject to a corporate income tax. Table 3.2 shows that 20 countries cut their top marginal personal income tax rates in recent years, by an average of over ten percentage points. In many cases, these tax cuts were financed by broadening the tax base. For example, taxes on fringe benefits were

Table 3.2.   **Basic rates of corporate income tax of central government**

Country	Top marginal rates of central government personal income tax[1]			Basic rates of corporate income tax of central government[2]		
	1986	1990	1995	1986	1991	1995
Australia	57	47	47	49	39	33
Austria	62	50	50	30	30	34
Belgium	72	55	55	45	39	39
Canada	34	29	31.3	36	29	29
Denmark	45	40	34.5	50	38	34
Finland	51	43	39	33	23	25
France	65	57	56.8	45	34/42	33
Germany	56	53	53	56	50/36	45/30
Greece	63	50	40	49	46	35/40
Iceland	38.5	33	38.2	51	45	33
Ireland	58	53	48	50	43	40
Italy	62	50	51	36	36	36
Japan	70	50	50	43	38	38
Luxembourg	57	56	50	40	33	33
Netherlands	72	60	60	42	35	35
New Zealand	57	33	33	45	33	33
Norway	40	20	13.7	28	27	19
Portugal	61	40	40	42/47	36	36
Spain	66	56	56	35	35	35
Sweden	50	20	25	52	30	38
Switzerland	13	13	11.5	4-10	4-10	4-10
Turkey	50	50	55	46	49	25
United Kingdom	60	40	40	35	34	33
United States	50	28	39.6	46	34	35

1.   Canada, Finland, Iceland, Norway, Sweden, Switzerland and the United States also have personal income tax levied by sub-central government.
2.   Austria, Canada, Finland, Germany, Italy, Japan, Norway, Portugal, Switzerland and the United States also have sub-central corporate taxes. Rates rounded to nearest percentage point. Many countries also have special rates for firms with fewer profits and for particular sectors.
Source: Owens, 1996.

increased in Australia, Finland, New Zealand and the United Kingdom, and the deductibility of mortgage interest payments was limited in Finland, Ireland and the United Kingdom. Reforms in the United States removed a range of deductions. Corporate taxes have also fallen. Cuts in central government corporate income tax rates since the mid-eighties have averaged around 10 percentage points. As with the personal income tax reductions, the tax base has broadened with various tax relief schemes (targeted at particular regions or sectors, investment credits and property-related tax-shelters) being limited or abolished in Australia, Austria, Finland, Germany, Iceland, Ireland, Portugal, Spain and the United States (Owens & Whitehouse, 1996). Unfortunately, much of the simplification achieved during the 1980s has been lost as a consequence of the renewed tendency among policy makers to use tax incentives to achieve economic and social policy goals.

Effective tax rates differ from statutory rates because of various tax relief schemes. Jorgenson & Landau (1993) show, in a study of corporate tax rates in nine countries, that marginal effective corporate tax rates, a much contested concept,[1] have tended to increase since the 1980s (See Table 3.3). However, when combined with taxation on corporate earnings at the personal level, effective rates have been decreasing. In particular, corporations in the United Kingdom, the United States and Canada benefit from a relatively low effective tax rate.

Table 3.3.   **Marginal effective tax rates on corporate earnings**[1]

	Year	Effective tax rate at the corporate level	Effective tax rate at corporate and personal level combined	Memorandum item: Statutory corporate tax rate
Australia	1980	41.8	23.4	46.0
	1990	14.6	28.1	39.0
Canada	1980	16.9	20.0	..
	1990	25.9	19.3	..
Japan	1980	3.1	15.6	52.6
	1990	6.1	23.0	54.7
Germany	1980	15.2	32.9	62.2
	1990	4.6	28.6	58.1
France	1980	−28.8	74.1	50.0
	1990	−34.4	65.4	37.0
Italy	1980	−91.6	58.5	36.3
	1990	−72.8	58.2	46.4
Sweden	1980	−22.5	37.9	39.6
	1990	1.0	27.8	30.0
United Kingdom	1980	−31.4	30.7	52.0
	1990	28.0	13.8	34.0
United States	1980	14.4	22.5	49.5
	1990	24.0	19.1	38.3

1.   The effective tax rate at the corporate level is defined as the ratio between the difference of pre-tax real rate of return and the post-corporate tax real rate of return and the pre-tax real rate of return. The effective tax rate at the corporate and personal level combined is the ratio between the difference of the pre-tax real rate of return and the post-tax real rate of return of the saver. The pre-tax real rate of return is assumed at 10 per cent.
Source: Jorgenson & Landau, 1993.

Other taxes such as social security contributions can also affect entrepreneur-ship, yet it depends on how the entrepreneur assesses risk. It has been argued that the growth of self-employment has been assisted by the lower social contri-butions the self-employed pay. An OECD Study (1994b) compared the average rates of contribution for those who are self-employed (i.e., owners of unincorpo-rated businesses) and those who are employed at a common level of income. A survey across countries shows that in most countries the self-employed pay far lower contributions than would be paid by employees and employers combined. These differences in social security contributions must be seen in the context of the special (usually separate) and less attractive social security benefit regimes which normally apply to the self -employed; in particular unemployment insur-ance or unemployment benefits are rarely extended to cover the self-employed who become unemployed.

The burden posed by inheritance taxes can diminish entrepreneurial activity by making the transfer of company ownership prohibitively expensive. Therefore, in order to facilitate inter-generation transfers of businesses and other assets either at death or as gifts, most countries operate systems under which spouses and direct heirs are tax exempt or relatively lightly taxed. There are also a number of other special tax provisions specifically designed for small businesses: inheri-tance and gift taxes in the UK, and capital gains taxes in Canada, France, Germany, the UK and the USA all have such provisions. Leadbeater (1997) points to the usefulness of employee-buyouts in succession planning where retiring owners have been encouraged to sell their company to its employees. Buyouts could take place within the framework of Employee Share Ownership Plans whereby the owner, in selling to his employees, obtains a capital gains tax concession.

Low tax rates are not the only factor affecting the amount of entrepreneurial activity. The relative tax rates on different types of activities (unincorporated versus incorporated) can favour one form over the other. A particular concern of the small business community is that the difference in relative tax rates is not to its advantage. As can be seen in Table 3.4, personal income tax rates tend to be progressive and corporate rates tend to be flat-rate taxes. Depending on their earnings, unincorporated firms may or may not pay higher taxes than corpora-tions. Further complexities in the tax system render comparison of tax burdens difficult. The corporate tax understates the actual tax on corporate earnings because these may be taxed both at the corporate level and again as personal income when the profits are distributed to shareholders. In many countries this problem has been recognised, and the amount of tax due on profits is reduced when they are distributed, either by reducing the corporate tax or personal taxes. For example, the US tax code is fairly neutral with respect to the choice of legal form of a business with, in particular, the possibility of using S taxation which offers almost full elimination of double taxation (OECD, 1994c). In Sweden, tax

Table 3.4. **Personal income tax and profits tax**

July 1992

	Personal income tax rate (per cent)		Corporate tax rate (per cent)
	Lowest bracket	Highest bracket	
Australia	20 (< A$ 20 700)	47 (> A$ 50 000)	39
Austria	10 (< Sch 50 000)	50 (> Sch 700 000)	30
Belgium	26.75 [25] (< BF 245 000)	59 [55] (> BF 347 000)	39
Canada	27 [17]	48 [29]	General 41 [28]; Manufacturing 36 [23].
Denmark	52.1 [22] (< DKr 162 300)	68.7 [40] (> DKr 231 800)	34
France	0 (< FF 18 690)	56.8 (> FF 254 170)	34
Germany	19 (< DM 8 153)	53 (> DM 120 042)	36 for distributed profits; 50 for undistributed profits.
Greece	18 (Dr 390 000)	50 (> Dr 1 689 000)	35
Iceland	39.8 [32.8]	39.8 [32.8]	45
Ireland	27 (< Ir£ 14 590)	48 (> Ir£ 14 590)	40
Italy	10 (< L 6 800 000)	50 (> L 337 700 000)	52 [36]
Japan	15 [10]	66 [50]	57 [38]
Luxemburg	10	10	42 [33]
Netherlands	13 (Gld 42 966)	60 (> Gld 85 930)	35, but 40% on the first Gld 250 000
New Zealand	24 (< NZ$ 30 875)	33 (> NZ$ 30 875)	33, but 38% on non-resident companies
Norway	38.7	51.7 [23.7] (> NKr 233 000)	28 [0]
Portugal	15 (< Esc 810 000)	40 (> Esc 4 860 000)	39.6 [36]
Spain	20 (Ptas 600 000)	56 (> Ptas 9 550 000)	35
Sweden	31 [0]	51 [20]	30
Switzerland	6 [1] (> SF 18 000)	44 [13] (> SF 595 200)	13-39 [4-10]
Turkey	25 (< TL 12 million)	50 (> TL 192 million)	46
United Kingdom	20 (< £ 2 000)	40 (> £ 23 700)	Reduced rate: 25% for profits below £ 250 000
United States	17 [15] (< US$ 35 800)	36 [31] (US$ 86 500)	38 [34] Reduced rates (central government): 15% US$ 0-50 000; 25%: US$ 50 000-75 000

Note: The rates in [ ] are the rates for the central government only.
Source: OECD, 1994c.

reform has addressed the differences in tax rates and introduced a universal corporate tax rate of 30 per cent which applies equally to incorporated and non-incorporated enterprises. However, this more equal treatment of small and large enterprises has come at the cost of a considerably more complex tax code. Perhaps the discrimination perceived by smaller firms would be better addressed through lower rates.

Administrative and compliance costs

Although the tax burden remains a concern, attention has turned to the costs for the government of managing the tax system (administrative costs) and for firms and individuals of complying with tax laws (compliance costs). For example, a recent study in Australia found that more than 70 per cent of all enterprises considered the frequency and complexity of changes to federal tax rules as a major concern (Bickerdyke & Lattimore, 1997). Costs of compliance may take the form of monetary costs (payment to tax advisors or the wages of employees engaged in tax work) and time costs (the time spent in dealing with tax matters). Complex tax systems also open the door to tax avoidance which can further distort economic activity. In some countries such as Spain, it is agreed that compliance is not an issue considered important by firms because enforcement is weak (OECD, 1998c).

Estimates of administrative and compliance costs involve difficult problems of measurement. Differences across countries must, therefore, be interpreted with caution, yet available evidence suggests they can be quite significant. Administrative costs generally refer to budget outlays for the *Internal Revenue Service* or *Tax Department* and cover all taxes levied. Estimates suggest administrative costs amount to 1.5 per cent of GNP for the UK (Sandford, 1989); 2.5-3.0 per cent for Germany; 1.8 per cent for Norway; and 1 per cent for Sweden (Malmer *et al.*, 1994). Compliance costs, accounting of the time and resources spent in complying with major taxes (personal and corporate income tax, social security constitutions, value-added tax, etc.), tend to be as high as administrative costs: 2.5 per cent of GNP for New Zealand[2] and 1.5 per cent for the Netherlands (Allers, 1994).

Furthermore, evidence suggests that compliance burdens are regressive. Research by the US SBA (*Small Business Administration*) has concluded that, in 1992, the average annual cost of regulation, paperwork and tax compliance amounted to US$5 000 per employee in firms with fewer than 500 employees and US$3 400 per employee in larger firms.[3] On the other hand, it was found that firms, when surveyed, agreed that they would have had to collect much of the required information for other purposes or found the information useful (GAO, 1996). However, all agreed that the tax system's ambiguity, frequent changes, expiration clauses and layers of federal and state regulation remain the main sources of the high compliance burden on businesses. By breaking down aggregate compliance costs by number of employees in Dutch firms, Allers (1994) shows that while the mean cost per firms increases with the size of firm, the cost per employee decreases sharply with the number of employees. When the owner/manager is included in the number of employees the compliance cost per head for small firms is nearly 20 times higher than for big businesses (see Table 3.5). The estimates which include all taxes confirm results from other studies (e.g., Sandford, 1989).

A number of countries have introduced policies to address tax complexity. The UK government has acknowledged that the "language of tax" is itself a hurdle and has therefore decided to rewrite tax legislation in simple, understandable language. Similar projects have begun in Australia and New Zealand. Also in Australia, the burden of complying with *fringe benefit taxation* (FBT) has been eased, *i.e.*, by abolishing the demand for record-keeping by companies with small FBT liabilities. More significantly, by mid-1998 the government intends to establish a single registration process for the *Taxation Office, Securities Commission, Bureau of Statistics* and the *Insurance and Superannuation Commission* whereby duplication of reporting can be reduced (OECD, 1998a).

Noting the regressiveness of compliance costs governments have been looking for ways of relieving the burden on smaller firms. This has led to relief from the requirement to register, to reductions of tax liability (special concessions) and to modified administrative requirements. Among the relief in the last category are options to furnish returns less frequently, to account for tax on a cash basis and the possibility to calculate tax liability on a provisional or estimated basis or on the basis of a proxy (e.g., predetermined percentage applied to purchases and/or

Table 3.5.   **Average compliance costs of income tax on the self-employed**

(Netherlands, 1990, Gld 1 000)

Number of employees	Number of firms in sample	Mean cost per firm	Mean cost per employee	Mean cost per head
0-4	174	9	7.1	4.3
5-9	107	15	2.3	2.1
10-19	141	19	1.3	1.3
20-49	220	36	1.1	1.1
50-99	161	56	0.8	0.8
100-499	179	80	0.4	0.4
500+	71	320	0.2	0.2
Total	1 053	–	–	–

Source: Allers, 1994, Table 5.14.

sales) (OECD, 1994c). Countries are also increasingly using information technology as a means of reducing the compliance burden. Electronic filing is now possible in a number of countries such as Canada, the Netherlands and the United States. For example, the Dutch Ministry of Finance estimates that approximately 5 per cent of taxpayers are choosing to file their returns on diskettes provided by the Revenue Service. The Australian Tax Office is also introducing similar technology. Again in the Netherlands reducing the costs of compliance with taxation and regulation has become a major focus of attention and is part of the programme *"Towards Lower Administrative Costs"* (OECD, 1998d).

One of the fundamental sources of tax complexity is the use of tax subsidies and tax relief to achieve a wide array of economic or social objectives. Tax measures are attractive tools because they can be implemented through an existing administrative system and there is, therefore, no need to establish a new, costly system of providing benefits or services. These measures include tax credits to promote employee training, tax credits for R&D, special provisions to small corporations to help them access financing exemptions for the self-employed and special tax provision to create enterprise zones. However, the problem with tax incentives is the complexity they introduce into the tax system. Tax subsidies require definitions of the eligible activities, accountability requirements and other administrative procedures – and these generate administrative expenses for government and compliance costs for business. Therefore, there may be a trade-off between using the tax system to correct market failures and favour particular social goals, on the one hand, and the objective of reducing compliance costs, on the other. In order to better account for the costs and benefits of tax measures, many governments have developed measures of tax expenditure whereby the cost of subsidies operated through the tax system is addressed. A recent OECD study examines tax expenditure measures in 14 countries (OECD, 1996b).

Late payment

Late payment is a problem which particularly concerns small-scale firms, both because of their vulnerability to cash-flow constraints and because of their frequently weak bargaining position with respect to purchasers. Survey work shows that 40 per cent of European businesses believe their growth to be stifled by late payments. Twenty-eight per cent believe they could increase exports if paid more rapidly and 33 per cent hold that late payment threatens their survival (1996 *European Payment Habits Survey*, cited by Jan-Erik Paulden in a public hearing on late payments organised in Brussels by *Directorate-General XXIII of the European Commission* on 7 October 1997). The problem is not restricted to the private sector. Delays in payment for publicly procured goods are common in many countries, with some, such as the Republic of Ireland, having introduced legislation on prompt public sector payment of commercial debts. A number of governments have introduced legislation on late payments in the private sector, and the European Commission has also issued guidelines. Legislation can offer such measures as statutory rights of interest on late payment and the right to sue late paying firms (as proposed recently by the UK Minister for Small Firms). Nevertheless, obstacles are present in the implementation of legislation. For example, many small firms cannot afford to sue negligent purchasers and, indeed, agreeing not to sue can become a source of competitive advantage (as these firms may be favoured with future contracts).

Intellectual property rights

The absence of protection of intellectual property rights (IPR) can be a serious barrier to entrepreneurship. Despite the potential benefits offered by research and the development of new products and services, firms are reluctant to invest in R&D because the results of such spending – technological discoveries, new products, techniques – can fall easily into the hands of rivals due to the difficulty associated with attaching ownership rights to these results. Arrow (1962) argued that because R&D results in information which is "non-appropriable", the amount of R&D which the market will produce will fall short of what is socially optimal. Empirical studies have confirmed that the social returns from R&D are higher than private returns (see OECD, 1992b for a review of the evidence). For a more general and comprehensive review of innovation see OECD (1996h).

Governments attempt to increase innovation by creating systems to protect intellectual property. Intellectual property policy is intended to set an equilibrium between two objectives: first, rewarding or compensating creators and inventors for innovation; and second, promoting the interests of business and the public at large in securing access to science, technology and culture. This implies granting innovators the rights that are necessary to recoup their investment without stifling competition for an unduly long period of time. For example,[4] patent systems promote the creation of new technology by providing a limited monopoly to inventors. Patentees receive the exclusive right during a certain period of time (usually 20 years) to use the new technology in the territory covered by the agency that delivers the patent.

Intellectual property rights differ across countries. With regard to patent systems, while most countries give the priority to the so-called "first-to-file", in some others, notably the United States, the system favours the "first-to-invent", regardless of the application sequence. Although the first-to-invent rule may seem more equitable since patents are supposed to reward innovation, the US system has proven to be litigation prone because, in the case of a conflict, applicants are forced to engage in conflict proceedings to prove which of the applicants was first to invent. In addition, there appears to be a wide divergence in the costs of obtaining and maintaining patents. It is estimated that the cost of obtaining European patent protection (in France, Germany and the United Kingdom) is three times higher than the cost of obtaining the same patent in Japan and the United States (see Table 3.6). It could be as much as five times higher if full territorial European coverage is sought for the patent. However, the enforcement costs of intellectual property rights through litigation are considered extremely high in the United States as compared to Europe. An IRDAC (*Industrial R&D Advisory Committee of the European Commission*) (1996) report recommends some levelling of these costs through reducing enforcement costs in the United States while lowering the costs of patenting in Europe.

The patent system was originally developed for individual independent inventors. Today's inventions are almost always generated within specific institutional environments – firms, university departments and institutes, hospitals, government research establishments, etc. The system has had to adjust to this situation. Patent laws generally regulate: who owns an invention made by an employee and thus who receives the patent rights, and whether or not employees should receive a reward over and above their normal salary for making a successful invention for their employer. Under UK law, for example, inventions made in the course of employment belong to the employer. In contrast, under German law, they belong to the employee and, if necessary, have to be claimed by and transferred to the employer (OECD, 1997a).

An area where the government may positively influence entrepreneurship is in the allocation of patent rights derived from the government funding of R&D. Generally, governments contract to obtain all rights to any invention made by publicly funded R&D. However, since 1980, US federal law allows beneficiaries (universities and businesses) to elect to retain title to inventions produced under such conditions, in order to encourage exploitation. Even if the private body

Table 3.6. **Comparative costs of patent applications**

(in DM)

	European patent	US patent	Japanese patent
Patent office fees	8 250	3 304	2 000
Representation expenses	25 771	9 000	12 859
Total	34 221	12 304	14 859

Source: IRDAC, 1996.

obtains the patent, the government retains several rights. These rights include a license to use the invention and, if the private body is not diligently proceeding to commercialise the invention, the government can force the private body to license the patent. In Japan, where the government held all patent rights arising from sponsored research, the situation changed in 1994 – with private companies allowed to retain at least 50 per cent of the rights.

Notes

1. METRs have a number of short-comings. First, the marginal investor is very difficult to identify in practice and, second, the outcomes are highly sensitive to the assumptions upon which METRs are based. Finally, METRs do not take into account the behavioural responses of taxpayers (*i.e.*, tax planning).

2. Reported by the New Zealand Delegate to the *Consumption Tax Group* at its meeting on 9-10 July 1996.

3. These figures are estimates for 1992 based on many assumptions, including those about the business share of total regulatory costs, the industry sector shares of the business costs and employee wages. These assumptions were needed in the absence of hard information and the resulting estimates are subject to considerable uncertainty.

4. There are also other kinds of property rights. In addition to patents, there are copyrights which relate to literary or artistic work and also extend to engineering drawings, computer software. Design rights relate to shapes and configurations. Trademarks relate to words or symbols applied to products or services to identify source or sponsorship. Plant varieties protection provide rights to plant varieties based on the model of the *International Union for the Protection of New Varieties of Plant*. Trade secret protection protects confidential information and does not require registration or formalities.

Chapter IV

Solving Problems of Financing

The financing gap

Whether to create a new business or to expand an existing one, entrepreneurs need financial resources to stay competitive, to introduce new technologies and to grow. One of the major difficulties they face is access to capital. Most small firms are financed by family, friends, personal savings or banks. Theory suggests that a debt financing gap, or credit rationing, may exist if banks do not have sufficient information about potential borrowers (Stiglitz & Weiss, 1981). On this view, banks choose to ration credit because raising interest rates results in an "adverse selection" towards risky borrowers, which reduces expected profits. Thus, potential borrowers can be refused loans even if they are prepared to pay interest rates in proportion to risk. Credit rationing may be particularly severe for new, small or innovative firms because statistically they are more likely to fail than larger, stable firms and as a result are perceived to be riskier. Banks often reduce their risk exposure by demanding collateral, but small and young firms are less likely to have collateral to offer as security. Therefore, collateral-based lending may cause many promising projects to be abandoned for lack of financing. While rates paid by different borrowers vary, they are not widely dispersed. However, since it is not known what the appropriate interest rate dispersion should be, it is not certain that a narrow range of interest rates reflects a financial market imperfection.

Closing the debt financing gap and increasing the availability of financing for new and small firms is an issue at the top of policy agendas throughout OECD countries. For example, in Spain, 43 per cent of firms cited the cost of financing as a main short-term constraint on expansion while 32 per cent cited it as a long-term constraint. Moreover, among SMEs, only 47 per cent felt that they had sufficient access to finance to be able to carry out their plans over the next 3 years. Yet, when surveyed, small businesses in other countries do not view the availability of debt financing as a problem. In the United Kingdom, the *Department of Trade* organised several regional conferences to learn more about the issues which affect small businesses. One of the most striking features of the conference was the relatively low level of concern expressed about the cost and availability of financing (DTI, 1996).[1] Similarly, the *National Federation of Independent Business* in the United States noted that the most surprising result in its survey of the problems of greatest concern facing its members was the relatively low importance given to the problems caused by obtaining loans: obtaining long-term and short-term loans ranked 63rd and 64th respectively in 1996 (Dennis, 1996a). Nor did other surveys of entrepreneurs in Sweden and Australia highlight a problem of obtaining debt financing (OECD, 1998 b and 1998c). Also in the Netherlands a recent survey showed that only 18 per cent of respondents cited either the cost or the availability of financing as a main long-term constraint (OECD, 1998d).

The results of these surveys may reflect inaccurately the situation of many enterprises. Most firms are small, family-owned enterprises which do not plan to grow and do not seek to raise debt financing. However, the smaller, and more dynamic subset of new and high growth firms may have pressing financial needs which have not been met by the banking community (and may be better addressed through equity financing). The surveys may also be inaccurate because potential or previously existing enterprises which have not been created or which have failed are unlikely to be included in the sample. Some governments are concerned that there may be a problem for new and innovative firms which cannot raise collateral. Indeed, in high-tech ventures much of the value of a firm may be tied up in the knowledge and talent of the entrepreneurs and staff. Indeed, the frequent requirement for owner/manager/entrepreneur to provide personal guarantees to banks in order to support the financing of their firms can be a significant disincentive. Many OECD governments have therefore taken measures to bridge the perceived debt financing gap which faces smaller businesses. For example, loan guarantee programmes have often been introduced to assist small firms obtain debt financing (See Box 4.1).

Government loan guarantee schemes can be viewed as attempting to overcome the disadvantages faced by apparently more risky projects by transferring some, though typically not all, of the risk to the public sector. Public-sector costs are usually contained by having banks themselves administer the loans. In most programmes of this type, the subsidy component is not through the interest rate, which is usually some conventional market rate plus a small premium, but rather through the costs that the government incurs in the event of a default. The success of such a programme depends on holding down the number of defaults while, at the same time, providing loans that firms would not be able to obtain in the commercial market.

The evidence gathered for the programmes described in Box 4.1 suggests that the impact has been limited by two factors. First, in many cases assistance has been given to firms which already had access to conventional sources of debt

---

Box 4.1. **Loan guarantee schemes in Canada, United Kingdom and France**

In Canada, the *Small Business Loan Act* (SBLA) provides lenders with a government guarantee, currently at 85 per cent, against losses on loans. The loans are provided by private sector lenders (*e.g.*, banks, credit unions, insurance and loan corporations) and virtually all small businesses are eligible to borrow under the programme provided their annual revenue does not exceed C$ 5 million. Programme results in 1994 show that about 40 per cent of loans are made to very young businesses, 3 years old or less, and that the overall lending approaches C$ 3.5 billion. In 1993, the SBLA made about 13 000 loans. The default rate has averaged 5 to 7 per cent of loans made since 1961 yet about 30-40 per cent of SBLA loans would have been made without the programme (Riding, 1996).

In the United Kingdom, the *Loan Guarantee Scheme* (LGS) gives the bank a guarantee for 70 per cent (85 per cent in disadvantaged areas) of the principal. In general, eligible firms are those with less than 200 employees although, depending on the type of business, factors such as turnover, numbers of outlets and vehicles are taken into account in establishing what is a small firm. In 1987, a total of 1 270 loans were made. During the first two years of the scheme (1981 and 1982) almost 40 per cent of the firms had defaulted. After the introduction of programme reforms to encourage greater selectivity by the banks the default rates fell to about 15 per cent (Barret *et al.*, 1990).

In France, a financial institution (*Société Française de Garantie de financements des Petites et Moyennes Entreprises* – SOFARIS) with 12 regional offices was created in 1982 to manage several loan guarantee programmes. SOFARIS generally guarantees up to 50 per cent of the loan. If the loan is financing an enterprise start-up, the guarantee increases to 70 per cent and if the loan is used to implement an R&D project, the guarantee increases to 60 per cent.

---

finance, or the programmes have been used by banks to reduce risk on loans they would have made in any case. Only 60 per cent of borrowers in the Canadian SBLA programme reported that they would not have obtained a bank loan without the programme (Riding, 1996). This finding was confirmed by lenders, who reported that almost 50 per cent of SBLA loans would have been granted in the absence of the programme. Similarly, in the United Kingdom, Barret *et al.* (1990) showed that over half of the financing would have been raised from other sources in the absence of the programme.

Second, there is evidence that some small firms which received the loan guarantees displaced existing enterprises by forcing them to down-size or even to close. In the United Kingdom, Barret *et al.* found that 30 per cent of new jobs created by the firms receiving the LGS loan represented employment displaced from other businesses. Since the displacement was low for firms that supplied a new product or service and was also much lower in manufacturing than in retailing or services, reforms were introduced to exclude firms involved in activities causing high displacement, such as in retailing, catering and motor vehicle mainte-

Table 4.1.   **Financing methods for European SMEs**
Per cent

	Overdraft	Leasing/HP	Factoring[1]	Equity held by		Loans
				Institutions	Individuals	
Austria	37	32	4	1	1	70
Belgium	50	23	3	8	11	58
Denmark	72	19	5	5	7	33
France	42	33	21	7	4	55
Germany	55	49	2	1	0	66
Greece	40	23	6	3	5	67
Ireland	78	45	7	7	5	43
Italy	86	29	24	6	4	28
Luxemburg	36	18	6	12	6	40
Netherlands	81	29	2	6	17	49
Portugal	20	3	0	14	14	45
Spain	11	42	8	8	5	52
Sweden	9	26	2	2	3	63
UK	71	47	6	9	6	45
Average	54	35	10	5	5	49

1.   Factoring: the sale of accounts receivable for immediate cash.
Source: Grant Thornton, 1996.

nance. However, it should be noted that one of the subsidiary benefits of loan guarantee schemes can be the training it provides bankers in assessing risk (rather than lending on the basis of standardised formulae).

Finally, it should be noted that although the loan guarantee schemes described in Box 4.1 are well established, the numbers of loans made have been modest compared with bank loans to small businesses more generally. This could suggest that the private-sector financing of small firms is working efficiently after all. Dennis (1996a) points to greater competition in the United States which has made it easier to obtain loans. Commercial banks, the traditional suppliers of the bulk of loan funds, have been challenged by finance, leasing and credit card companies. European firms also have access to a wide range of debt financing tools (see Table 4.1).

Equity financing

Equity financing is also an important source of funds and is available through both public and private equity markets. Public equity markets (*i.e.*, registered stock exchanges) are established institutions in most OECD countries. It is relatively costly to issue equity on these markets because of rigorous reporting requirements and as a result it is only viable for large companies seeking to raise sums on the order of several million dollars. For example, a NASDAQ (*National Association of Securities Dealers Automated Quotation System*) stock offering of US$25 million would cost over US$2 million in fees. NASDAQ has recently launched the SmallCap market targeted at small firms with offering values of US$1 million which require fees of approximately US$10 000 (NASD, 1996, 1995). Similarly, the cost of equity financing in Australia is out of line with the capital needed for expansion in most smaller enterprises (OECD, 1998a).[2]

Alternatively, private equity markets, where unlisted equities are traded between firms and institutional or individual investors, are increasingly becoming significant sources of financing in several OECD countries. Private equity includes non-venture and venture investments made by professional equity managers.[3] Non-venture investments are those made in companies which are stable, profitable businesses. By contrast, venture capital is issued by young firms, typically those developing innovative technologies, and is considered highly risky (see Table 4.2).

Private equity financing is particularly important in the United Kingdom and the United States.[4] Why have private equity markets proven to be more dynamic in some countries than others? Many point to strong "equity cultures" in the United States and the United Kingdom to explain their success. However, a recent study demonstrates that the dynamic US private equity market is a classic example of how organisational innovation aided by regulatory and tax changes can expand a particular market (See Box 4.2). In particular, the government's role in modifying pension regulations and capital gains taxes is thought to have ignited growth in private equity markets.

Table 4.2.   **Geographical distribution of venture capital: international comparison**

US$ million

	Amount raised	Number of deals
United States, total	**10 023.4**	**1 502**
United Kingdom	3 775.7	1 715
France	1 078.2	1 186
Germany	908.1	769
Netherlands	753.1	320
Italy	647.7	198
Sweden	533.4	172
Spain	245.1	158
Switzerland	161.3	32
Belgium	138.4	158
Europe, total	**8 575.0**	**5 181[1]**

1.   This includes LBOs while the US statistics do not.
Source: Venture One, 1997 and European Venture Capital Association, 1997.

Box 4.2.   **Development of the private equity market in the United States**

The early stages: 1946 *to* 1969. Organised and professionally managed investments in private equity can be dated to 1946 and the formation of the *American Research and Development* (ARD) *Corporation,* a publicly traded investment company. Although the company was regarded as a modest success (*i.e.,* raised US$ 7.4 million in its first thirteen years) there was no effort to imitate it. Some private venture capital companies were formed during the period to manage the venture capital investments of wealthy families. In response to public concern that private equity capital was in short supply, Congress took steps to promote venture capital investments by individuals through the creation of *Small Business Investment Companies* (SBICs). Despite channelling record amounts of equity financing to small, fast-growing companies (*i.e.,* 692 SBICs managed US$ 350 million), the programme had a spotty record and in 1966 it was greatly reduced.

Seeds for future growth: the 1970s and the Limited Partnership. Private equity professionals saw an opportunity to improve upon existing arrangements through the formation of venture capital limited partnerships. Limited partnerships were attractive to many private equity professionals as a way of addressing the problem of compensation. Under the Investment *Company Act of* 1940, managers of publicly traded venture capital firms could not receive stock options or other forms of performance-based compensation. Also, limited partnerships were attractive as a way of avoiding SBIC-type investment restrictions and attracting investors more sophisticated than the retail shareholders of publicly traded SBICs. Between 1969 and 1975, approximately 29 limited partnerships were formed raising a total of US$ 376 million.

By 1977, public concern had focused once again on the shortage of capital available to finance new ventures. A significant reform which was introduced pertains to the "prudent man" provision of *Employee Retirement Income Security Act* (ERISA). Pension fund managers had long regarded venture capital investments as a potential violation of their fiduciary responsibilities. Between 1976 and 1978, venture capital partnerships raised less than US$ 5 million a year from ERISA pension plans. In 1978, it was ruled that investments in securities issued by small or new companies and venture capital funds were permitted, provided they do not endanger an entire portfolio. In the first 6 months of 1979, they raised US$ 50 million from such plans. Significant reforms also took place on the tax side. The *Capital Gains tax* (CGT) was cut from 49.5 per cent to 28 per cent in 1978.

Explosive Growth: the 1980s and 1990s. The evolution of the limited partnership in combination with the favourable regulatory and tax changes spurred the flow of capital to the private equity market. Commitments to private equity partnerships during 1980-82 totalled more than US$ 3.5 billion, two and one-half times the commitments to private equity during the entire decade of the 1970s. Over the next three years, commitments surged to more than US$ 4 billion annually. Since 1988, commitments have followed a cyclical pattern, reaching a low of US$ 6.4 billion in 1990 and a high of US$ 19.4 billion in 1994.

Source: Fenn *et al.,* 1995.

An important factor in the development of venture capital in the United States was the emergence of institutional investors as the primary source of funds, particularly pension funds, insurance companies and banks. In the

United States and other countries, including the United Kingdom, Ireland, Japan and Denmark, the revision of rules governing investment by pension funds allowed them to undertake higher-risk investment, including venture capital operations. As a result, pensions have become the largest single source of venture capital funding in these countries, with a third or more of the total. Judging from the US experience, the level of the capital gains tax rate is also an important determinant of investment flows to the private equity market. Although a large percentage of private equity capital provided by pension funds is tax-exempt, the funds provided by other investors (venture capitalists, private investors, entrepreneurs) are not.

The quantitative importance of the venture capital industry as a source of risk capital should be kept in view. In most countries, formal venture capital companies supply only a small proportion of all new funds raised by firms. For instance, in the UK – the European country in which venture capital is most highly developed – the venture capital industry supplied only some 2.9 per cent of new funds raised by small firms between 1987 and 1990 (and of course a much smaller share of new funds raised by all firms). Indeed, there are understandable reasons why many entrepreneurs do not wish to seek venture capital. They may fear a loss of control of their businesses and may be reluctant to share the benefits of attractive projects. Few ventures will grow at the rates required by venture capitalists and, the intensive monitoring of venture capital investments constitutes a high fixed cost. This raises the size of deal required by venture capitalists, frequently excluding many smaller projects. The qualitative importance of the industry may be greater however, given the advice it affords and the examples provided of entrepreneurial success. Efforts to expand the industry by augmenting venture capital funds have often failed on account of a shortage of competent venture capitalists. The lack of viable projects is also a frequent complaint of the venture capital industry.

An important outstanding policy issue is whether there is an equity financing gap, analogous to the debt financing gap.[5] Perhaps in response to perceptions that smaller firms and particular types of investments have difficulty attracting adequate equity financing, governments have, with varying degrees of success, provided direct assistance to equity in the form of tax subsidies and financial assistance (see Box 4.3). Ireland provides an interesting example of "moral-suasion" to benefit the venture capital market. The Irish government had initially considered passing legislation requiring pension funds to invest a percentage of their assets in venture capital. However, it was decided instead to issue a guideline suggesting that pension funds could invest additional funds in venture capital in order to bring their total assets invested in venture capital to 2 per cent by 1999. This effort has been credited with increasing venture capital funding in 1994 (OECD, 1996c).

Box 4.3.   **Government programmes to stimulate venture capital in the United States**

In the United States, *Small Business Investment Companies* (SBICs) are SBA-licensed venture capital firms which account for 10 to 15 per cent of venture capital investment. SBICs are allowed to match their investments with SBA loans and enjoy certain tax benefits. In exchange they are subject to certain limits on the size of the companies in which they invest, as well as on taking controlling interests. SBICs managed to channel record amounts of equity financing to small, fast-growing companies back in the 1960s, but also suffered from poor quality of managers. Tighter supervision followed the shocking revelation in June 1966 by the deputy administrator of the SBA that 232 of the nation's 700 SBICs were problem companies because of dubious practices and self-dealing and that the SBA was likely to lose US$ 18 million as a result. By 1977 the number of SBICs declined to 276 (Fenn *et al.*, 1995). Their presence remains important in those states where there is a significant potential for promising new firms but availability of venture capital is low. SBICs therefore play a complementary role to venture capital partnerships.

The UK government has recently introduced *Venture Capital Trusts* (VCTs) which are a type of quoted investment vehicle similar to investment trusts, the shares of which are listed on the London Stock Exchange. VCTs are to invest in unquoted companies with gross assets of less than £ 10 million. Investors in VCTs receive several tax incentives: tax relief at 20 per cent on the money invested and any dividends or capital gains are free of tax. The intention to launch VCTs has been announced by several firms, but thus far the overall level of interest in the programme has fallen short of the government's goals.

Labour-sponsored investment funds (LSIFs) have been created in Canada to raise funds from individual investors of whom 50 per cent are union members. The objective is to obtain equity positions in targeted businesses in order to stimulate the economic development of the regions in which the funds are located and create and maintain jobs locally. The Canadian government (in Quebec, the provincial government) allows tax credits of 20 per cent of the individual's investment up to a maximum investment of C$ 5 000. Three studies have evaluated the performance of Quebec's LSIF. Suret (1994) criticises the *Fonds de Solidarité* of the *Fédération des Travailleurs du Québec* (FTQ) because it under-invested in regional firms and, in the absence of the fund, individual investors, private investment companies and banks could provide adequate venture capital if the FTQ did not exist. In addition, the bulk of the portfolio was invested in government bonds, publicly traded stocks and the money market. Another report was more positive (Lamond *et al.*, 1994) and acknowledged increased investment in the region's businesses.

The importance of exit mechanisms to the provision of private equity financing

An important and sometimes overlooked issue in the viability of private equity markets is the provision of efficient "exit mechanisms" – the method by which investors and entrepreneurs (or a company's management) "cash in" their investments. Exit routes include private sale, share repurchase by the company or issuing stock via a public offering. A public offering generally results in the highest valuation of a company and is thus often the preferred exit route. Indeed, one of the most important determinants of returns on venture capital investments is the market valuation of the company's first sale of stock, known as an *initial public offering* (IPO). In addition to their direct role as exit vehicles, IPOs serve as benchmarks for pricing other types of exit. IPOs, therefore, play an important role in the functioning of all venture capital exits.

A private sale is also a welcome exit mechanism for investors as it provides payment in cash or marketable securities. Entrepreneurs, however, may not view a private sale as positively because the company may be merged with or acquired by a larger company and thus lose its independence. The third exit route, buy-backs, is used primarily when the investment has been unsuccessful.

The use of various exit vehicles differs across OECD economies. In the United States and Canada, public offerings are the most common exit vehicle, whereas in Europe private sales and buy-backs predominate. IPOs of venture-backed companies in the United States were US$11.8 billion in 1996, more than ten times the amount in Europe (Venture One, 1997; EVCA, 1997). Differences are also apparent in the duration of the process from start-up to the initial public offering on the stock market or acquisition by another company. While it is difficult to measure accurately, market sources indicate that the average time is 5 years in the United States, significantly longer in Europe and about 17 years in Japan. Indeed, a number of participants in the European venture capital market see the limited possibility to exit through sales on stock markets to be a critical hindrance to the full development of the European private equity capital industry (OECD, 1996c and 1996g).

The use of IPOs as an exit route in North America has been facilitated by the NASDAQ, the best known of the second-tier markets, which was created in 1971 as a nation-wide market for trades in young, innovative companies. Second-tier markets provide easier access to public securities markets through less stringent admission requirements and lower continuing costs than those for first-tier markets. The success of NASDAQ has been substantial, and it serves as a benchmark for all other second-tier markets. In 1994, there were a total of 4 902 companies quoted, compared with 2 570 on the first-tier *New York Stock Exchange* (NYSE). Many companies which could be listed on the NYSE, such as Microsoft, Intel, MCI and Apple Computer, have chosen to remain on NASDAQ rather than move to a first-tier market. Japan also has a second-tier market, JASDAQ (*Japan Association of Securities Dealers Automated Quotation system*), which, after a modest beginning, had a major relaunch in 1984. This market is similar to NASDAQ in that it is an alternative market operated under separate management from the main stock exchange.

Second-tier markets were set up in European countries in the 1980s, yet have performed relatively poorly. They have attracted few companies and few inves-

Table 4.3. **Number of companies, admissions and liquidity in second-tier markets, 1992**

	Number of companies	New companies admitted	Liquidity[1]
USA (NASDAQ)	3 850	432	138.2
Japan (JASDAQ)[2]	477	55	25.5
Eur12 Total	1 104	31	21.1

1. Liquidity is defined as the turnover/capitalisation ratio.
2. Japan figures are for 1993.
Source: Bannock, G. & Partners Ltd., 1994, p. 105-106.

tors, and therefore suffer from low liquidity (see Table 4.3). This may be due to the fragmented nature of European markets, which reflect differences in the currency, language, accounting standards, regulatory rules and taxation of the country in which each is located. Bannock (1994) pointed to two other related issues. First, none of the second-tier markets in Europe is alternative in the sense of being under separate management from the first-tier market. This leads to the second-tier market being seen as inferior to the main market, with companies moving up to the first-tier as soon as possible, which undermines the second-tier markets. Second, institutional investors are less important in Europe (with the exception of the United Kingdom).

In recent years, various ideas have been floated regarding the possible creation of a pan-European stock market which would be separate from the first-tier markets. The *European Association of Securities Dealers* (EASD) has negotiated with institutional and government bodies the creation of EASDAQ which became operational in September 1996. Meanwhile, other second-tier markets such as the UK's AIM, France's *Second Marché*, Germany's *Neuer Market* and Italy's METIM have also started up.

Seed financing

Most start-ups obtain their finance through informal sources of capital.[6] In particular external formal equity financing is used by only a small proportion of new entrepreneurs. This is the case in the United States, but even more so in Europe.[7] Most seed funds, which are used to start businesses, come from the personal savings of the entrepreneur, or those of family and friends. An important policy issue is therefore to understand how this informal resource allocation functions and how government action influences it. This is particularly important in that a number of governments have sought to add to these main funding sources.

Assets per household vary between different OECD countries. There is certainly no clear cut correlation between these household assets and the ability of would-be entrepreneurs to finance their new venture. Yet there is anecdotal evidence that in some countries such as Sweden the limited capacity of households to accumulate capital due to solidarity-based wage policies and high social contributions and income taxes has been an obstacle for entrepreneurship development. Beyond the value of household assets available, the form in which these

---

Box 4.4. **Micro-credit in the United States**

Amounts less than about US$ 10 000 cannot be raised with commercial banks as the transaction costs are too high to make for commercially viable lending. So-called microenterprise loan funds have stepped into this niche. These loan funds are unregulated, typically non-profit organisations that provide credit and management assistance to the owners of microenterprises (most commonly defined as enterprises with up to 5 employees). Microenterprise loan funds were introduced to the US as an enterprise development approach in the mid-1980s. It is estimated that there are more than 100 such funds operating at present (Shorebank Advisory Services, 1992). Micro-enterprise development is an approach which often targets women, minorities, low-income individuals, displaced wage-earners, and the under- or unemployed. To this end this approach focuses very much on creating local entrepreneurial capacity to foster indigenous economic growth and job creation within communities. The American models have been strongly influenced by experiences in less-developed countries. These experiences include the *Grameen Bank* in Bangladesh, *Bank Rakyat* in Indonesia or US *Accion International* and FINCA throughout Latin America.

Credit-Funds in North-America address market niches similar to those addressed by such schemes in developing countries. The principal bottleneck for entrepreneurs is access to credit rather than the high interest rate charged (OECD, 1996d). In addition to financial resources micro loan funds provide information and knowledge as part of their services. Also important is the network of peers and local contacts which come as part of a successful micro-credit scheme. Moreover successful micro-credit schemes appear to target certain kinds of entrepreneurs, as for example the *Women's Initiatives for self-employment* (WISE) in San Francisco or the *East Side Community Investments* in Indianapolis which has focused on local day care providers (East Side Community Investments, 1990).

It is difficult to get an accurate quantitative picture of the impact of micro-credit funds on job creation or other local development goals. Micro-credit programmes stress a number of qualitative, long-term gains rather than easily measurable short-term objectives such as business creation. Improved evaluation of such programmes and the dissemination of best practices is therefore still a critical challenge for policy-makers.

---

assets are held – whether in real estate, liquid financial assets, in pension funds, etc. – will influence the capacity to finance a start up from own savings.

Moreover finance through the wider network of family and friends is crucial. Some governments, such as that of the Netherlands, have tried to promote this informal capital market through schemes for tax exemption. Informal financing networks also point to the importance of social capital. If there are strong relationships of trust between people in a community the transaction costs of capital allocation can be reduced, allowing for more entrepreneurial projects to obtain informal finance for example from local business angels at lower cost. Local institutions such as chambers of commerce, business associations and networks of entrepreneurs have an important role to play in this connection (Kaufmann & Kokalji, 1996).

Another option for policy makers is a more direct intervention in the supply of seed capital. For example in Germany capital is made available for start-ups within the framework of the *Eigenkapitalhilfe-programme* (EKH). The resources in this scheme are allocated via commercial banks. Such a system allows a relatively cost-efficient coverage of a wide range of enterprises but owing to risk aversion on the part of banks entails a tendency to fund largely low risk projects. This illustrates the kind of complicated trade-off between for example the cost efficiency of the chosen distribution mechanisms and the extent to which public resources will be eventually channelled to the most entrepreneurial and job generating projects. Other examples of micro-credit are provided in Box 4.4.

There is one important overall lesson for policy makers. Though the market for venture capital and secondary equity markets have a significant role, most start-up finance is informal. This facet of entrepreneurship finance is often overlooked as it is unspectacular and the policy conclusions are not easy to grasp. Yet it is here where the least effort has been made and where additional policy consideration could yield valuable results. For example, as described in Chapter 6, policy makers could examine means of increasing the supply of investment related information to informal investors at the local level.

Notes

1. Large scale national surveys of small and medium sized firms in the United Kingdom, on the other and, have found that external finance is widely seen as an important constraint by business managers, although its importance appears to vary with the business cycle and interest rates. Whilst a 1991 survey found that the cost and availability of finance were the most important of a wide range of factors constraining growth (SBRC, 1992), they were attributed less importance in 1995 at a time when interest rates were falling and demand constraints had increased (Cosh and Hughes, 1996).

2. The cost of public listing is A$ 250 000 to A$ 500 000 whereas firms on average are looking for A$ 500 000.

3. Private equity investments are also made by angel investors – wealthy individuals – and by institutional investors. By some estimates, the angel capital and informal private equity markets are several times larger than the private equity investments of professional equity managers.

4. The formal venture capital market seems to be quite developed also in the Netherlands, and the amount of investments made, relative to GDP, is similar to those in the United States. Yet the venture capital market in the Netherlands is investing a significantly smaller proportion of its funds in seed and start-up projects (OECD, 1998d). In Sweden it appears that the supply of venture capital is now rapidly increasing though from a low level (OECD, 1998b).

5. Theoretical work argues that rationing can occur in the equity markets similar to the market failure that occurs in the credit market. At higher prices, a higher proportion of unprofitable entrepreneurs offer equity, leading investors to withhold funding (Hellman and Stiglitz, 1995).

6. For example a survey of nascent entrepreneurs in about 750 households in the United States showed that only 14 per cent have asked a financial institution for funds and that another 5 per cent were in the process of asking financial institutions for funds (see Reynolds, 1997).

7. The part of seed finance of Venture Capital Finance in Europe is both relatively and absolutely much lower than in the United States. Start-up and early phase financing in Europe via external formal equity is the exception and not the rule (see EVCA – European Venture Capital Association – Yearbooks).

Chapter V

Optimising Human Resources

Since 1992, the OECD has undertaken extensive study of the many causes of unemployment. For example, wage formation, labour adjustment, education and training and benefit systems have all been reviewed. The following section touches only briefly on these topics as it affects entrepreneurship. For a more in-depth analysis, see other OECD publications:

- OECD (1994), *The OECD Jobs Study: Facts, Analysis and Strategies*, Paris.
- OECD (1994), *The OECD Jobs Study: Evidence and explanations*, Paris.
- OECD (1995), *The OECD Jobs Study: Implementing the Strategy*, Paris.
- OECD (1996), *The OECD Jobs Strategy: Enhancing the Effectiveness of Active Labour Market Policies*, Paris.
- OECD (1997), *Implementing the OECD Jobs Strategy: Lessons from Member Countries' Experience*, Paris.

Increasing labour market flexibility

The flexibility of wage setting differs greatly across OECD countries and depends on various factors. Non-wage labour costs are also important and they have been touched upon in Chapter 2. Compensation flexibility has proven important to companies in the United States, particularly among start-up companies in high-tech industries which often turn to stock-based compensation plans to attract and motivate employees while conserving cash and generating capital. Venture capitalist lawyer Rosati (1997) explained that in Silicon Valley's competitive environment, stock options represent an important supplement to overall employment packages. These enable emerging companies to compete for talent with larger, more established companies. Because these options are often granted at a time when companies are growing and positioning themselves for the future, their stock prices are low and the potential for appreciation is very high. Stock options are also becoming more common in large, existing companies as a method of fostering entrepreneurship among employees. Many other countries do not allow equity options in lieu of wages due to the incentives these create to avoid taxes.

Although intended to protect employees, rigid labour regulations can adversely affect job creation by obstructing the creation of new activities and when particularly severe may diminish entrepreneurship. When surveyed, employers cite employment protection as one of the main reasons for restricting their hiring in countries where conditions are strict, but seems less important in countries with more flexible legislation (OECD, 1994a). For example very restrictive labour market legislation appears to be a particularly strong barrier to entrepreneurship and job creation in Sweden and Spain (OECD, 1998 b and 1998c). In

---

Box 5.1. **Self-employment programmes**

As part of a range of active employment programmes, self-employment programmes encourage the beneficiaries of *unemployment insurance* (UI) to formulate a business idea and create their own jobs. The beneficiaries continue to remain eligible for unemployment insurance benefits for the duration of the UI term. At least eighteen OECD Member countries currently offer such programmes to their unemployed, though their size varies from country to country.

Self-employment programmes tend to be very small with fewer than 5 per cent of beneficiaries opting to participate. Evaluations of self-employment programmes have shown that, like many other active employment programmes, dead-weight is present (Wilson & Adams, 1992). That is, a significant number of participants would have created a business in the absence of the programme. As an employment generation strategy, these programmes do not contain a large multiplier effect as the self-employed do not hire large numbers of additional workers (OECD, 1992a). Those without workers represent the bulk of the self-employed. However, self-employment assistance is a cost-effective alternative to paying unemployment insurance benefits even when accounting for dead-weight effects as one US study has done (Benus et al., 1994). Studies in the United States and the United Kingdom show that a higher percentage of programme participants than non-participants succeed in finding long-term employment, even if their businesses fail (Benus et al., 1994; Tremlett, 1993). Because of an overly generous programme to encourage the unemployed to create their own jobs, the programme in France proved to be far too expensive. The French programme gave the participant a lump-sum payment roughly equal to the amount of UI benefits they would have collected if they had stayed in the UI programme (instead of a periodic payment). Participants were again eligible for UI benefits if their business failed. This aspect of the programme was removed in 1996 as part of a larger programme reform. Two evaluations of Canada's "*Self-Employment Incentives*" programme show other important benefits: self-sufficiency for participants and households; large community economic development impacts; small but non-trivial job creation; and provides opportunities for socially excluded groups (Wong et al., 1994; Graves et al., 1996).

Germany, employment protection has been waived for new and small enterprises in order to assist their start-up and growth because such regulations are more likely to be a constraint for small enterprises which face greater problems of divisibility, including greater uncertainty and volatility in regular personnel turnover. This benefit – while helpful to small enterprises which stay small – poses a dilemma for growing companies. That is, they help small businesses by exempting them but as a business grows it graduates out of the class were the concession is offered, and thus suddenly faces higher costs.

Also, labour market regulations often include social security benefits which can augment the preference for salaried employment. Becoming an entrepreneur is a daunting prospect because of the element of risks involved and becomes even more so if leaving salaried employment means giving up advantages such as healthcare coverage, pensions, invalidity insurance and *unemployment insurance* (UI). These are benefits which may not be available to the entrepreneur in the early years of his firm. For example, UI systems are generally only available to wage and salaried employees. The unemployed may be reluctant to become entrepreneurs because it would mean that they would "lose" unemployment insurance benefits. To overcome these obstacles many OECD countries* have created *Self-Employment* or *Micro-Enterprise programmes* which allow the beneficiaries of unemployment insurance to create an enterprise and continue to receive UI benefits. Programme evaluations have shown that, if carefully designed, micro-enterprise programmes are a cost-effective alternative to income support (see Box 5.1).

Necessary investment in education and training

There is increasing awareness of the importance of providing the option of entrepreneurship through the education system and of involving the more qualified (*i.e.*, graduates) in the process of entrepreneurship. According to a *Business Longitudinal Study* in Australia, 34 per cent of business decision-makers had tertiary education, of whom about two-fifths had management qualifications. This was considered low owing to the central importance of managerial decision making. The survey indicated that the best-educated do not often go into business and that the education and training system gives insufficient emphasis to developing the types of skills required by managers. The lack of diversity in available management skills seems to be another weak point which the education and training system has failed to address (OECD, 1998a).

---

* The list includes Australia, Belgium, Canada, Denmark, Finland, France, Germany, Greece, Ireland, Italy, Luxemburg, the Netherlands, Norway, Portugal, Spain, Sweden, the United Kingdom and the United States.

Entrepreneurship has to be promoted as a real career alternative for young people. Young people have a low probability of being self-employed or business owners, although they are particularly likely to say that they would be self-employed if given the choice (Blanchflower, 1996). Facilitating this choice can be helped through the design of curricula presenting career information to young people and introducing them to concepts of self employment. Research conducted by Ohio State University shows that two thirds of entrepreneurs come from homes in which someone has owned a business. This indicates that the transmission of entrepreneurial culture and know-how can affect career outcomes. Work on manufacturing firms has found that both managerial and educational qualifications have a significant influence upon firm formation rates (Gould & Keeble, 1984). Other studies conducted on a broader range of firms indicate that educational qualifications fail to predict the likelihood of self-employment, but do have an effect on the success of business ventures (Daly, 1991; Curran & Burrows, 1989; and Blanchflower & Oswald, 1990). The introduction of self-employment concepts in educational systems has already been experimented with in the United Kingdom, the United States, Canada and South Africa. Beyond aiming to stimulate entrepreneurship directly, the major objective of this kind of education is to help develop enterprising attitudes and to teach self-reliance. Programmes should provide entrepreneurship awareness (in its general sense) to all ages and groups, both in schools and universities.

A growing number of universities and colleges, especially in the United States, the United Kingdom and Canada teach entrepreneurship. This is the result of the recognition that graduates can be oriented towards careers in independent business management and not only towards traditional employee careers within large organisations. Studies (Vickery, Pilkington & Read, 1990) have shown that an increasing number of MBA students have chosen to run their own business, while research on graduates of Babson College and Harvard University revealed that subsequent self-employment and business creation was positively correlated with the number of entrepreneurship/small business classes taken while students (although the direction of causality is unclear). More research is required on the effectiveness of entrepreneurship education.

Training specifically targeting start-ups needs to be practically oriented and to provide concrete support in establishing new businesses. The impediments to starting a business are greater for some groups than others. Young people, for example, often face age discrimination, difficult access to capital and limited life and work experience generally, while other groups such as women, aboriginal populations and ethnic minorities can face specific hurdles in setting up a business. To better respond to these difficulties, the provision of services is most effective when targeted (see Box 5.2). Targeted assistance in such fields as the assessment of business ideas, the accessing of technical information, marketing, and other business skills, allows the better tailoring of services to needs. Of

---

Box 5.2. **Targeted training and assistance: the case of youth**

In general, young entrepreneurs experience more severe problems than adults in setting up a business, especially in securing start-up capital and coping with business expansion. Age plays an important role in the decision to enter entrepreneurship, due to capital constraints, to the lack of networks, and a more limited experience of work. These are some of the elements that explain the need for helping youth to see entrepreneurship as a real career alternative.

In a number of OECD countries, a significant number of successful businesses fail to find successors. While the age distribution of owners of craft or small and medium sized businesses in many countries will lead to the retirement of numerous entrepreneurs – in Germany alone, about 200 000 business owners are due to retire during the next five years (Muller, 1997) – too few young people consider entrepreneurship as a viable option.

The IG Spa (*Imprenditorialità Giovanile*) in Italy is an illustration of an effective response to the needs of youth start-ups and one of the most important examples of State action in the promotion of youth entrepreneurship. Set up in 1994, the agency – now a joint stock company – was entrusted with the management of *Law* 44 which had previously been the responsibility of the governmental *Committee for the Development of Entrepreneurship among young people*, a branch of the *National Treasury*. Eighty-four per cent of IG Spa's capital is currently held by the Italian Treasury, with the remainder provided by private partners. IG Spa supplies a complete range of services responding to the specific needs and difficulties of young entrepreneurs between the ages of 18 and 35. IG Spa's work covers all aspects of business creation, beginning with the promotion of entrepreneurial culture among young people through work with local authorities and the diffusion of information in schools and universities.

The agency provides finance through low interest loans and grants, as well as mentoring over the period of repayment of the loan and other start-up services (assistance with the business plan, assessment of business ideas, etc.). Whilst financial support is a major element of the programme, technical assistance plays an important role, allowing the newly-created SMEs to attain a survival rate of 81 per cent after 4 years. Training is administered by qualified management and vocational training institutions. The agency's mentoring strategy is another of its main features. The mentor is an established firm that provides assistance, first voluntarily and then commercially. *Law* 44 functions on the premise that entrepreneurship is best learned from other entrepreneurs. The relationship between IG Spa and the mentors is regulated by a contractual agreement whereby the agent enjoys discretion as far as planning and implementation is concerned while IG Spa sets overall objectives.

Since its implementation in 1986, *Law* 44 has evaluated 4 900 business plans of which it has approved 1 200. To date, more than 800 businesses have been financed with the creation of around 23 000 new jobs.

---

particular importance may be training in the preparation of loan applications. Aside from the increased likelihood of obtaining funds, informed and clearly articulated deliberations with lenders often lead to the refinement of investment concepts. An example of targeted assistance is the "An Income of Her Own Program" implemented in the United States and New Zealand. This programme targets young women between the ages of 16 and 20 and especially those at risk of social exclusion. The Canadian Aboriginal Business Programme showed that providing an integrated and targeted package of support can bring successful results. Since 1989 the Programme has provided financial and advisory support to over 5 000 firms. Programme investments of over C$ 300 million have catalysed further investment in the aboriginal private sector.

Chapter VI

Focusing on the Local Dimension of Entrepreneurship

A range of factors determining the extent and success of entrepreneurship have a local dimension: they are either strongly affected by local phenomena and/ or they are best supported by initiatives conceived and implemented locally. For example, the success of entrepreneurs and local financial institutions are often interdependent, while entrepreneurship frequently spreads through imitation, which can be spurred through proximity. Entrepreneurship can also be fostered through locally-based instruments such as business incubators and extension services. Indeed, relative to central initiatives there are particular advantages in supporting entrepreneurship through local measures: actions can be better tailored to the specific needs of an area and its businesses, and the involvement of a wider range of actors can bring a mix of competencies to the issue. Furthermore, a number of acute social problems – such as unemployment among minorities, and distressed urban areas – are highly concentrated geographically and require, among others, a local response involving the stimulation of entrepreneurship (indeed, in such areas the divergence between private and public returns to entrepreneurship may be particularly high). Moreover, it is at the local level where the need for policy co-ordination is perhaps greatest.

The fact that the extent and likely success of entrepreneurship is frequently tied to the local milieu demands creative policy thinking from both local and central governments. Indeed, given that a variety of location-specific factors affect entrepreneurship, a policy which fails to account for regional and local differences will likely be suboptimal. Furthermore, increased international economic integration adds to the policy challenge. This is because internationally mobile factors may be less rooted in local communities than in the past, and thus may have less incentive to invest in their prosperity (Rodrik, 1997). Faced with adverse local economic developments, globalisation has made it easier for firms simply to outsource or relocate.

Spatial variations in entrepreneurial activity

Chapter 2 referred to evidence showing that some regions in OECD countries have annual firm birth rates that are two to six times higher than other regions. Before addressing specifically local issues, it may be instructive to consider why entrepreneurship should be more prevalent in some areas than in others. David J. Storey (1994) identifies six significant influences on new firm formation (a concept related to but somewhat narrower than entrepreneurship) which can vary from region to region. These six factors are: *i*) demographics, as areas with young populations tend to start more firms and rates of start-up are generally higher in urban than in rural environments; *ii*) unemployment, which through different routes can both encourage and diminish start-up rates; *iii*) wealth, with wealthier areas expected to produce more start-ups owing to higher levels of demand and greater availability of capital; *iv*) the educational and occupational profile of the workforce, which may have contradictory effects as persons with superior qualifications will more likely find employment but may also have superior means with which to create their own enterprises; *v*) the prevalence of small firms, it being argued that employees in small firms will aspire to own other small firms; and *vi*) the extent of owner-occupied housing, with property being a frequent source of start-up capital for entrepreneurs. Some of these factors are interdependent. For instance, the educational and occupational profile of a population is likely to correlate closely with unemployment and housing variables. Infrastructure endowment, which is related to investment demand, is also likely to play a role, as is a region's history and culture.

Clusters of firms and entrepreneurship

The regionalisation of entrepreneurial activity can also reflect the phenomenon of "clustering". Clustering is the apparent tendency of firms in related lines of business to concentrate geographically. The fame of high-tech clusters such as California's Silicon Valley and England's "Silicon Fen" in Cambridge, has given many the impression that clusters are a recent phenomenon linked to R&D. This is misleading. Even in the early twentieth century the bulk of manufacturing in the United States was clustered in the North East of the country. The Italian region of Emilia-Romagna is home to a cluster which dates back to the 1960s and which produces a range of goods, notably in light industries and mechanics, mainly in small, family-based companies. The degree to which economic activities are clustered is often impressive. For example, according to one estimate there are around 380 clusters of firms in the United States operating across a broad spectrum of service and advanced manufacturing industries. Together they employ some 57 per cent of the workforce of the United States and produce 61 per cent of the country's output (Rosenfeld, 1996). Local industrial districts account for some 30 per cent of total employment in Italy and in 1994 produced 43 per cent of Italy's exports.

Clusters in different areas involve varying degrees of interaction between the firms involved, ranging from fairly loose networks of association through to multifaceted interrelationships involving a mix of co-operation and competition (which can often afford greater competitiveness for all parties). Numerous Italian clusters for instance involve a greater degree of specialisation and interaction between members of the cluster than is the case in Silicon Valley. The economic forces driving clustering, and the nature of the benefits derived therefrom, vary with the scale of the agglomeration in question. Some clusters have proven very resilient, able to adapt to new competitive pressures and remain at the cutting edge of their industry, generating jobs and wealth in the areas where they are located (see Box 6.1).

Beyond the observation that business clusters often enjoy commercial success, there are reasons why clusters are of particular relevance to entrepreneurship. First, the high degree of specialisation which clusters can permit allows individual entrepreneurs to start firms which concentrate on only a small part of a given industry. In other words, a low degree of vertical integration in firms belonging to clusters can also lower barriers to entry for entrepreneurs. Secondly, as clusters often contain many buyers and sellers in different parts of the production chain, the pressure to innovate is great, while conditions conducive to innovation are often present. As innovation can take many forms, a fertile environment is thus created for entrepreneurship. Thirdly, in many clusters there is considerable vertical mobility in the labour market. Blue-collar workers can eventually establish their own ventures, in part, as mentioned above, because of the lack of vertical integration constraints. Knowing that the possibility exists of graduating to a position of company owner is likely to encourage workers to adopt problem-solving and entrepreneurial attitudes in the workplace.

In broad terms, the agglomeration of firms and their suppliers permits the creation of locally concentrated labour markets. The clustering of firms can likewise encourage specialisation and division of labour between firms (offering greater scale economies for individual firms), attract buyers and sellers, and reduce the unit costs of activities undertaken collectively such as marketing. The clustering of firms may also facilitate access to finance and reduce the unit costs of technical services provided to members of the cluster (such as in design, accountancy, technical advice, etc.). By operating in close proximity firms can also more easily subcontract to competitors those orders that exceed their own capacities, because proximity among firms allows greater knowledge of the reliability, work standards and overall capabilities of various potential contractors. This may allow firms to retain valued customers.

Box 6.1. **Silicon Valley's competitive advantage**

Silicon Valley in California and Route 128 in Massachusetts, located on opposite coasts of the United States, are typically viewed as industrial counterparts and comparable centres of electronics entrepreneurship. But Silicon Valley is by far the more dynamic of the two and appears better able to seize new market opportunities and develop new technologies. Silicon Valley recovered rapidly from the major competitive challenge in the mid-1980s posed by Japanese production of cheap and reliable high-memory semiconductors, a challenge which displaced one in five Silicon Valley semiconductor workers. In response, firms in Silicon Valley introduced a stream of customised high value-added semiconductors, computers, components and software-related products. By the end of the 1980s Silicon Valley had clearly surpassed Route 128 as the national centre of computer systems innovation. Silicon Valley is now home to one-third of the 100 largest technology companies created in the United States since 1965. The market value of these firms increased by US$ 425 billion between 1986 and 1990, dwarfing the US$ 1 billion increase in the value of Route 128 counterparts.

The divergent performance of the Route 128 and Silicon Valley clusters cannot be attributed to regional differences in real estate costs, wages, taxes or defence spending. A more significant consideration is the large number of small firms organised in a horizontal network dominating Silicon Valley. In contrast, Route 128 has been dominated by a small number of corporations that internalise a wide range of productive activities. This difference has made Silicon Valley more responsive to change because the network's decentralisation encourages the pursuit of multiple technical opportunities with many groupings and regroupings of skills, technology and capital. This structure also promotes flows of information and collective technological learning. Vertically-organised corporations, by contrast, often find themselves locked into obsolete technologies while their hierarchical structures limit their ability to adapt quickly. Moreover, vertical integration deprives the regional economy of the infrastructure needed to increase start-ups and help them grow. Other factors have likewise played a critical role in Silicon Valley's success: the area is home to around a third of America's independently-raised venture capital; major centres of learning and specialised research operate in close proximity; and the prominent role of immigrant entrepreneurs reflects the presence of a cultural climate tolerant to immigration. Indeed, cultural factors, though elusive, appear central to Silicon Valley's success. Tolerance of failure, meritocratic outlook, a disposition to collaborate, and a positive view of change are just some of the often-cited components of Silicon Valley's cultural foundation.

Source: Saxenian, 1994 and *The Economist*, 29 March 1997.

Agglomeration also facilitates the flow of ideas and information. These flows occur both formally and informally, for example when employees change employer, through contacts with common suppliers, through social exchanges and so on. Such information flows represent positive externalities derived from proximity. These interrelationships are sometimes overlaid by common membership of artisanal and commercial associations, mutual credit guarantee schemes, labour associations, various community-based institutions and even political parties, all of which can serve to facilitate communication and create a climate of trust.

By allowing companies to stay small, while enjoying the advantages of size, clusters permit firms to focus on their fields of competitive advantage. Consequently, enterprise in the clusters is often characterised by rapid product and process innovation, swift diffusion of new techniques, a marked diversity of products, and high standards of design and quality. However, interest in the clustering and networking of firms also reflects the social success associated with clusters in such locations as Silicon Valley and parts of Italy. Workers are often well organised. And labour standards and conditions of work are generally high, with an emphasis also placed on training. In many cases, the ability to supply highly differentiated high-value-added products to high-income markets has permitted the maintenance of both high wages and low unemployment in the vicinity of the clusters.

Does the clustering of firms have implications for policy? Most clusters, especially large or region-wide agglomerations, have not occurred as an outcome of public policy. It is also probably unwise for policymakers to attempt to create clusters. The clustering of firms has complex determinants, which greatly constrains effective policymaking. Moreover, there are numerous possible sources of inefficiency in such a course of action. For instance, resources may be expended to encourage firms into high-cost locations, while firms which do not benefit from the policy may have their competitiveness diminished if they have to pay for the policy. However, policymakers can lock-in some of the benefits of existing or embryonic clusters by ensuring suitable institutional conditions. For example, amongst other actions, promoting the establishment of suppliers' associations and learning circles, facilitating contacts among participants in the cluster and ensuring effective extension services can all increase the benefits to firms of belonging to a cluster. Firms should have access to such institutional arrangements whether they belong to a cluster or not. However, it is likely that the benefits of such arrangements will be magnified by cluster membership. Conversely, the cost-effectiveness of provision may be greater when supplying to a clustered rather than a dispersed group of firms.

Attracting outside investment may help stimulate a cluster if it can bridge capability gaps. An array of new supplier/purchaser linkages may be created thereby. The outside investor may also possess superior product and/or process standards, which are likely to feed through into the production practices of other firms in the cluster (particularly suppliers). The provision of adequate infrastructure is important in consolidating a cluster. However, waste may occur if the supply of infrastructure is expanded in the expectation of an increase in a cluster's size. The cluster may fail to expand (indeed some clusters have collapsed), while the infrastructure supplied has an opportunity cost. Even an embryonic cluster is likely to offer locational advantages to other firms. Disseminating information about the cluster throughout the business community of a region or country may attract new firms (although a variety of other considerations will impinge on the location decisions of firms).

In Italy, a significant role in the creation of clusters has also been played by trade associations. Their ability to act as a catalyst not only stems from the large number of association representatives dealing with the problems of member firms, but also relies on a well established reputation earned through long experience in providing services (including book-keeping, preparation of pay-packets, etc.) to small firms. Such associations have branched out still further, now promoting professional training courses, establishing associations for the purchase of raw materials, assisting companies to participate in trade fairs, co-ordinating the demand for credit with banks to secure low-interest loans, and so forth.

Social capital and entrepreneurship

Practitioners and analysts working on entrepreneurship usually place considerable importance on the development of social capital (the complex of institutions, customs and relationships of trust conducive to co-operation) and a culture supportive of entrepreneurial endeavour. Indeed, there is growing evidence that a lack of social capital is a constraint on growth (Knack & Keefer, 1997; Moesen, 1997). As described below, local conditions and initiatives appear central to the development of social capital.

A commercial environment characterised by mistrust will require that entrepreneurs invest in mechanisms to defend against the potentially opportunistic behaviour of counterparts. These added transaction costs may deter some forms of entrepreneurial initiative. Similarly, in low-trust economies the time spent by entrepreneurs in monitoring the behaviour of workers and partners may be considerable, and is time unavailable for innovation (Knack & Keefer, 1997). Recent work in Italy suggests that social conditions in local communities influence attitudes brought to the workplace, especially as concerns the willingness to co-operate (Brusco, 1996a). In economies with little social capital resources may be employed unproductively on a range of services and behaviours to protect property rights. Government policy may also have added credibility in high-trust economies, and the quality of policy may be superior in localities with a strong civic tradition and a high degree of political participation. Indeed, it is noteworthy that entrepreneurship can thrive in areas with above average costs of labour, land, housing, transport and taxes. This suggests that, while such economic variables are extremely important, other considerations – such as social capital – can also be vital.[1] The presence of social capital may likewise help explain the success of some immigrant entrepreneurs living in neighbourhood communities (see Box 6.2). Furthermore, globalisation, by augmenting competition and adding to pressure for specialisation, by creating uncertainty and by shortening product life cycles, can create incentives for various forms of inter-firm collaboration. Such collaboration is likely to be facilitated by the presence of social capital.

As a public good, there is a natural role for public authorities in promoting social capital. However, scant attention has been given to the policy dimension of this issue. Nevertheless, despite the somewhat elusive and underexplored nature of the subject, there does appear to be scope for change through policy. For example, it has been suggested that providing tax exemption for community organisations will encourage social capital. In Japan, institutional design seems to have been essential in developing forms of inter-firm collaboration often viewed as an inherent cultural asset. Among post-war institutional developments of this sort was legislation to promote small-firm associations and prevent unfair subcontracting practices. Similarly, public authorities can enhance trust by, for instance, establishing systems of arbitration which avoid costly and lengthy court procedures and help identify parties which betray trust (Brusco, 1996a).[2] In New Zealand, efforts by the *Trade Development Board* (TRADENZ) to foster networking among firms have given rise to gradual but significant processes of inter-firm

---

Box 6.2.   **Enclaves of immigrant entrepreneurs**

Members of minority groups are often concentrated geographically in neighbourhood enclaves. The reasons for this vary. For example, in some countries and regions immigrants may constitute a large share of the minority population. Migrants may have family and other ties to persons who have already migrated, towards whom they will naturally gravitate. The perception of hostility toward members of minority groups may also lead to their local concentration. The neighbourhood can thus cushion the immigrant's incorporation into the country by providing both a community and employment.

Evidence suggests that such enclaves can strengthen immigrants' capacity to compete in the broader market as entrepreneurs by providing information networks, sources of credit, a loyal consumer base and a steady supply of workers (Light, 1988). Researchers have noted that immigrant businesses often expand into under-served markets where demand is unstable or uncertain and frequently make significant contributions to the local economy. Immigrant entrepreneurs have revitalised many neighbourhoods. For example, Cubans are widely credited with redeveloping Miami's Little Havana and transforming Miami into a thriving economic gateway to South America (Portes & Bach, 1985).

---

collaboration. The TRADENZ programme has witnessed firms changing their output mix, becoming more specialised and inter-dependent, after deliberations with industry counterparts have revealed scope for co-operation and convinced entrepreneurs that collaboration and inter-firm learning are practicable. A different form of social capital may stem from proximity to a seat of higher learning, which can foster a supportive attitude among the local population towards high-tech endeavour. Evidence also suggests that social polarisation and economic inequality diminish social capital, underlining the importance of policies to reduce such disparities.

Social capital can derive from public programs discussed in this study which bring together and increase the frequency of exchanges among potential business partners. How best to undertake the complicated and imprecise task of developing social capital and cultural support for entrepreneurship will vary from one area and historical tradition to another (indeed, an increase in associational activity may even prejudice economic efficiency if the concerns of narrow interest groups are advanced thereby). For this reason, and because of the need for direct interaction among the parties concerned, local initiatives will be critical to the achievement of positive change.

Locally-based policies and programmes to foster entrepreneurship

A trend devolving resources and decision-making power to regional and local levels has occurred since the late 1970s. As a result, local and regional governments in OECD countries have developed an array of enterprise development programmes with a variety of objectives and target groups. Some of the programmes aimed at attracting inward investment are discussed in the penultimate section of this chapter. Other programmes offered by national, regional and local governments aim at indigenous development. They include efforts to improve enterprise dynamics, particularly start-ups, by tapping into latent entrepreneurial ability, improving the regional business climate and facilitating collaborative behaviour. Efforts have also been made to increase the level of innovation. This section reviews key policies and programmes to support entrepreneurship which are best designed and managed locally. Some of the issues addressed, such as credit guarantee associations, have already been considered in Chapter 4. The intention here is thus to explain how the local dimension relates to such schemes.

Finance. The success of entrepreneurs and local financial institutions are often interdependent. Banks and other financial bodies which service the local economy will gain from the presence of a buoyant corporate sector. In turn, physical proximity to financial institutions may be important in facilitating access to finance for segments of the business community, especially small firms.

Credit Guarantee Associations. As described in Chapter 4, banks may ration credit, particularly for innovating firms and start-ups perceived to be risky. The extent of this problem may vary from one geographic area to another depending, for example, on the sectoral, size and demographic profile of the population of borrowing firms. One policy response to capital market imperfections of this sort is to attempt to reduce information asymmetry by increasing the supply of relevant information. One means of doing so is for small firms to form consortia to guarantee their own loan applications. In addition to affording a guarantee for lenders, this would capitalise on information held by the firms themselves. The effective operation of such credit guarantee associations is necessarily a local undertaking. An advantage of guarantee associations is that evaluation of the loan risks may be done more effectively by association members working in the same industry, while peer pressure may help effect repayment. There are many possible institutional arrangements with credit guarantee associations, although a key issue is the size of the group. Peer pressure and the ability to screen proposals thoroughly may be greatest with a small group, which underlines the importance of the local dimension in such schemes (however, with small groups the scope for risk sharing is also reduced).

The establishment of a loan guarantee consortium may involve significant initial costs for the firms concerned. Many of these costs will not be borne by subsequent members of the consortium.[3] Therefore, to counter the under-supply of such schemes public support in their establishment is likely to be required. Such support will be most relevant in areas where set-up costs are likely to be high, for example where there is no previous experience of such schemes. This form of public-sector-driven institutional change must be undertaken by or with local authorities.

Regionally-based mutual guarantee schemes have been created in several countries. In every German *Länder*, there exists at least one credit guarantee institution. Such institutions often specialise in a particular industry. They are chartered as limited liability companies, with capital provided by the banking system and by the guilds of trades and trade chambers. Federal and state governments share the responsibility for guaranteeing up to 70 per cent of the loan amount. The losses experienced between 1984 and 1988 averaged about 2 per cent of the total loan amount, lower than the default rate on regular bank loans (Harm, 1992). Similarly, in Italy, regional loan guarantee consortia have been created throughout the country.

Venture capital. In the case of formal venture capital, many countries are home to venture capital companies with a nation-wide outreach. However, start-up investments frequently come from local venture capitalists. This follows from the fact that start-ups require a high degree of interaction between entrepreneurs and venture capitalists (the often-cited rule of thumb is that such investors prefer to invest within a 1-2 hour travel time from their homes).

Capital provision by so-called "business angels" is generally organised informally, and reliable statistics are scarce. However, in the United States this source of informal venture capital is thought to be at least twice the size of the formal venture capital pool, though individual deals are much smaller (Wetzel, 1987). The angel capital market is fragmented and localised, and in the absence of organised intermediaries the match-making process is difficult. Potential angels hesitate to publicise their willingness to invest, and entrepreneurs are not keen on revealing what they believe to be innovative ideas (Dennis, 1996b). There is also evidence from the United Kingdom that informal investors in small firms would make additional investments if presented with suitable investment proposals (Mason & Harrison, 1994). In these circumstances, an information barrier exists which could be lowered through appropriate public policy, with benefits for the economy at large. The lowering of such information barriers requires the collection, processing and dissemination of information with a high local content. For example, an initiative has been launched in the United States to create an *Angel Capital Electronic Network* (ACE-Net). This is a nation-wide Internet listing of small innovative companies, with access restricted to subscribers.

Extension and information services. Extension and information services are often key to the creation and development of enterprises (extension services provide firms with direct technical assistance in a range of business functions). Owing to the degree of interaction required with beneficiaries, the provision of extension services is necessarily local. There are a number of reasons why extension services may be needed. Many small firms often have an insufficient internal division of labour to permit the development of specialised skills in-house in different business functions. For instance, the firms may be too small for in-house R&D, specialised financial management, sophisticated marketing and so forth. Some of these services may therefore need to be contracted-in. But because the required volume of services is often small, and some of the services themselves indivisible (for instance, many engineering consultancies would not consider servicing the minor daily advisory requirements of a small enterprise), the market may undersupply substitutes for the skills lacking in some small firms. Perhaps more importantly, many small firms will not always know what information they best require to address a particular competitive challenge (and the benefits of certain options, such as investment in information technology, may be hard to envisage for the uninitiated). Consequently, in a given area there may be too low a level of effective demand for certain necessary services to allow private suppliers to emerge. The provision of these services by a public body can foster an awareness among potential private sector suppliers of the importance of the services offered. The public provision of these services may only need to be temporary therefore. In addition, some of the services provided by extension services may have the character of public goods.

Extension services can provide training in a variety of useful fields. For example, banks often respond to the charge that they are creating a debt gap by citing inadequate planning, documentation and investment appraisal amongst small firms. Banks may themselves have an interest in training entrepreneurs in record keeping, basic business administration, finance and related fields. Such training could serve to limit this form of informational deficiency. However, where banks fail to act there is a role for public authorities in providing – or at least initiating – training and advisory services.

Anecdotal evidence suggests that effective industrial extension services are important but rare. Extension services must be proactive and staffed by engineers, technologists and other specialists able to quickly assess the needs of firms. This personnel should also be able to work with busy entrepreneurs, as needed, in implementing technological and managerial suggestions for productivity and quality improvements. Japan has a long experience in affording public assistance to the modernisation of small business. To this end an extensive network of *Kohsetsushi* centres was created after the Second World War. The centres provide advice and services to help small companies overcome technical constraints and adopt new technology. There is at least one centre in each of Japan's 47 prefectures, with a total of 170 centres nation-wide. The centres are administered by regional and municipal governments. These also provide the bulk of funding, which in 1992 amounted to US$910 million. Estimates suggest that around 30 per cent of small firms use the centres in any one year. The centres have been criticised for promoting technologies which are not "leading edge". However, others have also cited this as an advantage in that it allows *Kohsetsushi* staff to offer advice and solutions immediately applicable to current manufacturing practices (OECD, 1995c).

In the United States, the *Manufacturing Extensions Programme* (MEP) is a nation-wide network of locally managed manufacturing extension centres dedicated to helping smaller manufacturers improve their competitiveness by adopting modern technologies. The programme was initially designed to transfer advanced technologies developed at the government's *Advanced Manufacturing Research Facility* in Maryland and at other government research institutes. However, once established, the centres quickly realised that most small firms in the United States did not need advanced technologies and that most firms would be better served by off-the-shelf technologies (Shapira *et al.*, 1995). One survey showed that 73 per cent of the manufacturers who used the service believed that MEP assistance had positively affected their overall business performance (GAO, 1995b). However, the survey also asked companies that could have used a MEP why they had made limited or no use of the services. About 82 per cent reported that they had not used the services because they were unaware of these programmes. In the United States manufacturing extension organisations can learn from each other's experiences through the *Modernisation Forum*. This nation-wide association is open to not-for-profit organisations that provide technical assistance and services to small- and medium-sized companies in the manufacturing sector.

Business incubators and science parks. Business incubators aim to assist new entrepreneurs with business start-ups. They typically seek to: provide preferential conditions, usually with respect to workspace, for a specific industry or type of enterprise; pool resources in terms of services, facilities, and equipment, and concentrate geographically the supply of utilities. After the first critical years of the new business the young firm leaves the incubator making room for another start-up. While incubators are concerned with creating jobs directly, they can also have long-run indirect job creation effects which are difficult to measure. For example, incubators can be critical in encouraging imitation. A few successful start-ups can help local communities recognise that entrepreneurship is within their abilities. Business incubators can also help promote the clustering of firms by bringing them into physical proximity. In areas where crime is a constraint on business, such as in southern Italy and parts of the Russian Federation, incubators can likewise provide a safe haven for legitimate entrepreneurship.

The economic characteristics of the location in which an incubator is established will greatly affect its operation and its usefulness. Business incubators should maximise synergies with the local business environment. In the United States, for example, most incubators have an affiliation with the nearest *Small Business Development Centre* (established in every state by the federal government's Small Business Administration). The areas chosen as incubator sites should ideally provide access to markets for products or services (as small firms within an incubator stand to benefit from trade and networking with larger companies outside), a degree of business expertise in the community, diverse financial resources, and local commitment to the incubator programme. In the United States and elsewhere the operation of many incubators is overseen by an advisory board comprising representatives of the local business community. Prior to establishing a business incubator it may be necessary to improve the local climate for entrepreneurship so as to encourage demand for the services an incubator would provide. In this vein, a 1994 evaluation of science parks in the United Kingdom found that a critical issue was to increase the supply of high-tech firms (Westhead & Storey, 1994). Incubators can also improve operating revenues by extending services to the local business community. In Australia, for instance, larger incubators frequently offer telephone answering services to local "home businesses". Furthermore, in many countries local governments play an important role in the financing of business incubators, heightening the significance of the nexus with the local economy.

The popularity of incubators has become widespread. For example, there are now over 100 incubator schemes of different sorts around the United Kingdom and some 550 incubator programmes in the United States. Local authorities and business associations in Australia consider business incubators a useful instrument for nurturing a more entrepreneurial climate while reducing the failure rate of small enterprises (the failure rate within the first year is an estimated 8 per cent among companies in incubators, compared with a national average of 32 per cent). Both the public and private sectors have participated in establishing and running business incubators. However, a potential problem in the operation of business incubators is that industries set up on their premises may remain there, excluding new entrants.

An important issue in the functioning of business incubators is the nature of their interaction with institutions of higher education. The clustering of start-up firms – particularly high-technology firms – around the university centres of Boston in the United States and Cambridge in the United Kingdom are cases in point. Many institutional permutations are possible, some involving a greater degree of involvement of the academic community in business development than others. In such cases, suitable divisions of labour between academic activity and enterprise development have to be found, for instance as between applied and general research. A related tension stems from the fact that industry often operates with short-term time-frames, while universities may pursue longer-term research objectives. In addition, where universities and the land they occupy are publicly owned, legal and administrative difficulties may arise from the establishment of rent-charging property-based incubation schemes. The presence of important centres of technical learning may also mean that entrepreneurs engaging in high-tech ventures will be less likely to feel like outsiders and may more often encounter interlocutors (such as bank managers) familiar with the problems they face.

During the 1980s, many sub-national governments, facing decreasing revenues and increasing unemployment, looked to technological development to revive their local economies and create jobs. A popular strategy was the creation of science parks. Science parks differ in size and structure across OECD countries but share several characteristics. While most establishments in a science park are engaged in high-tech activity, basic research and mass production are uncommon. Science parks are also expected to generate new high-tech firms through spin-offs or other forms of new investment. Most science parks feature links with a research facility. Regional and local authorities often support science parks through the provision of infrastructure and land, tax breaks and tax holidays, and other incentives. Japan has one of the most ambitious plans for hi-tech development. In 1983, the Technopolis Law was enacted to create 26 regional hi-tech centres to relieve pressure on Tokyo. In Australia 16 science parks have so far been created and a further four are under construction (OECD, 1998a).

The overall impact of policies to support science parks is difficult to ascertain because few have been evaluated. Failure rates appear to be high with about a half of all parks in the United States closing down. In addition, a number of science parks have been criticised because the parks' growth has occurred largely through attracting firms from outside the region rather than through new-firm formation. A survey of UK science parks found that two-thirds of the parks' enterprises had previously been located elsewhere (Amirahmadi & Saff, 1993). When successful, science parks can generate economic development and high job creation which spill over the borders of the park. Successful parks have been located close to metropolitan areas which offer high-quality infrastructure such as good transportation linkages and a reputable university. Government assistance is also required during the start-up phase and often for several years afterwards. For example, the *Research Triangle Park*, one of the largest science parks in the United States, took more than a decade to become viable at a significant cost to the state. Of the A$ 100 million of public funds invested in Australia's science and technology parks, only one park is cited as a success. One of the main reasons for this could be the unwillingness of universities to transfer intellectual property rights to potential entrepreneurs among their staff. Therefore, the promise offered by policies to establish or promote science parks must be viewed cautiously in view of their costs. Careful analysis is required by public authorities prior to any outlay of funds.

Promotion of business networks. As already mentioned, the success of enterprise clusters in Emilia-Romagna has attracted the attention of policy makers and given rise to support initiatives aiming to replicate aspects of the Italian experience. One of the first such initiatives was the *Danish Network Programme*. Support to networking has since become widespread, with examples in Europe, Australia and the United States. A number of these networks do not rely primarily on physical proximity among the actors concerned, making use of information technologies which allow interaction at a distance. Business networks have also gone beyond collaborative relationships between firms, coming to encompass agreements with research bodies, education and training institutions and public authorities. The underlying objective of all such networks is to foster innovation, strategic alliances and information sharing. Various of the networks also seek to exploit specific scale economies present in collective action. The potential benefits of networking are evidenced in the fact that, in reorganising their supply chains, a number of large companies encourage forms of networking among their suppliers.

In July 1991 the Danish government announced the success of its Network Programme, with 3 000 companies having been drawn into active participation. A mid-term survey showed that 42 per cent of the networks had increased their sales, 67 per cent had reduced costs and 75 per cent believed that they had become more competitive (Gelsing & Knop, 1991). Further, 94 per cent said they would continue to collaborate after subsidies had ended. Three new network programmes were created in 1991. However, as the programmes in Denmark have drawn to a close, the full extent of their impact is unclear. There is evidence that the networks cannot survive without ongoing government assistance, and several were abandoned when subsidies ended. This programme has served as a template for a subsequent and somewhat modified programme in Norway. And later work in New Zealand has built on the Norwegian experience, but with a greater emphasis on financial autonomy. Indeed, at the instigation of a local technological institute, a co-operating group of 65 small firms in the Twente area of the Netherlands has established an independent private company to undertake the networking function (Pyke, 1997).

Area-based initiatives can also facilitate linkages between small and large firms. The *Plato* programme in Ireland and Belgium illustrates how co-operation between large and small businesses at the local level can enable small entrepreneurs to obtain guidance from management experts. Such linkages are important if direct investment in a given area is to have significant multiplier effects for the local economy. Furthermore, for policymakers concerned about the footloose nature of foreign direct investment, the establishment of inter-firm linkages with an outside investment may provide incentives for the outside firm to maintain its current location.

One-stop shops and administrative simplification: To facilitate start-ups central and local governments have participated in the creation of "one-stop" shops where enterprises can obtain all necessary permits as well as regulatory information and details of support services, programme entitlements and so forth. One example includes the *Business Links* programme in the United Kingdom. The establishment of one-stop shops has been a response to the frequent complaints from business of difficulties in obtaining public support supplied by a multitude of government organisations. For example, a regional survey showed that the State of Wisconsin has at least 400 different enterprise programmes providing some 700 kinds of services (Center for the Study of Entrepreneurship, 1993). However, knowledge of these programmes was not widespread.

Skills and training: Many entrepreneurs operate in localised labour markets that may vary significantly in the skills demanded and supplied. Evidence from company surveys suggests that the quality of skills supplied may be important in facilitating entrepreneurial activity (SBRC, 1992; Cosh & Hughes, 1996). Labour market assessments and targeted training initiatives seek to improve the match of skills supplied with business requirements. It can be argued that this is best carried out at local or regional levels where agencies can better take account of varying business needs and how to meet them. Recent work by the OECD *Local Economic and Employment Development Programme* documents a wide range of initiatives that aim to provide significant adaptation to spatially distinct labour market circumstances (OECD, 1998f). In the United Kingdom, for example, *Training and*

Enterprise Councils (TECs) and *Business Links* were set up in the firm belief that locally based agencies are best placed to design and implement appropriate training and skills development policies.

The policy initiatives that can be undertaken in this area fall into three main categories: First, regional or local monitoring mechanisms to identify skills shortages and audit training activity; secondly, measures to improve the operation of the local labour market both by helping firms identify their requirements and by providing guidance, job search and placement for job seekers; thirdly, support for training initiatives tailored to the perceived needs of local entrepreneurs, for example in management development, information technology, marketing, sales and finance. The provision of training for potential entrepreneurs in the essentials of starting and running a business also has a role to play.

Entrepreneurship and schemes for community development. In many countries, publicly-sponsored schemes operate to encourage enterprise as part of broader socially-oriented programmes, such as those aimed at countering the problems of distressed urban areas. For instance, President Clinton has endorsed the creation of a network of community development banks to channel private capital to the most disadvantaged areas. This initiative includes the use of funds for small business development. Also in the United States, *Small Business Investment Companies* provide venture capital using a mix of private and public funds. And the 1994 *Riegle Community Development and Improvement Act* aims at creating a secondary market for loans to small companies. This legislation also established the *Community Development Financial Institutions Fund* which is intended to increase the availability of finance for the development of selected areas. A number of States also operate *Capital Access Programmes* (CAPs) in which public authorities assume a portion of loan risks and thereby encourage private banks to lend to small firms.

The *South Shore Bank* in Chicago provides an interesting example both of creative banking and of the interdependence between financial intermediaries and the local economy. Faced with a deteriorating economic and social environment, with adverse effects on the bank's profitability, *South Shore* established a programme in the early 1980s aimed at generating savings for loans to small firms and the redevelopment of derelict housing. With federal assistance in the early stages the programme lent almost US$100 million between 1981 and 1987, playing an important role in reviving the local economy and the bank's fortunes. Indeed, the experience of the *South Shore Bank* encouraged the introduction of funding legislation aimed at promoting community development financial institutions in the United States.

In a number of countries partnerships organised at the local level have also been effective in stimulating entrepreneurship as part of a strategy for local economic regeneration. Particularly innovative among these have been the partnerships developed in Ireland (see Box 6.3). It must be stressed however that

---

Box 6.3.   **Entrepreneurship and locally-based partnerships in Ireland**

Entrepreneurship in Ireland has been strongly affected by a lack of indigenous industry and a large agricultural sector mainly controlled from England. Post-independence policies promoted inward investment, but not necessarily indigenous entrepreneurship. Various analyses confirm the division of the economy between small, relatively uncompetitive Irish firms, largely serving the domestic market, and a dynamic foreign sector. Observers have stressed the need for a long-term, broadly-based strategy to develop indigenous industry and entrepreneurship. The small business policy of the Irish government seeks to encourage expansion among existing indigenous SMEs, and promote links between foreign multinationals and local SMEs, but also recognises the importance of building a culture of entrepreneurship.

In disadvantaged urban and rural areas where entrepreneurial culture is generally weak, *Area-Based Partnerships* play an important role in helping new entrepreneurs, particularly the unemployed and other target groups, establish small businesses. Mainstream organisations such as the *County Enterprise Boards* aim to develop strong, competitive SMEs. However, the local partnerships play a somewhat broader role, linking enterprise creation with employment and the fight against social exclusion.

The task of the partnerships is to reconsider the problems of unemployment within their jurisdictions and devise effective responses to them. Legally the partnerships are independent corporations under Irish company law. Their boards group representatives of local community interests, including the unemployed, representatives of the national social partner organisations of labour and business, and local or regional representatives of the national social welfare, training, or economic-development administrations. Through this structure, the partnerships often have de facto authority over a significant share of the local activities and expenditures of core agencies of the national government. In addition, they have the right to provide services and build institutions not contemplated by the statutory bodies.

In six years of operation, urban partnerships have developed innovative techniques for retraining and placing the long-term unemployed and building potentially self-sustaining firms that provide both training and jobs. They have also established new programmes to help early school leavers and single mothers, and to encourage community policing and the management of housing estates by their tenants. These innovations, moreover, are accompanied by local proposals for adjustments to the rules governing eligibility for social welfare benefits whose purpose is to make participation in the new programmes broadly affordable and attractive, and to remove the disincentives that often deter the most needy from exploring entrepreneurship and training programs (for example by allowing them to keep medical care benefits, school meal tickets, etc.).

Source: OECD, 1996e.

---

while entrepreneurship is valuable in combating certain social ills, the justification for public spending in support of entrepreneurship must be based on explicit cost-benefit analysis and careful consideration of possible market failures.

Entrepreneurship and regional development policy

Marked regional and local disparities in income and employment exist in all OECD countries. Amongst other constraints, depressed regions generally have fewer examples of successful entrepreneurs. This is an important drawback in that much entrepreneurial endeavour is imitative. Since the late 1970s, and propelled by major restructuring and job losses in primary industries such as steel and coal, local and regional governments in OECD countries have developed an array of enterprise support programmes (such as those described in this chapter), especially in the most depressed areas. The promotion of entrepreneurship as a means of combating unemployment and poverty reduction has a number of benefits. The demonstration effect of entrepreneurship and of an active approach generally addresses issues of dependency and passivity often cited in debates over traditional forms of welfare. Entrepreneurial activity may also have external benefits such as raising the degree of competition in a given market. The encouragement of entrepreneurship in an area in decline may also have advantages over some long-standing programmes of subsidy to ailing industrial subsectors: for example, entrepreneurship can facilitate structural change, while the costs to the state of supporting an industry in decline may be incurred indefinitely. Furthermore, the reliance on private initiative as a source of employment creation is all the greater at a time of increasing pressure on public expenditures. Atlantic Canada provides an interesting example of a regional programme, based on media and educational initiatives, to promote entrepreneurship (see Box 6.4).

Indeed, some other frequently-employed means of countering regional decline appear far from satisfactory. For instance, a common method for creating jobs in poorer regions is to lure existing firms from other regions. As incentive packages become increasingly generous in spite of dubious results, there is concern that these efforts amount to a costly poaching exercise with little or no economy-wide impact. For example, the State of Alabama, caught in a bidding war with other states to win a Mercedes car plant, offered tax breaks and other subsidies amounting to US$200 000 per job created (Meyerson, 1996). It is not uncommon for companies to hold out for the best incentive deals they can get from regional officials anxious to attract large plants and enterprises, successfully playing one off against the other. One auto-maker launched negotiations with UK government officials holding out the prospect of a US$700 million engine plant if it could match the investment aid offered by Austria (Wolffe, 1996). In an attempt to counter this trend, legislation is being introduced in some regions to curtail the bidding war and "claw-back" public funds when companies fail to deliver on their job creation promises or move out of the State.

Attention has also been paid to taxation, which can be burdensome in some areas because of multiple national, regional and local taxes. In a survey of US businessmen, local property taxes and regional taxes on business income were

---

Box 6.4. **An entrepreneurship development strategy: Atlantic Canada**

Atlantic Canada has a combined population of 2.4 million: 45 per cent of which lives in rural areas. The unemployment rate is the highest in Canada and the region is heavily dependent on government support, federal transfer payments and natural resource-based industries. In the 1990s, the policy of attracting outside companies to relocate or build branch plants was abandoned in favour of a more endogenous development within the region based on policies to enhance entrepreneurship.

The strategy included subsidies to assist start-ups and to help to develop existing firms. It also included entrepreneurship awareness programmes to provide information on the role of small enterprises in the community, to promote entrepreneurship as a viable employment and career opportunity and to raise the profile of entrepreneurs in the community. Entrepreneurship awareness programmes were delivered through media campaigns and education programmes. Media campaigns included television programmes about entrepreneurs and business management and an advertising campaign. Viewers were provided with follow-up telephone numbers and addresses. Education programmes added enterprise training to the curriculum and targeted three groups: school children; students of vocational schools and community colleges; and university students.

As a result of the education programme, some 50 000 students were enrolled in full entrepreneurship classes in secondary school in 1995. High school students in 1995 were almost twice as likely to have been exposed to courses with entrepreneurship-related content as high school students in 1990. The share of students with a strong intent to own their own business has remained constant at approximately 20 per cent. However, the percentage of students with low intent fell from 42.7 to 40.7 per cent. The media campaign is also considered to have had a positive impact. The "intent to start a business within the next two years" of the general population increased from 7 per cent in 1991 to 14 per cent in 1995.

Source: ACOA, 1996.

---

high-priority concerns among business people (Dennis, 1996*a*). These concerns have not escaped the attention of sub-national authorities which compete with each other – often in a mutually disadvantageous manner – by lowering the tax burden.

The imperative of programme evaluation

Too frequently there is no systematic evaluation of programmes supporting entrepreneurship, small enterprise and local development. Good intentions are sometimes equated with good economics. It is incumbent on public authorities supporting such programs to encourage a culture of evaluation and benchmarking and to adjust programmes or alter the policy mix where findings suggest that this is required. The need for proper evaluation is highlighted by the scale of resources expended by local and regional authorities on various forms of business support. For example, the estimated net cost to government of programmes supporting industry that were managed locally, regionally or through other sub-central institutions was over US$8.3 billion in 1993 (some 36 per cent of the net cost of all such support programmes) (OECD, 1997d). The net cost to government of spending on industry-related programmes with a regional development orientation was some US$15.4 billion in 1993. The total magnitude of expenditures on all forms of local and regional business development initiatives far exceeds these figures. Proper evaluation, then, is a necessary component of such sizeable outlays.

Evaluation must be built into support programmes from the outset. This requires, *inter alia*, clear initial specification of objectives, outputs and expected impact. Structured design, monitoring and evaluation must be part of an integrated framework. Furthermore, a clear mission statement – to serve as an evaluation baseline – is important for providing guidance in areas of potential operational conflict such as, to take the case of business incubators, between the promotion of economic development and the achievement of financial autonomy. Where possible, the collection of long-run data sets comparing firms and persons benefiting from assistance with similar non-beneficiaries would be particularly valuable. Proper evaluation will also facilitate necessary comparisons of the costs incurred in some programmes against the costs of other forms of public support for enterprise and job creation, and local economic development. Inter-regional comparisons, important for identifying best-practices, are similarly hindered by deficiencies in evaluation.

Evaluation is not without difficulties. Indeed, it is not uncommon to encounter resistance to evaluation. It must be emphasised therefore that evaluation, if appropriately structured, can afford a powerful management tool. Evaluations conducted mid-way through the life of a programme can, for instance, provide guidance for the remaining period of implementation. The evaluation process can also be technically demanding. It may be difficult for example, in the case of an *ex post* evaluation, to isolate the various factors which have determined the impact of a given programme. Evaluations may also be costly. Indeed, economies of scale and scope may apply, which underlines the importance of co-operation with central levels of government. Furthermore, local and regional institutions can benefit when central authorities disseminate evaluation findings nationally.

Notes

1. Indeed, there are at least grounds for conjecture that the high standards of wages and conditions of employment prevailing in some industrial districts are not just a consequence of this form of industrial organisation but may even constitute a *requirement* of innovation-based competition. The point is that innovation occurs in people's minds. The volunteering of ideas cannot be compelled, but requires willing collaboration. The exchange of ideas also requires trust. An environment in which perceptions of fairness and distributive justice are common is likely to be more conducive to innovation than one characterised by mistrust and the desire for retribution. For an examination of the managerial implications of this view see Kim & Mauborgne (1997).

2. The term "trust" should not be taken here as referring to a belief in the moral quality of another's intentions, but rather to the predictability of generally constructive behaviour. In the words of a leading theorist "Trust is a repeated game in which everyone has something to gain".

3. These costs are benefits to the firms joining an established consortium. In the language of economics, these benefits have the character of a "public good". That is, once they have joined, latecomers cannot be excluded from these benefits, while their use of these benefits does not decrease the availability of the benefits for others. The "public good" problems associated with loan guarantee consortia were pointed out by Hughes (1992).

Chapter VII

Entrepreneurship in the New Social Economy

Between the state sector and the market, there is a whole set of organisations governed by types of legal status that differ from one Member country to another. They are involved in manufacturing, processing and/or distribut[...] services, for the benefit of their members or for the comm[...] organisations differ from the public and private sectors in their [...] *Employment in NGO* they operate. Broadly speaking, they belong to the "third sector" by virtue of their common origin: meeting needs that are not met, or are only partly met, by the public sector or the market. They can also be defined as the product of individual or collective initiatives meant to introduce new practices or break through bottlenecks for which traditional systems and established norms have no satisfactory solution (Lorthiois, 1996).

At the international level, this sector includes many different kinds of organisation. However, an increasing number, especially those set up since the 1970s, are run on a commercial basis. Over the years, with the changes that have occurred in all spheres of the economy and the new style of management in public affairs, the more innovative of these organisations have become new economic agents.[1]

The growing importance of the non-profit sector (NPS)

In the absence of an internationally agreed definition of the not-for-profit sector,[2] due to the very varied nature of the organisations claiming to belong to this sector and the wide range of statutory frameworks, national or otherwise, that govern Non-Profit Organisations (NPOs), it is hard to assess the economic importance of the NPS. Despite the obstacles, however, an analysis by Johns Hopkins University of 13 countries including 8 OECD Member countries, highlights some interesting figures[3] from the tables reproduced here in Figures 7.1 and 7.2. They show that, depending on the country concerned, the NPS accounts for a percentage of total employment that ranges from 1 per cent (Hungary) to 7 per cent

Figure 7.1. **Employment in the non-profit sector**

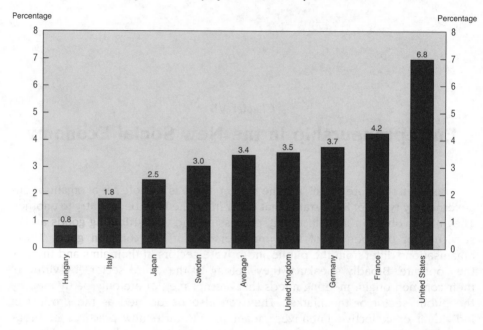

1. Non-weighted average (by country population) in order to avoid the predominance of the United States.
Source: Archambault, 1996*b*.

(United States). The operating expenditures of the sector as a percentage of national GDP varies within about the same range. Figure 7.3 shows that, for all eight countries, private earnings (users' shareholdings, subscriptions, sales and income from investment) are the main source of income, accounting for 47 per cent. Public funding amounts to 43 per cent of the total, and private or business donations only 10 per cent. However, this average conceals wide disparities, as can be seen from Figure 7.4. In France and Germany, unlike the other countries, government funding predominates.

In Europe, several countries are showing increasing interest in the NPS, as is suggested by recent research by INSEE (*Institut National de la Statistique et des Études Économiques*) in France and by new regulations in Italy and Belgium for organisations with a social scope. The European Commission has launched a vast horizontal work programme which seeks, among other things, to link local development and employment initiatives to the NPS.

Figure 7.2.   **Operating expenditures of non-profit sector as per cent of GDP**

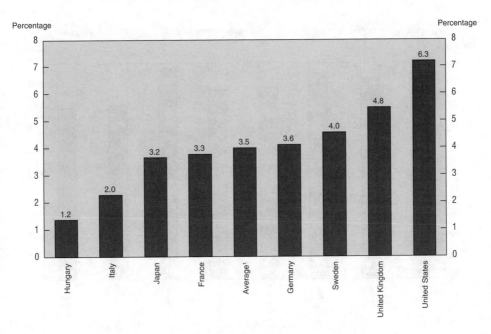

1.   Non-weighted average.
Source: Archambault, 1996*b*.

The new social economy and its entrepreneurs fit into the competitive economy but also rely on government funding, depending on the project in hand, *e.g.*,

- Activating hitherto unused or under-used material and immaterial resources. This applies to "social enterprises" that generate new skills and new jobs, their chosen aim being to integrate those in greatest difficulty into the local and regional labour markets.
- Creating new, high-quality services at prices affordable to as wide a section of the community as possible. Examples of this are NPOs that run public-interest activities connected with social action, coaching for school children, care for the elderly, environmental protection, cultural development, etc. Besides mobilising funds and support from a range of sources, they give direct or indirect responsibility to users or beneficiaries of the operations undertaken, cutting government intervention costs by preventive action or consciousness-raising.

Figure 7.3. **Sources of non-profit sector revenue**

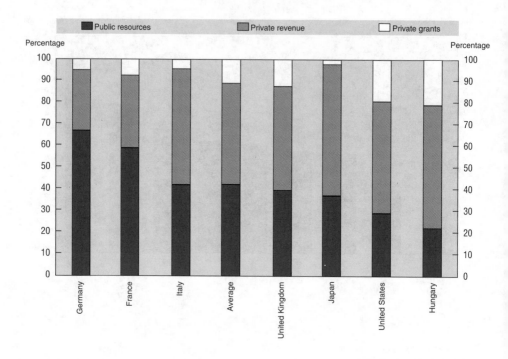

Source: Archambault, 1996*b*.

– Fostering local development by pooling information, skills and financial resources through formal or informal networks of affiliated organisations, increasingly by means of the new information technologies. These initiatives range from setting up a development agency with support services for new businesses to creating financial instruments that gather local savings to meet the financing needs of project initiators whose needs are not addressed by the rather standardised services offered by conventional loan institutions. They usually involve banks, the authorities and international or regional organisations in partnerships geared to attaining particular goals.

This spirit of enterprise is in a way a two-sided affair. It affects demand and supply simultaneously, by mechanisms connected either with government policy and ongoing policy changes, or with the market, through competitive supply. The

Figure 7.4. **Resources of the non-profit sector**
Eight country average

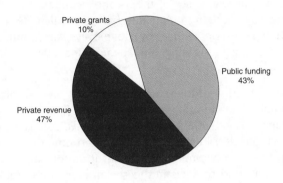

Source: Archambault, 1996*b*.

increasing overlap between these new enterprises, the public sector economy
and the market economy calls for examination.

Applying the business approach to the NPS[4]

The approach of the NPS is not very different from a straightforward business
approach. The starting point that triggers the initiative is the identification of a
collective need, whether this concerns a social group, professional group, ethnic
community or territorial community. However, NPS business activities are conducted for the common good (Maiello, 1997). While the entrepreneur can be
regarded as a risk-taker who combines resources in a coherent and efficient way,
innovates, creates new services, products or processes, makes a long-term commitment by defining goals and generates profits over and above the current
allocation of resources (European Commission, 1997; LEDA, 1996), his/her coun-
terpart, the social entrepreneur, seems to bring all the same skills into action
except for the capacity to distribute financial profits.

As NPOs and social enterprises (see example of Italy's social co-operatives,
below) increasingly seek to solve social problems (European Commission Per-
spectives Unit, 1996; and Ben Ner & Gui, 1993), the pressure on them tends to
increase and demand greater professionalism. The importance of the quality
factor in services rendered by the NPS places it in competition with the private
sector, at least in some fields. For example, NPOs must learn how to manage their

structure just like a private business and must obtain significant, easy-to-interpret, readily accessible results (Girard & Neuschwander, 1997). In the vast field of local development, where the social meets the economic (OECD, 1996*f*), NPOs stimulate demand (by changing latent needs into explicit demand) and/or provide an innovative good or service by developing or running local or interregional networks or by harnessing human and financial resources for mutual benefit.

As regards the granting of loans for projects that are "atypical" according to the banks' recognised standards, a wave of new financing organisations has emerged in Europe.[5] The INAISE *network* (*International Association of Investors in the Social Economy*) was founded in 1989. It has its head office in Brussels, and gives institutional form to this movement. At present it unites some forty newer financial organisations that fund projects in the social, environmental and local development spheres and which are considered to have a high job creation potential. All these financial institutions provide backup services for job creators, cutting by 20 to 30 per cent the risk of the new enterprises failing after three years in operation. The latest of these new financial institutions is the *Caisse Solidaire Nord Pas-de-Calais*, backed by several French banks. Since October 1997 it offers the general public a form of saving that is designed to create jobs; these are fixed-time accounts paying 2 per cent interest at most. Other financial bodies, in particular in Belgium and Switzerland, take in local savings, sometimes with co-operation from banks (mutual funds, savings accounts); with these savings they fund loans at market price or below, for social/environmental projects that generate employment. Savers in this case forego part of the income on their capital. The *Caisse d'Économie de Québec*, in Canada, affiliated to the *Mouvement Desjardins* (the province's first co-operative bank) gives priority to loans for collective entrepreneurship (associations, etc.) and to long-term unemployed people wishing to become self-employed or start a business. In its 26 years of activity, this bank has proven its ability to make profits (above the average for the other 1 300 *Caisses Desjardins*) by creating an alternative relationship with borrowers – settling problems, meeting needs – and relying on numerous local networks.

In Canada and the United States, non-profit organisations have set up enterprise networks (the Flexible Business Network) to support economic development and help SMEs conquer new markets (Corporation for Enterprise Development, 1988). The French *"Boutiques de Gestion"* management shop network has been in operation for eighteen years, during which time it has assisted 45 000 business start-ups and has helped create some 6 000 jobs per year (1996 annual report submitted by the *Comité de Liaison des Boutiques de Gestion* to the French ministry for employment and solidarity). It especially focuses on young entrepreneurs (12 per cent of their business creating customers are under 26) and women, through information campaigns and individualised training. The Austrian organisation ÖSB

Box 7.1. **Local development in deprived areas: United States and Mexico**

Community Development Financial Institutions – CDFIs in the United States

Community Development Financial Institutions (CDFIs) are financial intermediaries with a local development mission: they provide very small loans. There are four kinds of CDFI: *i)* local development banks, *ii)* local credit unions (often co-operatives founded by immigrants a century ago), *iii)* local development funds (which just act as intermediaries to attract investors), and *iv)* micro-loan programs. They use their financial capacities to make direct or indirect loans and investments that commercial banks will not make, and they finance training and advice for business or real estate ownership, and other local development services. The *South Shore Bank* of Chicago is one of the best known CDFIs. It began by investing in an underprivileged area of Chicago with a 98 per cent black population, and then extended itself to cover other communities, outside the State of Illinois. It is also involved in programmes for Eastern Europe.

The *Community Development Banking and Financial Institutions* Act of 1994 created the *Federal* CDFI *Fund*, managed by the *Treasury Department*, to grant subsidies, loans and technical assistance to duly selected lenders. The government also offers non-repayable tax credits to those investing capital in CDFIs; these credits should amount to US\$ 48 million for the period 1997-2002.

Mexico: Privatisation recipe for employment and social development

In November 1991, the Mexican government set up the *National Solidarity Programme*, which provided for the creation of the *National Support Fund for Solidary Enterprise* (FONAES) and the transfer of the BANRURAL portfolio to the *Secretariat for Social Development* (SEDESOL).

FONAES was founded six years ago, with the aim of backing entrepreneurial initiative and so give a boost to equitable, sustainable development in Mexico. FONAES is particularly active in areas where poverty is passed on from generation to generation, owing to isolation or resource scarcity. During its first five years in existence, FONAES created and monitored nation-wide 26 000 enterprises set-up as social co-operatives, taking over from financial institutions that did not wish to venture onto this terrain. It works on the principle of offering the poorest people opportunities to assert themselves and organise themselves in production communities to improve their living conditions. Two hundred and fifty thousand jobs have been created this way. Designed to combat poverty, FONAES is helping to develop a network of new social enterprises using such instruments as venture capital, guarantee funds and financing funds.

---

was set up on the same basis; it now advises the *Federal Ministry of Social Affairs* on ways to develop active labour market policies and support business formation.

These few examples barely indicate the abundance of ongoing initiatives in the social economy. The social enterprises that are now emerging in most OECD countries deserve special mention. A social enterprise is defined as an economic entity whose main aim is to integrate low-skilled, high-risk people into the labour market after a period of learning on the job that lasts between 4 months and 2 years, depending on the national background and the beneficiaries' particular situation. These firms pay reduced social security contributions or receive financial support from the government for staff employed on this basis. Italy's social co-operatives are one example of the social and entrepreneurial innovation models that have developed in Europe. Their social objectives are to enhance the employability of people with severe to very severe problems, or with no skills or qualifications – young people especially. But they also have the economic aims of keeping a balanced budget, planning investments, etc. They develop by multiplying their production activities through subsidiaries, in much the same way a private enterprise would introduce a new product or service. In Italy today there are 2 500 social co-operatives with about 50 000 employees and some 15 000 voluntary staff; they achieve annual sales of about L 2 000 billion (Maiello, 1997; Agnelli Foundation, 1997).

As they industrialise or grow by branching out, social enterprises are confronted with the laws of the market and with their stakeholders' demand for results (in particular public sector contributors). This tension forces promoters of these initiatives to use forms of sponsorship fairly similar to the promotion techniques used in the private sector.

Box 7.2. **Examples of social enterprises in Scotland and Germany**

In *Scotland* the *Wise Group* is a non-profit-distributing company employing and training unemployed people to install insulation, energy-efficient heating and home security systems, and to carry out environmental improvements in low-income neighbourhoods. It operates in Scotland, Derby and Newham. In 1995, it employed 234 people and recruited nearly 800 trainees. During their eight-week induction period, trainees receive benefits plus £ 10 sterling; then they are paid a proper wage for the remaining 44 weeks of their contract. Having employees work for wages rather than benefit is a crucial feature of the *Wise Group*'s success. As well as a "rate for the job", this programme provides a contract and employee status. The most recent figures available show that two thirds of trainees found a job at some point after leaving the Group. The percentage of people still employed or self-employed at 3 and 6 months after leaving were 43 per cent and 46 per cent respectively. This is significantly higher than the results achieved in comparable areas by the *Training for Work* programme, which was then the main government scheme for the long-term unemployed.

In *Germany*, the *Sozialbetriebe* (social enterprises) of Lower Saxony produce goods and services for the market and hire the long-term unemployed in order to assist their re-integration into the labour market. More than 50 companies employ 1 000 people in such varied fields as catering, environmental protection, recycling and manufacturing.

An intricate mix of the commercial and non-commercial

In every Member country, history, culture, regulations and tax systems have shaped a fabric of organisations that are neither public nor private, but which have productive activities intended to harness resources to satisfy needs. Treated as suppliers of collective goods and services, NPOs traditionally only supplied a residual demand, funded by obligatory levies. However, now that calls for tender or proposals are the general rule, the authorities "purchase" or contract out services to NPOs in order to spread "good practice" on a large scale (transferring and adapting experiences that prove positive in terms of cost effectiveness). This means that, increasingly, NPOs and the private sector[6] compete with each other in markets organised by the state.

Active labour market policies now tend to transfer public services to the private sector and to NPOs (see documents prepared for the European Council of Labour and Employment Ministers, November 1997). They delegate to these organisations the task of helping job seekers back into the world of work, helping them find a job or become self-employed. In the selected organisations, these beneficiaries find themselves in real job situations while also receiving training in situ. Of the young or unemployed people benefiting from these programmes, the percentage who enter or return to employment afterwards varies between 40 per cent and 80 per cent, depending on a number of variables: the general unemployment rate, the beneficiary's degree of handicap (social or health problems, etc.), the skilfulness of the support structure in negotiating partnerships and fitting into the local environment, etc. From the decentralisation standpoint, the federal or nation-state is devolving more and more of its powers to lower government echelons, which then become responsible for providing services, identifying operators capable of carrying them out, or even issuing proposals for the supply of such services.

The NPOs also produce commercial goods and services (sold at a price that is intended to at least cover production costs) but also non-commercial services, provided either free or at a price unrelated to the cost, the difference being made up by subscriptions, subsidies, etc. – funding sources that are external to the market. Some NPS activities are "economic" (i.e., profitable from the producer's point of view if the target customers have sufficient income), while some are "social", for beneficiaries who cannot pay the market price (Vienney, 1994). In other words, the NPOs become partners to both state and market, producing goods and services both for the general interest and for the market.

But the motivations that prompt NPOs to produce and develop new methods of production go far beyond any defining features of the public and private sectors (Manfredi, 1997). Standards of supply were referred to earlier in connection with funding by banks – a supply that does not always match the demand from new types of enterprise – and innovations introduced by the new financial institutions. Similarly, collective needs are segmented in a way that the authorities find hard to take into account, since they have to provide for the general interest. This opens up a whole new field for the NPOs' operations. Close to the grass roots, they can interpret and anticipate the needs of the most vulnerable groups and further their integration into social and professional life. Closely in touch with the general interest but aware of the dangers of forgetting that specific situations and needs keep on increasing, the NPOs reveal new demands. And once the new demands have been formalised, they can be presented to public sector decision makers through the NPOs' partnership with these bodies.

Interactions with public policy

For several years now, experts have been reconsidering the contribution of the NPS to the production of collective goods and services. Rather than attributing the existence of the NPS to the failings of the state or the private sector, S. Salamon introduces a new argument, highlighting the business-like approach of the sector in the way it has anticipated new demands to be met. These new demands emerged as a result of changes in society (*e.g.*, the greater participation of women in the labour market, longer life expectancy, the need to update skills for better access to the labour market) and helped by movements calling for more sustainable forms of development (a movement to which the NPS has generally contributed). At first, finance was not forthcoming, either from the market or the authorities, as it seemed it would be hard for some of these projects to achieve solvency. Moreover, needs connected with quality of life or security were not necessarily identified straight away as demands that might become effective in the long run. One example is the community services programme in France. After experimenting in this sphere for many years, the French state has decided to increase its investment by means of a youth employment programme that relies particularly on NPOs to develop new opportunities for expanded economic viability in this new branch of industry (through help for business creation, financial packages).

The NPOs are hotbeds of ideas and experiments, and they are able to get innovative policies adopted at the central, regional or local government levels. In recent years, for example, the US government, in partnership with the NPS and the private sector, has introduced a series of job creation measures for the long-term unemployed and introduced specific programs to revitalise deprived areas. In advancing the concept of *"Workfare"*, it has in effect institutionalised initiatives stemming from associations and local communities, focusing on career design and participation in an active society. One good example in the United States is a pilot project to promote self-employment among people on welfare, run by a non-profit organisation and adapted from French and English programmes for unemployed people starting up in business. This led to regional legislation in advance of the new active labour market policies, whose effective introduction dates from July 1997, when the Federal welfare budget was devolved to individual States.

Questions outstanding

A number of questions remain unanswered, however, especially as concerns the law on competition (unions of NPOs and limited calls for tender in some countries or regions with regard to NPOs or co-operatives may contravene regulations). Distortions may also arise in this connection, as when public contracts include clauses with social criteria such as the obligation to provide training and jobs for the long-term unemployed, marginalised young people, etc. In another example, the French government recently made it obligatory for enterprises in France tendering for government building contracts to adopt a commercial status. Similar projects are being considered in other countries.

Other quantitative and qualitative studies are needed to provide better guidelines for public policy, along the lines of the *Zamagni Commission* in Italy, whose task is to study the best ways for NPOs to fit into the economy and how they can be made viable. In Ireland, the government has commissioned the *National Economic and Social Forum* to reflect on how the social economy can be included in the "plural economy" (OECD, 1996f); the Forum has drawn attention to the danger of marginalising NPOs. In Belgium, a new status has been created for non-*profit associations* (ASBLs): that of a "company with a social purpose". This brings greater rigour and responsibility to their management; it is intended to limit certain abuses identified in the management of associations which, even if they cannot make profits, can offer considerable perks to some of their members. It also clarifies the question of associations that offer commercial services: although operating in a competitive market, they have to identify precisely the social purposes to which they allocate their resources.

The success of the NPOs is due, so far, to their ability to innovate and remain competitive in developing and supplying high quality goods and services, at reduced cost. The comparative advantage of the non-profit sector also lies, no doubt, in its ability to reduce transaction costs. In co-operation with the authorities and the private sector, it can work for the common good more easily than an entrepreneur driven by the profit motive. Recent developments seem to support this assumption although not all NPOs have progressed in the same way. In summary, entrepreneurship in the social economy adds extra value to the production of goods and services by its ethical approach and its contribution to social cohesion and sustainable development.

Notes

1. In this chapter, we analyse organisations which, in terms of the rules and regulations in force in the countries concerned, are not regarded as business firms with regard to all their activities but are considered entrepreneurial. However, other organisations that today belong to the competitive sector but which have social aims and invest in the social economy/third sector (some co-operatives, new financial institutions) are also dealt with. They show that some activities, especially activities connected with the emergence of new societal demands, can be run on a commercial basis.

2. According to research by Anheier & Salamon (1997), there are three classifications of the economy that account for the NPS in a more or less satisfactory way. These are ISIC, the system set up by the *United Nations*; NACE, the *Eurostat* nomenclature of economic activities; and NTEE, a US taxonomy of tax-exempt organisations. Criticisms of the ISIC system focus on the fact that it excludes NPS organisations that derive more than 50 per cent of their income from public finances. NACE, although it has added two further categories to those of ISIC (research and development, and leisure and culture), ignores that part of social programme implementation that has been transferred from government to the NPS. Like ISIC, it also underestimates the contractual status of conventions or partnership agreements between NPS organisations and the authorities. The NTEE, for its part, classifies organisations by the missions they adopt at the time of their foundation.

3. The *Johns Hopkins* evaluation of the NPS, although it proceeds from a common definition of this sector, covers a very disparate collection of organisations which have to be seen in relation to the history, legislation and government policy of each country. Significantly, no other attempt at quantification is currently available internationally. In 1993, the *System of National Accounts* (SNA), to which many OECD Member countries refer, was revised and began to include non-profit institutions under the heading of non-commercial transactions. All the same, the SNA gives neither a complete overview of the NPS nor does it provide detailed figures which capture the advancement and gradual transformation taking place in this sector.

4. Reference is made to NPS organisations which motivate this sector to be innovative and entrepreneurial. This movement is not necessarily representative of the whole not-for-profit sector; notable differences exist within the same sector of activity and from country to country.

5. The status necessary to carry out their activities does not necessarily enable us to identify them as being non-profit organisations; categories in trade registers are of no use for identifying structures that claim to be part of the social economy. Indeed, some demand that a specific new status be created for "non-profit financial instruments of social interest" (INAISE, 1997).

6. The notion of a non-commercial service is only of relative value in this context, since private sector firms consider services to the public sector as services to be billed in the usual way.

References

LES PLACEMENTS ALTERNATIFS ET SOLIDAIRES" (1997),
Alternatives économiques, hors série, Paris.

ACOA (1996),
"The Implementation of an Entrepreneurship Development Strategy in Canada: The Case of the Atlantic Region", OECD, Paris.

ALBERTINI, J.M. (1996),
Le chômage est-il une fatalité ?, PUF, Paris.

ALLERS, M.A. (1994),
Administrative and Compliance Costs of Taxation and Public Transfers in the Netherlands, University of Groningen.

AMIRAHMADI, H. and SAFF, G. (1993),
"Science Parks: A Critical Assessment" in Journal of Planning Literature, Vol. 8, No. 2, November.

ANHEIER, K. and SALAMON, L.M. (1997),
Defining Non-profit Sector, A cross-national analysis, Manchester University Press, UK.

ARCHAMBAULT, E. (1996a),
Le secteur sans but lucratif, Édition Economica, Paris.

ARCHAMBAULT, E. (1996b),
Revue internationale de l'économie sociale, No. 261, 3rd trimester, Paris.

ARROW, K. (1962),
"Economic Welfare and the Allocation of Resources for Invention" in The Rate and Direction of Inventive Activity: Economic and Social Factors, University Press, Princeton.

AUBRY, M. (1997),
Inffo Flash, No. 481, 14 September, Paris.

BANNOCK, G. & PARTNERS LTD. (1994),
European Second-Tier Markets for NTBFs, Graham Bannock & Partners Ltd., London.

BARRET, S., COLENUTT, D, FOSTER, R, GLYNN, D., JAFFER, S., JONES, I. and RIDYARD, D. (1990),
An Evaluation of the Loan Guarantee Scheme, Research Paper No. 74, Department of Employment Group, London.

BATIFOULIER, P. (1995),
L'économie sociale, Que sais-je, PUF, Paris.

BAUMOL, W.J. (1993),
Entrepreneurship, Management and the Structure of Payoffs, Massachusetts Institute of Technology, Massachusetts.

BEN NER, A. and GUI, B. (1993),
   The Non-profit Sector in the Mixed Economy, University of Michigan Press.

BENUS, J., JOHNSON, T.R. and WOOD, M. (1994),
   "A New Reemployment Strategy: Final Report on the UI Self-Employment Demonstration", Occasional Paper 95-4, US Department of Labor, Washington, D.C.

BICKERDYKE, I. and LATTIMORE, R. (1997),
   "Reducing the Regulatory Burden: Does Firm Size Matter?" Staff Research Paper, Industry Commission, Canberra.

BIRCH, D. (1979),
   The Job Generation Process, MIT programme on Neighbourhood and Regional Change, Cambridge, Massachusetts.

BIRCH, D., HAGGERTY, A. and PARSONS, W. (1996),
   Entrepreneurial Hot Spots: The Best Places in America to Start and Grow a Company, Cognetics Inc., Massachusetts.

BIRCH, D., HAGGERTY, A. and PARSONS, W. (1997a),
   Who's Creating Jobs, Cognetics Inc, Cambridge, Massachusetts.

BIRCH, D., HAGGERTY, A. and PARSONS, W. (1997b),
   Corporate Almanac, Cognetics Inc., Massachusetts.

BLANCHFLOWER, D.(1996),
   "Youth Labour Markets in Twenty-three Countries: A Comparison Using Microdata", Center for Economic Performance Discussion Paper, No. 284, LSE, London.

BLANCHFLOWER, D. and OSWALD, A.J. (1990),
   "What makes a Young Entrepreneur", National Bureau of Economic Research, Working Paper No. 3252, University of Chicago Press, London.

BOYCKO, M. and SHLEIFER, A. (1996),
   Privatising Russia, MIT, Cambridge, Massachusetts.

BRUSCO, S. (1996a),
   "Trust, Social Capital and Local Development: Some Lessons from the Experience of the Italian Industrial Districts", Networks of Enterprises and Local Development, OECD, Paris.

BRUSCO, S. (1996b),
   "Global System and Local Systems", in Cossentino, F., Pyke, F. and Sengeneberger, W (eds.), Local and Regional Response to Global Pressure: The Case of Italy and Its Industrial Districts, Institute for Labour Studies, Geneva.

BRUSCO, S. (1983),
   "Distretti industriali, servizi alle imprese e centri di comparto", paper presented to the seminar "Innovazione Tecnologica, Ruolo della Piccola Imprese e Intervento del Governo Locale" held in Turin, 25 February 1983.

CAMPBELL, M. (1996),
   "Local Labour Market Management", Report to the Directing committee of the LEED Programme, November, OECD, Paris.

CANTILLON, R. (1755),
   Essai sur la nature du commerce en général, Ireland.

CASSON, M. (1982),
   The Entrepreneur: An Economic Theory, Martin Robertson, Oxford.

CECOP (1995),
   "L'entreprise sociale : une chance pour l'Europe", first European Conference on Social
   Co-operation, Brussels.

CENTER FOR THE STUDY OF ENTREPRENEURSHIP (1993),
   "Wisconsin's Entrepreneurial Climate Study", Marquette University, mimeograph.

CENTRE FOR COMMUNITY ENTERPRISE (1997),
   Making Waves, Working Document No. 3, Port Alberni, Canada.

CHARLEROI TRAVERSES (1996),
   Let's Go: Petite histoire du LETS, No. 105, January.

COMITÉ DE LIAISON DES BOUTIQUES DE GESTION (ed.) (1996),
   Annual Report.

CORPORATION FOR ENTERPRISE DEVELOPMENT (ed.) (1998),
   Annual Report, Washington, D.C.

COSH, A. and HUGHES, A. (eds.) (1996),
   *The Changing State of British Enterprise: Growth, Innovation and Competitive Advantage in Small
   and Medium Sized Firms*, 1986-95, ESRC Centre for Business Research, University of
   Cambridge.

COSTA-CAMPI, M.T. *et al.* (1993),
   "Co-operation entre empresas y systemas productivas locales en Espagna", IMPI,
   Ministry of Industry.

CURRAN, J. and BURROWS, R. (1991),
   Paths of Enterprise, Routledge, London.

DAVIS, S.J., HALTIWANGER, J. and SCHUH, S. (1993),
   "Small Business and Job Creation: Dissecting the Myth and Reassessing the Facts,"
   NBER Working Paper No. 4492.

DENNIS, W.J. Jr (1996a),
   Small Business Problems and Priorities, NFIB Education Foundation, Washington, D.C.

DENNIS, W.J. Jr (1996b),
   "Small Business Access to Capital: Impediments and Options", Testimony before the
   Committee on Small Business, House of Representatives, 28 February, Serial
   No. 104-62, US Government Printing Office: Washington, D.C.

DENNIS, W.J. Jr. (1995),
   Small business primer, NFIB Foundation, Washington, D.C.

DTI (1996),
   Your Business Matters: Government Response, Department of Trade and Industry, London,
   June.

DTI (1997),
   "Growth Constraints on Small and Medium Sized Firms", report prepared
   by Alan Hughes on behalf of the ESRC Centre for Business Research, University of
   Cambridge and PACEC for the Department of Trade and Industry, London.

EASTSIDE COMMUNITY INVESTMENT INC. (1990),
   Developing Self-Employment Opportunities through Family Home Day Care, Eastside Community Investment Inc., Indianapolis, Indiana.

ENJOLRAS, B. (1995),
   "Annals of Public and Co-operative Economics", Oxford/Cambridge.

EUROPEAN COMMISSION (1995),
"Stratégie européenne d'encouragement aux initiatives locales de développement et emploi", COM 273/95, Brussels.

EUROPEAN COMMISSION(1997a),
"Communication de la Commission sur la promotion du rôle des associations et fondations en Europe", DG XXIII, Brussels.

EUROPEAN COMMISSION(1997b),
Mise en œuvre de l'action pilote "Troisième système et l'emploi", Programme de travail, Brussels.

EUROPEAN COMMISSION(1997c),
Euro-info, July/August, Brussels.

EUROPEAN COMMISSION, EUROSTAT (1997),
"Le Secteur coopératif, mutualiste et associatif dans l'Union européenne", Brussels.

EUROPEAN COMMISSION PERSPECTIVE UNIT (1996),
Lessons for Territorial and Local Employment Pacts, first report on local development and employment initiatives, European Commission Forward Studies Unit, November.

EUROPEAN OBSERVATORY FOR SMEs (1995),
Annual Report, EIM Small Consultancy, Zoetermeer, The Netherlands.

EUROPEAN NETWORK FOR SME RESEARCH (1996),
Fourth Annual Report, EIM Small Business Research and Consultancy, the Netherlands.

EUROPEAN VENTURE CAPITAL ASSOCIATION (1997),
A Survey of Venture Capital and Private Equity in Europe, 1997 Yearbook, Zaventen, Belgium.

FAVREAU, L. (1997),
"L'économie sociale mise en perspective : renouvellement au Nord et émergence au Sud", University of Québec at Hull, Canada.

FENN, G.W., LIANG, N. and PROWSE, S. (1995),
The Economics of the Private Equity Market, Board of Governors of the Federal Revenue System, Washington, D.C.

FIALSKI, H. (1994),
"Insolvency Law in the Federal Republic of Germany" in Corporate Bankruptcy and Reorganisation Procedures in OECD and Central and Eastern European Countries, OECD, Paris.

FONDATION ROI BAUDOIN (1994),
"Développer l'entreprise sociale : Portraits d'aujourd'hui, Questions pour demain", Brussels.

GAILLOT, L. (1995),
"French Bankruptcy Law" in Turnarounds & Workouts Europe, Beard Group Inc., Washington, D.C., Vol. 4, No. 1, January.

GAO (1995),
Manufacturing Extension Programs: Manufacturers Views of Services, Report GAO/GGD-95-216BR, Washington, D.C.

GAO (1996),
Regulatory Burden: Measurement Challenges and Concerns Raised by Selected Companies, Report GAO/GGD-97-2, Washington, D.C.

GELSING, L. and KNOP, P. (1991),
"Status of the Network Programme: results from a questionnaire survey", National Agency for Industry and Trade, Copenhagen.

GIBB, A.A. (1997),
   "Entrepreneurship and Small Business Management: Can We Afford to Neglect them in the Twenty-first Century Business School?", British Journal of Management, Vol. 7.

GIRARD, A. and NEUSCHWANDER, C. (1997),
   Le Libéralisme contre la démocratie. Le temps des citoyens, Éditions la Découverte et Syros, Paris.

GOULD, A. and KEEBLE, D. (1984),
   "New firms and Rural Industrialisation in East Anglia", Regional Studies, Vol. 18.3.

GRANT THORNTON (ed.) (1996),
   European Business Survey, London.

GRAVES, F. and GAUTHIER, B. (1996),
   Evaluation of the Self-Employment Assistance Program, Human Resources Development Canada, Ottawa.

HALL, C. (1995),
   "The Entrepreneurial Engine", paper presented at the OECD "High-Level Workshop on SMEs: Employment, Innovation and Growth", held in Washington, D.C., 16-17 June, mimeograph.

HARM, C. (1992),
   The Financing of Small Firms in Germany, Policy Research Working Paper 899, World Bank, Washington, D.C.

HART, P. and OULTON, N. (1996),
   "Growth and Size of Firms", The Economic Journal, Vol. 106, September.

HELLMAN, T. and STIGLITZ, J. (1995),
   "A Unifying Theory of Credit and Equity Rationing in Markets with Adverse Selection" Research Paper No. 1356, Graduate School of Business, Stanford University.

HUBER, P. (1996),
   "Stylised facts of New Enterprise Formation in Central and Eastern Europe", conference document, Vienna.

HUGHES, A. (1992),
   "The 'Problems' of Finance for Smaller Businesses", Working Paper No. 15, Small Business Research Centre, University of Cambridge.

HUGHES, A. (1997),
   "Small Firms and Employment", Working Paper No. 71, ESRC Centre for Business Research, University of Cambridge,.

INAISE EPICEA (1997),
   "Les instruments financiers de l'économie sociale et la création d'entreprises", document prepared for the European Commission DG V, Brussels.

INDUSTRY TASKFORCE ON LEADERSHIP AND MANAGEMENT SKILLS (1995),
   Enterprising Nation, Australian Government Publishing Service, Canberra.

INSTITUTO NATIONAL DE ESTATISTICA (1997),
   Encuesta sobre innovacion tecnologica en las empresas 1994, Madrid.

IRDAC (1996),
   "IRDAC Opinion on Intellectual Property Rights", Industrial R&D Advisory Committee of the European Commission, Brussels.

JOHANISSON, B. (1989),
"Community Entrepreneurship, Leader for Local Economic Development", Note for the OECD-ILE Directing Committee, May, Paris.

JORGENSON, D.W. and LANDAU, R. (eds.) (1993),
Tax Reform and the Cost of Capital: An International Comparison, The Brookings Institution, Washington, D.C.

KAUFMANN, F. and KOKALJ, L (1996),
Risikokapitalmärkte für mittelständische Unternehemen, IFM, Bonn.

KIM, C. and MAUBORGNE, R (1997),
"Fair Process: Managing in the Knowledge Economy", Harvard Business Review, Cambridge, Massachusetts.

KIRCHOFF, B.A. (1994),
Entrepreneurship and Dynamic Capitalism, Westport, Conn., Praeger.

KNACK, S and KEEFER, P. (1997),
"Does Social Capital Have an Economic Payoff? A Cross-Country Investigation", *Quarterly Journal of Economics*, Vol. 112, No. 4.

KNIGHT, F.H. (1940, 5th edition),
Risk, Uncertainty and Profit, Houghton Mifflin, Boston.

LAMOND, P., MARTINEAU, Y. and ALLEN, D. (1994),
"Impact économique et fiscal des investissements du Fonds de Solidarité des Travailleurs du Québec (FTQ), 1984-1993", Institut National de la Recherche Scientifique (INRS), University of Québec.

LA PORTA, R., LOPEZ-DE-SILANES, F., SHLEIFER, A. and VISHNY, R.W. (1997),
"Legal Determinants of External Finance" NBER Working Paper No. 5879, National Bureau of Economic Research, Cambridge, Massachusetts, January.

LAVILLE, J.L. (1992),
"Services de proximité en Europe", Syros, Paris.

LEADBEATER, C. (1997),
"A Piece of the Action: Employee Ownership, Equity Pay and the Rise of the Knowledge Economy" Demos, London.

LEDA (1996),
"Culture d'entreprise, création d'emplois et nouveaux services", Document Ressource, European Commission, DG Employment and Industrial Relations, March.

LEIBFRITZ, W., THORNTON, J. and BIBLEE, A. (1997),
"Taxation and Economic Performance", Economics Department Working Paper No. 176, OECD, Paris.

LÉVESQUE, B and NINACS, W.A. (1997),
Background Document for the meeting "Stratégies locales pour l'emploi et l'économie sociale", Montréal, OECD-LEED/IFDEC, June.

LIGHT, I. and BONACICH, E. (1988),
Immigrant Entrepreneurs, University of California Press: Berkeley & Los Angeles, California.

LIPSKY, M. and RATHGEB SMITH, S. (1993),
Non-profits for hire: The Welfare State in the Age of Contracting, Harvard University Press, Cambridge, Massachusetts.

LOGOTECH, S.A. (1997),
"Étude comparative internationale des dispositions légales et administratives pour la formation de petites et moyennes entreprises aux pays de l'Union européenne, les États-Unis et le Japon", EIMS Project, 96/142, Athens.

LORTHIOIS, J.(1996),
Le diagnostic local de ressources, ASDIC, Edition W, Paris.

LOVEMAN, G. and SENGENBERGER, W. (1991),
"The Re-emergence of Small Scale Production: An International Comparison", Small Business Economics, Vol. 3.1.

MAIELLO, M. (1997),
Working document No. 3, Consorzio Gino Matarelli, Brescia, Italy.

MALMER, H., PERSSON, A. and TENGLAD, A. (1994),
Arhundradets Skattereform – Effekter pa skattesystemets driftskostnader, skatteplanering oc skattefusk, Stockholm. (English summary).

MANFREDI, F. (1997),
Economica Management, No. 3, Milan.

MARIE, C-V. (1992),
"Les étrangers non salariés en France, symbole de la mutation économique des années 1980", in Revue européenne des migrations internationales, Vol. 8, No. 1.

MANGHI, B. (1997),
"La solidarietà si fa impresa", Il Sole 24 Ore, Presentation of the Agnelli Foundation's Report, October, Milano.

MASON, C. and HARRISON, R. (1994),
"Informal venture capital in the UK", in Hughes, A. and Storey, D. (eds.) Finance and the Small Firm, Routledge.

MEAGER, N. (1993),
"Self-Employment and Labour Market Policy in the European Community", WZB Discussion Paper FS I 93-201, Berlin.

MOESEN, W.A. (1997),
"The Macroeconomic Performance of Nations and Regions: Cultural and Institutional Determinants", paper prepared for the conference "Employment, Economic Success and Cultural Values", held in Luxemburg, 27-28 November 1997, organised by Foundation Europe of Cultures 2002.

MULLER, H-W. (1997),
"Proceedings from the Conference on Youth Entrepreneurship", organised by the European Commission DG XXIII, held in Larissa, Greece.

MYERSON, A.R.(1996),
"O Governor, Won't You Buy Me a Mercedes Benz?", in New York Times, September.

NASD (1995),
The NASDAQ Stock Market: A practical guide to listing on the NASDAQ Stock Market, National Association of Securities Dealers, Washington, D.C.

NASD (1996),
Going Public, National Association of Securities Dealers, Washington, D.C.

OECD (1992a),
Employment Outlook, OECD Publications, Paris.

OECD (1992*b*),
  Technology and the Economy: The Key Relationships, OECD Publications, Paris.

OECD (1992*c*),
  "Private Sector Involvement in the Delivery of Social Welfare Services", LEED *Notebooks*, OECD, Paris.

OECD (1993),
  Regional Determinants Affecting Firm Creation, OECD Publications, Paris.

OECD (1994*a*),
  The OECD Jobs Study: Facts, Analysis, and Strategies, OECD Publications, Paris.

OECD (1994*b*),
  Employment Outlook, OECD Publications, Paris.

OECD (1994*c*),
  Taxation and Small Businesses, OECD Publications, Paris.

OECD (1995*a*),
  Employment Outlook, OECD Publications, Paris.

OECD (1995*b*),
  "Deregulation and Privatisation in the Service Sector", in OECD *Economic Studies*, No. 25, OECD Publications, Paris.

OECD (1995*c*),
  Boosting Business Advisory Services, OECD Publications, Paris.

OECD (1996*a*),
  "SMES: Employment, Innovation and Growth, The Washington Workshop", Paris.

OECD (1996*b*),
  Tax Expenditures: Recent Experiences, OECD Publications, Paris.

OECD (1996*c*),
  Financial Market Trends, No. 63, OECD Publications, February.

OECD (1996*d*),
  "Microcredit in Transitional Economies", document OCDE/GD(96)40, Paris.

OECD (1996*e*),
  Ireland: Local Partnerships and Social Innovation, OECD Publications, Paris.

OECD (1996*f*),
  Reconciling Economy and Society, OECD Publications, Paris.

OECD (1996*g*),
  "Venture Capital and Innovation", DSTI, document OCDE/GD(96)168, Paris.

OECD (1996*h*),
  Technology, Productivity and Job Creation, OECD Publications, Paris.

OECD (1997*a*),
  "Intellectual Property Rights: Patents and Innovation in the International Context", Paris.

OECD (1997*b*),
  Implementing the OECD Jobs Strategy: Lessons from Member Countries' Experience, OECD Publications, Paris.

OECD (1997*c*),
  Report on Regulatory Reform, Vol. 1 and 2, OECD Publications, Paris.

OECD (1997*d*),
"Public Support to Industry", The OECD Observer, No. 204, Paris.

OECD (1998*a*),
OECD *Economic Survey* – *Australia*, OECD Publications, Paris.

OECD (1998*b*),
OECD *Economic Survey* – *Sweden*, OECD Publications, Paris.

OECD (1998*c*),
OECD *Economic Survey* – *Spain*, OECD Publications, Paris.

OECD (1998*d*),
OECD *Economic Survey* – *Netherlands*, OECD Publications, Paris.

OECD (1998*e*),
Immigrants, Integration and Cities: Exploring the Links, OECD Publications, Paris.

OECD (1998*f*),
Local Management for More Efficient Employment Policies, OECD Publications, Paris.

OWENS, J. and WHITEHOUSE, E. (1996),
"Tax Reform for the 21st Century" in *Bulletin for International Fiscal Documentation*, Vol. 50, No. 11/12, November/December.

PERRET, B. and ROUSTAND, F. (1993),
L'économie contre la société, Le Seuil, Paris.

PIORE, M.J. and SABEL, C.F. (1984),
The Second Industrial Divide, Basic Books Inc., New York.

PORTES, A. and BACH, R. (1985),
Latin Journey: Cuban and Mexican Immigrants in the United States, University of California Press: Berkeley and Los Angeles, California.

PYKE, F. (1997),
"Networks, Development and Change", unpublished paper prepared for the International Institute for Labour Studies, Geneva.

REYNOLDS, P. (1996),
"Business Volatility: Source or Symptom of Economic Growth" paper presented at the "Entrepreneurship, SMEs and the Macro Economy" Conference in Jonkoping, Sweden; mimeograph, Babson College, Massachusetts.

REYNOLDS, P. (1997),
"Who Starts New Firms? Preliminary Explorations of Firms-in-Gestation" in *Small Business Economics*, No. 9: 499-462.

REYNOLDS, P. and STOREY, D. (1993),
"Regional Characteristics Affecting Small Business Formation", ILE Notebooks No. 18, OECD, Paris.

RIDING, A. (1996),
"On the Care and Nurture of the Loan Guarantee Programs", mimeograph, Carleton University, Ottawa.

RODRIK, D. (1997),
"Has Globalization Gone Too Far?", Institute for International Economics, Washington, D.C.

ROSENFELD, S.A. (1996),
"United States: Business Clusters" in *Networks of Enterprises and Local Development*, OECD, Paris.

ROSATI, (1997),
Interview with OECD, 6 June.

SANDFORD, C., GODWIN, M. and HARDWICK, P. (1989),
   Administrative and Compliance Costs of Taxation, Redwood Burn Ltd, Wiltshire, UK.

SAXENIAN, A. (1994),
   Regional Advantage: Culture and Competition in Silicon Valley and Route 128, Harvard University Press, Cambridge, Massachusetts.

SBRC (1992),
   The State of British Enterprise: Growth, Innovation and Competitive Advantage in Small and Medium-Sized Firms, University of Cambridge.

SCHUMPETER, J.A. (1942),
   Capitalism, Socialism and Democracy, Harper and Row, New York.

SHAPIRA, P., ROESSNER, D. and BARKE, R. (1995),
   "New Public Infrastructures for Small Firm Industrial Modernization in the USA", in *Entrepreneurship and Regional Development*, Vol. 7, No. 1, January-March.

SHOREBANK ADVISORY SERVICES (1992),
   Widening the Window of Opportunity, Strategies for the Evolution of Microenterprise Loan Funds, prepared for Charles Stewart Mott Foundation, July, Chicago.

STIGLITZ, J.E. and WEISS, A. (1981),
   "Credit Rationing in Markets with Imperfect Information", American Economic Review, Vol. 71, No. 3, June.

STOREY, D.J. (1994),
   Understanding the Small Business Sector, Routledge, London.

SURET, J-M. (1994),
   "Le fonds de solidarité des travailleurs du Québec: A Cost-Benefit Analysis", Fraser Institute, Vancouver, Canada.

TREMLETT, N. (1993),
   The Business Start-Up Scheme: 18 Month Follow-Up Survey, Social and Community Planning Research, London.

US SMALL BUSINESS ADMINISTRATION (1996),
   The State of Small Business 1995, Washington, D.C.

VENTURE ONE (1997),
   National Venture Capital Association: 1996 Annual Report, San Francisco, California.

VIENNEY, C. (1994),
   L'économie sociale, Éditions la Découverte, Paris.

WESTHEAD, P. and STOREY, D. (1994),
   An Assessment of Firms Located on and off Science Parks in the United Kingdom, HMSO, London.

WETZEL, W.E. Jr. (1987),
   "The Informal Venture Capital Market: Aspects of Scale and market Efficiency, in *Journal of Business Venturing*, Vol. 2.

WILSON, S. and VAN ADAMS, A. (1994),
   "Self-Employment for the Unemployed: Experience in OECD and Transitional Economies", World Bank Discussion Paper No. 263, World Bank, Washington, D.C.

WOLFFE, R. (1996),
   "BMW holds key to industrial future", in *Financial Times*, (6 October 1996), London.

WONG, G., PHELAN, F., DUGAN, B. and LIN, Z. (1994),
   Self-Employment for Unemployed Workers in Canada, Human Resources Canada, Ottawa.

Part II
LEARNING FROM OTHER COUNTRIES

Introduction

The five country case studies were undertaken in 1997 to provide further evidence for the study and to allow for the development of concrete policy recommendations to be tailored to the individual countries. These case studies were reviewed by the OECD's *Economic Development Review Committee* (EDRC) as part of the respective Country Surveys. Subsequently, they were published as chapters in: OECD (1998), OECD *Economic Surveys – Australia*, Paris; OECD (1998), OECD *Economic Surveys – Netherlands*, Paris; OECD (1998), OECD *Economic Surveys – Spain*, Paris; OECD (1998), OECD *Economic Surveys – Sweden*, Paris; OECD (1997), OECD *Economic Surveys – United States*, Paris. The countries chosen for in-depth study were dictated by the EDRC's calendar of country reviews and do not reflect a representative sample of OECD countries.

The OECD has an extensive programme to deliver technical assistance to formerly planned countries in transition to market-based economies. The chapter on entrepreneurship in Eastern Europe is the result of information collected during activities to promote private enterprise development in this region.

Chapter VIII

Australia

In several respects the Australian business sector cannot be considered as particularly entrepreneurial. The rate of enterprise creation has not stood out as high by international comparison, relatively few companies have grown beyond medium size and the industrial sector is still dominated by large resource-based – many foreign-owned – companies (see Box 8.1). As well, the fact that many well-known world-class inventions originating in Australia, such as xerography and the black-box flight recorder, have been commercialised elsewhere suggests luke-warm attitudes towards risk-taking. Such attitudes may have been nurtured by the sense of wealthiness engendered by rich natural resource endowments and, until

---

Box 8.1. **The Australian business sector: an overview**

The Australian business sector differs from that of most other OECD countries in the limited overall role of manufacturing and, within manufacturing, a strong reliance on the traditional resource-based industries. At less than 14 per cent, the share of manu-facturing value added in the economy is the lowest in any OECD country. As a corollary to this the service sector share is large and sharply increasing. In addition, the share of manufacturing value added which takes place in sectors classified as "high-tech" or "medium to high-tech" is the second lowest in the area. The *Business Longitudinal Study* shows a very high share of foreign ownership of larger companies (Table 8.1) particu-larly pronounced in the traditional and resource based industries.

Family-owned companies – a major source of entrepreneurial activity in many Euro-pean countries – make up a very large share of the Australian enterprises, and the share of companies which are relatively young is high across the size categories. However, women's share in top-management, on the other hand, is relatively high: in some of the rapidly growing segments of the service sector the share of female decision makers exceeds 20 per cent. Moreover, the level of formal education in top-management, particularly in small enterprises, is relatively low.

---

fairly recently, by a business environment shielded from foreign competition. However, over the last decade import protection has been substantially reduced, financial markets liberalised, industrial relations modernised, and competition in the non-tradeables sector stimulated through deregulation. The result is an environment more conducive to the development of a dynamic, entrepreneurial business sector, which is a key to higher incomes and better employment prospects. This chapter first documents various aspects of entrepreneurial phenomena in Australia, evaluates factors pertaining to the creation and growth of enterprises and concludes with a discussion of policy implications of the findings.

The state of entrepreneurship

A commonly used proxy for entrepreneurship is the economic importance of the small business sector. As in most other countries, small firms make up the bulk of enterprises in Australia: over 95 per cent of firms are SMEs (defined as those employing fewer than 100 persons in manufacturing and 20 persons in services). Moreover, they employ 56 per cent of the workforce, a share which has been increasing somewhat over the last decade. The main drawback of this measure is that to be meaningful it has to be evaluated at a rather disaggregated level since an aggregate measure is influenced by compositional changes. Indeed, a recent study attributes most of the higher share of SMEs in total employment to the increasing importance of the service sector (which typically operates in smaller units) and to decreases in the average size of industrial enterprises (Levesz & Lattimore, 1997). The same study concludes that one of the forces driving increases in self-employment are rises in the unemployment rate and other factors depressing the chances of finding paid work. However, while such "self-employment by default" may not primarily reflect entrepreneurial endeavour, it does arguably involve a significant element of individual risk-taking. Furthermore, over the period 1983/84 to 1994/95 there was virtually no difference in growth rates between the number of small and large enterprises[1] (Figure 8.1). Overall, it is difficult to draw any clear conclusions about the significance of entrepreneurship on the basis of size-related measures. Referring to small business and self-employment as a proxy for entrepreneurship may, moreover, be misleading since many of them are not particularly innovative or risk-taking.

Another indicator which may be relevant is the pace at which firms are starting up and closing down. This notion of turbulence has the advantage of not relying on definitions of firms' size, age, or growth. It attempts to capture the dynamic nature of entrepreneurial activity in the Schumpeterian sense of creative destruction. While little hard evidence is available for Australia, the Business Longitudinal Study allows a rough estimate of an annual start-up rate of somewhere

Table 8.1. **A snapshot of the Australian business sector**[1]

	Share of all enterprises in relevant category (per cent)
Age and ownership	
Companies less than 5 years old:	
1 to 19 employees	37.4
20 to 99 employees	26.4
At least 100 employees	13.8
Family-owned companies[2]	46.2
Foreign ownership[3]	24.3
Self-employment[4]	14.0
Management	
Decision maker having tertiary education:	
1 to 19 employees	33.2
20 to 99 employees	43.0
At least 100 employees	64.2
Female decision maker	9.5
Flexibility	
Coverage of award arrangements	52.2
Business improvement activities in medium-sized companies[5]	31.6
Having undertaken major changes[6]	
Product range	27.4
Market focus	20.7
Production technology	12.0
Management training	12.8

1. Data relate to 1996.
2. Companies with more than one proprietor, all from the same family.
3. Companies with at least 100 employees.
4. Share of total employment.
5. Companies with 20 to 99 employees, having introduced such activities as quality management or just-in-time inventory control within last three years.
6. Companies which estimate that they have undertaken "major" changes within the last three years.
Source: Business Longitudinal Study.

less than 13 per cent in recent years and a recent study shows that the exit rate is some 7 to 8 per cent. These figures are broadly comparable with other countries' experience, though differences in definition across countries make international comparisons difficult.

A sign of increasing entrepreneurial spirit may, however, be discerned from a sharp strengthening of export orientation of Australian companies in recent years. Given the small size of the domestic market, a business success often depends on its ability to tap the external market. Indeed, Australian exporters have in recent years been capable of gaining market shares in the rapidly growing South-east Asian markets, and they have on the whole performed more strongly in the

Figure 8.1. **Enterprises and employment by industry in Australia**

Average annual growth, 1983-84 to 1994-95

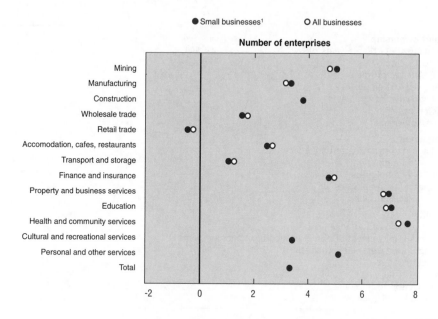

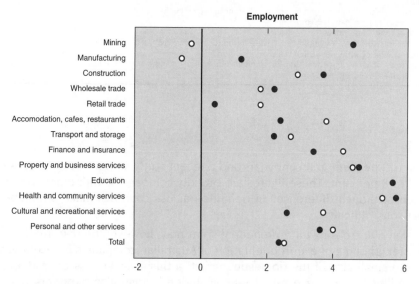

1. Less than 100 employees for mining and manufacturing, less than 20 for other.
Source: Australian Bureau of Statistics.

region than their European and American competitors (Figure 8.2). While some increase in export orientation is a normal consequence of an on-going integration of the Australian economy with the rest of the world and a strong share in the close-by markets would be expected – and, indeed, a weaker exchange rate has helped – a close inspection shows there is something special about the recent phenomenon. Studies found that even comparatively small and young enterprises are now successful exporters and active participants in cross-border networking, with their success built not only on uniqueness of their products or cost advantage but also on managerial competence, commitment to growth and a willingness to tailor their products to the local markets (McKinsey, 1993; Ministry of Foreign Affairs and Trade, 1995).

Another example of emerging entrepreneurial phenomena is a strong performance of companies backed by venture capital. A recent survey (Coopers & Lybrand, 1997) showed that between 1992 and 1996 average sales of venture-backed companies grew by 42 per cent per year and their profits by 59 per cent per year, compared with 6 per cent and 7 per cent, respectively, for the top 100 Australian companies.

The regional dimension. Entrepreneurial dynamism varies between states, though little formal analysis of such inter-state variations has been undertaken. Over the last decade, the average annual growth rate of the number of firms ranged from just over 2 per cent in Northern Territory and New South Wales to nearly 5 per cent in Queensland and Western Australia (Table 8.2), where construction and the service sector particularly stood out. The apparent entrepreneurial dynamism of the service sector of Queensland, however, may be slightly overstated. Semi-retired people have been known to move to this state and invest part of their superannuation money in self-employment in the service sector. As of recently, the incorporation of companies, as a proportion of all firms (1994/95), varies from 3.9 per cent in Tasmania to 11.7 per cent in Victoria, and the variation of the number of new registered firms relative to the labour force is of the same magnitude. Thus, while enterprise creation in Victoria has been low on average in recent decades, it seems to have picked up recently. This is related to both the impressive recovery of the state economy and to policies of deregulation, privatisation and tax cuts.

Within states, entrepreneurship is generally more prevalent in urban regions than elsewhere, but little hard evidence is available. One well-known form of regional specialisation relates to the existence of "clusters" where specialised, and often complementary, firms concentrate within a small geographic area. Clusters are recognised as potentially conducive to innovation and entrepreneurship, since they help overcome the disadvantage of small size in scale-intensive industries and enable groups of companies to internalise some of the externalities connected with marketing, training and R&D. Some information is available for

Figure 8.2. **Export performance in South East Asia**

Annual per cent change, 1986-95

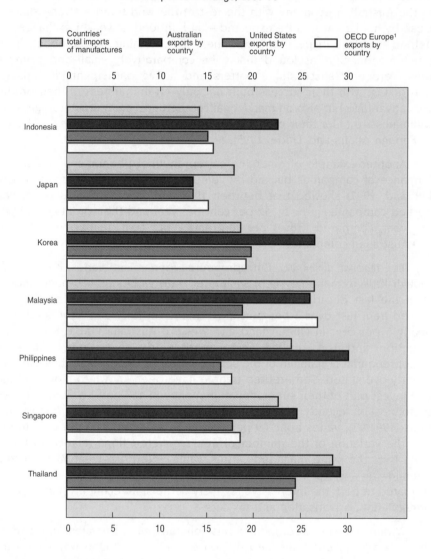

1. OECD Europe not including the Czech Republic, Hungary and Poland.
Source: United Nations and OECD.

Table 8.2.   **Enterprises and enterprise creation in Australia by States and Territories**

	Company incorporations	All firms (thousands)	Average annual rate of growth (1983/84 to 1994/95)	Labour force (thousands)	Company incorporation as per cent of all firms	Company incorporation per 1 000 members of the labour force
	(1)	(2)	(3)	(4)	(1), (2)	(1), (4)
New South Wales	29 119	262.3	2.4	2 709.1	11.1	10.7
Victoria	23 853	203.5	2.9	2 056.5	11.7	11.6
Queensland	14 251	156.2	4.8	1 385.2	9.1	10.3
South Australia	4 457	66.4	3.6	684.0	6.7	6.5
West Australia	7 526	86.4	4.8	759.6	8.7	9.9
Tasmania	735	18.8	2.6	205.6	3.9	3.6
Northern Territories	539	6.1	2.4	83.4	8.8	6.4
ACT	1 256	12.8	3.9	151.1	9.8	8.3
Total	**81 736**	**812.4**	**3.3**	**8 034.6**	**10.1**	**10.2**

Source: (1) Australian Securities Commission, *ASC Digest*, 1994/95; (2) & (3) Chapter 3 State Profiles, pp. 29 and 30, 1994/95; (4) *Labour Force Statistics*, 1991.

Queensland, where the government has identified some clusters in places such as Gladstone, specialised in aluminium and light metal, and Cairns, in tourism and agro- and food industries. Enhanced information on clusters would facilitate the ongoing discussion about restructuring service delivery, whether private or public, to these groups of inter-dependent firms – as recently discussed in OECD (1996b).

Factors affecting entrepreneurship

Culture. One of the rare opinion surveys in this regard reports that community opinion is not particularly positive about small business (Task Force on Leadership and Management Skills, 1995). Perception that the overall reward gained does not justify the effort or risk involved "may reflect a low risk tolerance or lack of entrepreneurial spirit within Australian culture, or perhaps a particular work ethic (or combination of these factors)" (Revesz & Lattimore, 1997). A lack of appreciation of the entrepreneurs may be partly attributable to the feeling that the natural wealth of Australia is the primary source of growth and well-being (Hartwell & Lane, 1991).

Entry and exit. Costs and procedural delays in setting up an enterprise are not significant in Australia (see Chapter 3, Table 3.1). On top of this, some accountants and lawyers – drawing on their obvious "economies of scale" – specialise in the sale of "shell-companies" whereby entrepreneurs, for a minor extra cost, can acquire a limited company without delay. This is one reason why the total number of Australian limited companies is close to one million – it is estimated that a significant part of these are not actively trading.

Also, the willingness to undertake entrepreneurial risk must be affected by financial and legal penalties in the case of personal bankruptcy and corporate insolvency. In Australia these are not particularly harsh by international comparison, although the three-year waiting period before discharge in the case of personal bankruptcy discourages risk-taking compared with the United States (Table 8.3). Indeed, in the United States "a good try" is reportedly encouraged, and many successful entrepreneurs have one or two bankruptcies behind them before they succeed. Also, persons affected by personal bankruptcy are legally barred from acting as directors in limited companies, and persons who have been directors in companies with particularly severe cases of insolvency can be barred from participating in the management of new companies.[2]

Table 8.3.   **Bankruptcy proceedings in five countries**

	Filing	Discharge clause
Australia	Entrepreneurs can voluntarily file for bankruptcy. For limited companies a number of procedures for liquidation and voluntary administration are in place.	Discharged after three years. For negligible amounts discharge can be granted after three months. Managers are not liable unless involved in improper dealing.
Germany		Currently, no discharge. Company managers incur civil liability and may also be liable for criminal penalties. Reforms to be enacted will discharge liability companies after seven years.
Sweden	Entrepreneurs can voluntarily file for bankruptcy. However, high-priority debt must be settled, and some additional costs are involved.	No discharge. Managers and owners of limited companies can be made personally liable for tax debts.
United Kingdom		Discharged after two years if the debt is lower than £20 000, and three years if the debt is greater.
United States	Entrepreneurs can voluntarily file for bankruptcy. Many bankruptcies are settled outside the courtroom.	Discharge effective immediately.

Source: Submissions from national authorities.

Cost of tax and regulatory compliance. Compliance costs are considered as a major impediment to entrepreneurship, and the burden of compliance has, therefore, been the target of recent central government efforts at deregulation and simplification. A recent report finds that the burden of compliance is considerably higher for companies which are either small or new in business, and compliance costs can therefore be said to bear particularly heavily on nascent entrepreneurship.[3] Indeed, the burden of compliance is listed as a primary concern of Australia's small and new enterprises.[4] Numerous studies have looked into this issue in the past and concluded that, except for some sectors subject to particular regulation and licensing rules, the main problems relate to tax compliance and, to some extent, superannuation.[5] Other kinds of compliance activities under survey related to unfair dismissals and health and safety standards. But enterprises generally rank them as less burdensome than tax compliance. Indeed, a recent study found that more than 70 per cent of all enterprises considered the frequency and complexity of changes to federal tax rules as a major concern, and for small and medium-sized enterprises this percentage was even larger (Bickerdyke & Lattimore, 1997). Two areas singled out as being particularly burdensome are the reporting in connection with the fringe benefit tax and wholesale tax. A recent survey of small business in Queensland concluded that compliance costs run as high as 40 per cent of the net operating profit of enterprises – a figure which is largely related to the imputed price of in-house work performed by the entrepreneur (Table 8.4). Moreover, for certain kinds of business taxation compliance costs reportedly run as high as 40 per cent of the taxes actually collected. However, in comparison with other industrialised countries Australia does not come across as having particularly high compliance costs. For example, total compliance costs in

Table 8.4.   **Compliance costs in small enterprises**[1]

	Construc-tion	Food retailing	Road transport	Auto repairs	Metal fabrication	Total
Annual hours spent on compliance	326	201	395	186	376	296
Annual cost per company (in dollars) *of which:*	9 688	9 570	31 214	8 053	11 923	14 026
fees and purchase of services (per cent)	26	49	72	44	31	52
in house efforts (per cent)	74	51	28	56	69	48
Costs as a share of turnover (per cent)	3	5	4	4	3	4
Costs as a share of profits (per cent)	29	37	42	32	24	32

1.   Survey covering Queensland companies with less than 20 employees.
Source: Deborah Wilson Consulting Services (1996).

UK enterprises in the 1980s were estimated at 1.5 to 2 per cent of GDP, while recent estimates for Germany are as high as 3 to 4 per cent (OECD, 1990). According to estimates by Bickerdyke and Lattimore (1997) the burden of compliance in Australia is likely to lie within this range. Finally, it should be noted that a large part of the burden of compliance relates to activities – accounting and auditing – which the companies would arguably have to undertake even in the absence of regulation and taxation.

Policy initiatives were taken recently to reduce the compliance burden of enterprises.[6] In particular, the burden of complying with the *fringe benefit tax* (FBT) has been eased, *i.e.*, by abolishing the demand for record-keeping by companies with small FBT liabilities. Also, a set of rather complex rules guiding the taxation of employer-provided parking and transportation was significantly simplified. More significantly, by mid-1998 the government intends to establish a single registration process for the *Taxation Office*, *Securities Commission*, *Bureau of Statistics* and the *Insurance and Superannuation Commission* whereby duplication of reporting can be reduced. There are also less concrete plans about co-operating with state and territory governments to establish single entry points to all levels of government through which business can obtain information on all official requirements and programmes.

Migration. The presence of migrants and temporary entrants to Australia adds an element of dynamism to the Australian business sector. For example, the recent surge in exports to South East Asia has been facilitated by the availability of people originating from this region. There is also evidence of migrants entering the labour market by starting small family-run shops and enterprises. As well, the generation entering Australia during the years following the Second World War is, reportedly, much more prone to start own enterprises than the average of the population. The 1996 *Labour Force Survey* shows that the share of self-employment among foreign-born persons was 15.4 per cent, compared with 14.3 per cent among native Australians. One of the only detailed surveys, using data for 1981, concludes that immigrants' propensity to become self-employed or employers is not significantly above that of others, although immigrants from South Europe seem to stand out somewhat (Table 8.5). Moreover, there has been a tendency for self-employed persons from Asia to move to Australia but – typically citing the higher economic growth and fewer regulations in this region – to continue doing business in their countries of origin. Since 1992 immigration visas have been granted to *Business Skill Class* (BSC) settlers who were previously self-employed business executives or investors, or who possess a proven ability to set up their own enterprise. Not surprisingly, more than 75 per cent of the BSC immigrants have been found to be in business within two years after their arrival (Business Skills Section, 1997).

Table 8.5. **Labour force status of workforce by region of birth, 1981**

Percentage share of labour force within each group

	Men		Women	
	Employer	Self-employed	Employer	Self-employed
Natives	6.2	10.2	4.5	7.6
All foreign-born	5.7	10.1	3.9	7.3
United Kingdom and Ireland	4.0	8.4	3.1	5.8
Germany	6.7	13.0	5.4	9.5
Greece	9.1	16.8	6.6	14.1
Italy	8.6	15.5	5.6	11.9
India	5.3	4.7	2.9	4.0
Vietnam	0.6	1.2	0.6	1.6

Source: Colins (1991).

Finance and risk capital. A lack of finance is often quoted as a major impediment to enterprise growth, particularly as regards small and new enterprises. In the absence of sufficient collateral banks lending to enterprises have to compensate for the higher risk through either significantly higher interest rates or restrictive lending practices. In the case of Australia, however, there is no evidence of banks being unduly restrictive *vis-à-vis* small and medium-sized enterprises and surveys of manufacturing companies indicate that the easing of financial constraints during the current economic recovery has, in particular, benefited small and medium-sized enterprises (Australian Business Chamber, 1996). According to a recent study the premium charged on short-term loans to small enterprises is typically fixed at around 200 basis points over the prime rate and varies little across clients. This implies that banks have, in fact, been cross-subsidising higher-risk loans among their small business clients. In any event, high risk enterprise start-ups and expansion may more appropriately be financed through equity capital, rather than borrowed funds.

As for equity finance, listing on the *Australian Stock Exchange* (ASX) is generally not an option to newly started enterprises, and on all accounts the costs of public listing – issuing a prospectus costs an estimated A$ 250 000 to 500 000 – are out of line with the capital needed for expansion in most smaller enterprises. Indeed, a 1995 study concluded that around 97 per cent of small businesses seeking external equity finance to fund their growth require less than A$ 0.5 million (National Investment Council, 1995). A second-tier stock market was established in the 1980s but was merged with the ASX after the stock-market crash in 1987. This explains the presence of many relatively small companies on the ASX. Nevertheless, the ASX does not stand out as particularly important as a way of acquiring new capital. The market capitalisation was around 70 per cent of GDP in 1994 – high in comparison with most continental European countries, but low relative to the United Kingdom and the United States – and the share of initial public offerings relative to total capitalisation is around 1 per cent, which is below most other OECD countries.

During the current economic expansion, venture capital firms have developed rapidly, but the stock of venture capital invested in Australian businesses, estimated at around A$ 1 to 1,5 billion, seems somewhat below OECD Europe relative to GDP (Figure 8.3, panel A) – though the European data include loans. Compared with these countries, a larger share of the venture capital investment goes into expansion and start-up than buy-outs (Figure 8.3, panel B). However, there is some indication that comparatively less capital is available early in the life-cycle of an Australian company compared with an American counterpart: an average venture capital-based company in Australia is nine years old compared with five in the United States. A recent study finds that venture capital-backed companies are generally successful. Some 56 per cent of those not already listed expect to become listed companies within the next five years, of which 67 per cent on the ASX and another 30 per cent on the NASDAQ in the United States.[7]

While the supply of venture capital at present seems somewhat low, there is no lack of funds which could, potentially, be made available for such equity investment. Regulatory restrictions on banks' investment in unlisted equity would limit their role as a source of venture capital.[8] But the capital under administration by institutional investors – notably superannuation funds – is considerable. In 1995 institutional investors controlled funds corresponding to some 76 per cent of GDP. This is above the average for OECD Europe, though significantly below levels in the United Kingdom and the United States. Nevertheless, there seem to be some problems with making these funds available for entrepreneurial investment concerning both suppliers and demanders of venture capital.[9] Venture capital firms normally do not find it profitable to invest less than two to three million dollars due to their fixed costs, i.e., related to monitoring of the investment, and in order to maximise the probability of success often demand share-holder agreements, effectively giving them control of the company. Venture capitalists are estimated to have insisted on management changes in about half of the companies in which they have invested. Finally, venture capital companies limit their investments to companies with a perceived profitability of some 25 to 35 per cent annual rates of return on the investment – up to 50 per cent in the case of start-up investment – earnings generally possible only in companies with unique products or processes.

Entrepreneurs, on the other hand, are generally reluctant to acquire funds at the cost of limiting their operational freedom and the risk of being put out of their

Figure 8.3. **Venture capital in Australia**

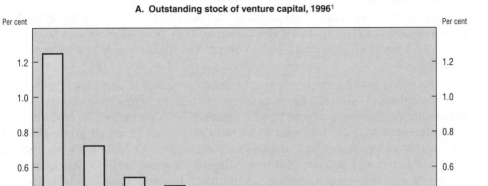

A. Outstanding stock of venture capital, 1996[1]

Per cent

GBR · NLD · FRA · SWE · **AUS** · NOR · DEU · DNK · FIN · ESP

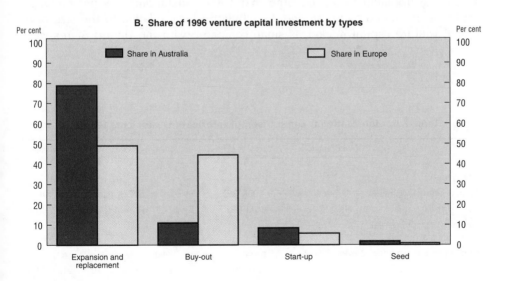

B. Share of 1996 venture capital investment by types

Per cent

■ Share in Australia   □ Share in Europe

Expansion and replacement · Buy-out · Start-up · Seed

1. Stock as a per cent of GDP. Australian data are for FY 1994-95.
Source: OECD (1996*a*).

own company. This aversion to outsider interference is particularly strong among the family-owned companies which account for a large share of companies in Australia. Furthermore, according to a recent study (Ernst & Young, 1997), small and young companies are often found to be not "investment ready", that is, they have not adequately separated the business from personal finances, and have achieved a level of accounting and information sufficient to attract professional investors.

The scope for financing expansion through injection of additional funds from the entrepreneur himself, persons close to him or informal investors (often referred to as "business angels") could arguably be more limited in Australia due to comparatively low household financial wealth.[10] On average gross financial wealth (net of claims on institutional investors) stands at around 75 per cent of GDP, compared with 200 per cent in the United Kingdom and 275 per cent in the United States. Even so, business angels have become increasingly visible in recent years. The typical profile of such an investor in Australia as in other countries is a wealthy senior executive or retiree with extensive business experience in the sector in which he invests. Recent studies show that it is fairly common for "business angels" to put their expertise at the service of the companies where they have invested (Productivity Commission, 1997). Also the size and the nature of individual "angel" investments are comparable with the experience from other countries (Table 8.6), with the maximum size generally believed to be around A$ 0.5 million. On the other hand, the outstanding amount of "angel" capital is estimated to be around A$ 1 billion which, relative to the size of the formal venture capital market, is small compared with the United States where

Table 8.6. **International comparison of informal investor characteristics**

	United Kingdom	Sweden	United States	Canada	**Australia**
Age (years)	53	54	47	47	45
Annual family income	UK 46K	60% > 500K SEK	$90K	$177K (Cdn)	$179K
Net worth	UK 312K	57% > 5M SEK	$750K	$1.36M (Cdn)	$2.1M
Previous entrepreneurial experience	57%	96%	83%	75%	75%
Number of investments	2 every 3 years	1 a year	2 every 3 years	1 a year	1 every 2 years
Rejection rate	7 out of 8	7 out of 10	7 out of 9	9 out of 10	3 out of 4
Average size of the investment	UK 10K	500K SEK	$58K	$207K (Cdn)	$193K (A)

Source: Ernst & Young (1997).

"business angels" provide at least twice as much equity capital as venture capital-ists. A study by the *Productivity Commission* (1997) finds that enterprises which gain access to informal equity perform better than average in terms of sales, employ-ment and innovation. To some extent, however, their superior performance reflects a selection bias.[11].

One further impediment for companies seeking small amounts of equity capital from private investors is the fact that Australian law stipulates that individ-ual enterprises may not contact more than 20 potential investors within a year unless each of them is willing to contribute more than A$ 0.5 million. In an attempt to overcome this – while, at the same time, enabling investors to take very small unlisted positions and providing exit mechanisms – the *Enterprise Market* has been established. The company is setting up an Internet-based match-making service for both primary and secondary offerings of non-listed equity. This service is scheduled to start in February 1998, by which time it is estimated that 1 000 companies and 2 000 to 3 000 potential investors will have joined.

The Government has also recently released proposals under the *Corporate Law Economic Reform Programme* aimed at facilitating capital raising by small and medium enterprises. In particular, companies would be able to raise up to A$ 2 million each year from up to 20 persons without issuing a prospectus, up to A$ 5 million based on an offer information statement rather than a full prospectus, and raise funds below the current A$ 0.5 million threshold from persons with a gross income of A$ 0.25 million or net assets of A$ 2.5 million without a prospectus.

Taxation. While the system of personal income taxation is broadly neutral with respect to risk-taking, some special problems could arguably relate to taxation of capital gains. In particular, financial entities which are tax exempt in their domestic markets and which are exempt from Australian taxation on gains and investments made directly, can be exposed to Australian taxation on gains made indirectly through a company or an entity treated as a company (*e.g.*, limited partnership). That is, tax paid by the company or limited partnership in respect of capital gains is not refunded to the exempt financial entity. While some argue there is a risk of limiting the flow of foreign funds into the nascent venture capital market, it is difficult to assess the extent of any effect. While scarcity of funds is not currently a problem, attracting foreign investors may still be beneficial for other reasons – *i.e.*, by introducing corporate governance practices which would lead to better company performances. Some easing of the capital gains taxation has been put in place for smaller enterprises. The most important elements are: *i)* a partial exemption of goodwill, half of which is now tax free up to a ceiling of A$ 2.2 million (indexed); and *ii)* enterprises with net assets of up to A$ 5 million are eligible to roll over capital gains where they are used to expand an existing business or acquire a new enterprise. It has been argued that further relief should be granted, *inter alia*, in the field of partly exempting capital gains on the transfer of intellectual property. However, the concessions put in place already make it easier for inventors to commercialise intellectual property; it is doubtful whether the benefits of further concessionary treatment would exceed the cost of a less coherent treatment of capital gains and the risk of increasing tax evasion.

Invention, innovation and R&D. At first glance, Australian companies seem to have an internationally rather low propensity to innovate and develop new products. For example, R&D spending by the corporate sector is far below the OECD average. Moreover, the *Department of Industry* (1996) found that, although Australian firms seem broadly in line with those in the advanced medium-sized OECD economies with regards to innovation through channels other than R&D, they lag in adopting advanced manufacturing technology and new management techniques. On the other hand, business R&D spending has increased strongly in recent years, surpassed only by Ireland and Southeast Asian economies (Australian Business Foundation). Also, Australia ranks high among OECD countries in inventiveness, as measured by the number of resident patent applications per 10 000 population as well as the growth in external patent applications (close to 20 per cent per year from 1981 to 1994). Altogether, typical Australian firms operate in sectors not characterised by very high research intensity, but they are, at a comparatively low cost, able to generate an internationally high number of inventions. There remains anecdotal evidence that many of these patents are either sold for commercialisation abroad, or generated in subsidiaries of foreign companies and transferred to the parent company.

Management skills. The quality of management is a vital determinant of the success of those firms and of their capacity to capture the value of innovation and technological development. There has been a general concern in Australia about the low level of management skills of entrepreneurs and managers, especially compared to its main trading partners (*Karpin report*). As measured by formal tertiary qualification, only 19 per cent of senior managers had a degree in 1995 compared with more than 60 per cent in Germany and France, and more than 80 per cent in Japan and the United States, while more than 50 per cent of front line managers had received no formal training for that role. This picture of poor Australian management quality has been reinforced by other studies. The *World Competitiveness Report* ranked Australian management as 12th out of 20 OECD countries in 1997 (and far behind other trading partners), though improving from 15th in 1993. According to the *Business Longitudinal Study*, 34 per cent of business decision-makers had tertiary education, of whom about two-fifths had management qualifications. Even though some progress has been made recently, proficiency of management and manager education attainment seem to remain poor by international standards, in sharp contrast with a quite good overall education attainment (13 per cent of the Australian population having a higher education degree, above the OECD average). It indicates that the best-educated people do not often go into business and that the education and training system gives insufficient emphasis to management education. Required management skills vary according to firms' stage of development, size, industry, or to whether they are independent or a subsidiary of large firms. The lack of diversity in management skills seems to be another weak point which the education and training system has failed to address.

Public programmes and policies

The main objective of overall policy toward the business sector has been *i*) to increase the degree of internationalisation of Australian enterprises, and, as a corollary to this, *ii*) to help raise their international competitiveness. The first has been achieved through the reduction in import tariffs, quotas and other barriers to trade mentioned above as well as the ongoing work on improved market access through APEC and CER *initiatives*. The second is pursued primarily through ongoing efforts to foster a good business environment, including by progressing market based reform, establishing stable macroeconomic underpinnings, and maintaining a competitive corporate tax rate. There are also a wide range of schemes and programmes, especially focused on promoting R&D and investment and providing export financing and insurance. A large part of the government outlays (see Table 8.7) relates to export promotion and finance. Almost all of the tax reduc-

Table 8.7. **Australian government support for the business sector**[1]

AS million

	Central Government		States[2] Outlays	Total
	Tax exemption[3]	Outlays		
Primary excluding mining	170	605	682	1 457
Manufacturing	1 114	750	924	2 788
Mining	400	119	138	657
Services	75	507	732	1 314
Total	**1 759**	**1 981**	**2 477**	**6 217**
Per cent of GDP	0.4	0.4	0.5	1.3

1. Financial year 1994/95. Central Government outlays: 1995/96.
2. Not including foregone revenue from payroll tax thresholds and exemptions. They are estimated at A$4.8 billion (1993/94).
3. Based on a different methodology the 1994-95 Tax Expenditure Statement estimated that overall tax expenditures were around A$1.1 billion higher.
Source: Industry Commission (1996) and OECD Secretariat.

tions, on the other hand, are connected with a 125 per cent tax break on certain R&D expenditure – down from 150 per cent previously [12] – and with a temporary 10 per cent investment allowance for tangible investments. Finally, at the state level, the considerable forgone revenue from payroll taxes almost exclusively supports small enterprises, which benefit from thresholds and exemptions, the extent of which varies from state to state. As for support more directly targeted towards promoting entrepreneurship and new business activities, several hundred programmes are in place. Generally operating at a very limited budget cost, most of them focus on correcting market failure by improving the flow of information or compensate small companies for lack of scale in area where economies of scale are presumed. Some of the more important schemes are listed below.

Encouraging new businesses. Like many other OECD countries, Australia maintains a programme for encouraging self-employment for previously unemployed persons. Basically, persons wishing to be self-employed are allowed to retain their unemployment insurance allowance for one year while starting the enterprise. The programme is judged as a success, since the dead-weight loss has been minimised and 82 per cent of all enterprises thus started survive after the termination of the programme. Another important recent initiative to help start up new ventures is the establishment of the *Innovation Investment Fund programme* (IIF). The IIF is based on the long running SBIC programme in the USA, and will create up to six new early stage venture capital funds focusing on commercialising R&D. The Australian Government will contribute A$ 130 million on the basis of A$ 2 for every A$ 1 raised by private sector venture capital funds licensed under the programme.

The *Pooled Development Funds* (PDFs) programme was established in 1992 to increase the supply of patient equity capital to SMEs. PDFs are venture capital funds investing in Australian SMEs which have total assets of less than A$ 50 million and where their primary activity is in either property development or retail sales operations. The incentives under the programme are that PDFs are taxed at concessional rates (being 15 per cent on income from investments) compared with the usual company tax rate of 36 per cent, and investors in PDFs receive both dividends and are capital gains exempt from tax. Under the programme, PDFs have raised over A$ 270 million.

Another way of facilitating the start-up phase, which has gained considerable attention in recent years, is the so-called business incubators, which provide rented office or workshop space to new enterprises for a limited period. Originally grown out of regional support schemes, incubators are typically owned by local authorities or non-profit corporate structures, and while they generally do not require ongoing funding an element of subsidisation is imbedded in the fact that some 70 per cent of them either own their own building or pay a symbolic rent. This implicit subsidy is, however, generally not passed on to the tenants in the form of rents exorbitantly below ongoing market rates. Rather, a considerable demand for "incubation" by small enterprises derives from short rental contracts, quick entry and exit and on the divisibility of the available space, all of which tends to make the costs of a "good try" manageable and provides for an easy exit. Local authorities and business associations perceive business incubators as a useful way of nurturing a more entrepreneurial climate while reducing the failure rate of small enterprises (the failure rate within the first year is an estimated 8 per cent among companies in incubators, compared with a national average of 32 per cent). This has, in turn, given rise to a spectacular increase in the number of such establishments. In 1997, 63 incubators operated in Australia, up from 39 in 1994, with a further 17 scheduled to be established in 1998. It should be noted that while Australian business incubators do tend to encourage similar enterprises to locate close to each other, specialised incubators remain rare. Indeed, only nine of them are industry specific, and only five are designated technology incubators.

Promoting R&D. The justification for public sector involvement in private R&D in Australia is based on the argument that private firms need to be compensated for the "positive externalities" or "spillovers" that result from their R&D investment; the conclusion from empirical evidence that R&D is a substantial driver of economic growth; and the pragmatic observation that Australian levels of private R&D are well below international norms for major developed economies. The Australian Government plays an active role in encouraging R&D through a general tax concession and other programs of a more targeted nature. Networking is encouraged, *inter alia*, to assist in technology diffusion.

The major single government institution involved in R&D activities is the *Commonwealth Scientific and Industrial Research Organisation* (CSIRO). It covers a broad span of scientific research and technology activities relevant to the manufacturing and resource sectors of the economy, as well as the environment. The Organisation receives annual Commonwealth Government funding of around A$ 500 million, which is, in principle, earmarked for generic research and administrative purposes. CSIRO derives an additional A$ 250 million from various sources, including some A$ 60 million from the business sector and A$ 40 million for research conducted in *Co-operative Research Centres* (CRCs).

CSIRO generates its private sector income through licensing technology and by undertaking contract and collaborative research. CSIRO participates in 56 of the 67 Co-operative Research Centres which are research, training and commercial development partnerships between universities, other public sector research bodies and industry. The CRCs' research is oriented toward commercial and/or environmental application and many of the Centres operate as formal networks, having geographically widely dispersed partners. These Centres may be seen as a complement to the regionally-based science and technology parks which derive most of their support from State Governments and universities. Finally, CSIRO actively encourages the spin-off of new companies and negotiates arrangements to bring intellectual property generated from publicly funded research results into newly started companies. Over the last decade, some 50 such technology-based companies have been created, of which few have failed.

Promoting information flows: Like other countries, Australia assists exports in a variety of ways, *inter alia* to promote the "export culture" which seems to be developing among companies. In the light of the rising importance of SME export-ers, incentives to networking and company linkages have gained increasing atten-tion. Recent reports show that companies engaging in formalised co-operation with others are likely to gain advantages in terms of technological innovation and productivity (Bureau of Industry Economics, 1995 and 1996). In addition to this, small and new exporters often co-operate with other enterprises in marketing and delivery in foreign markets. It is estimated that more than half of all exporting companies are involved in some kind of formalised co-operation (Table 8.8), and in recent surveys 22 per cent of all companies indicated that they would be interested in networking if they could find the right partner. Aiming at overcoming a perceived information asymmetry regarding potential partners, the central gov-ernment encourages inter-firm co-operation in several ways, most notably *AusIndustry's Business Networks Programme* (BNP). The basis of the BNP is a network formation process, in which brokers paid by the programme play an active role in close contact with state governments and local business associations. The central government essentially covers the costs of the matchmaking, but is normally not involved in the financing of the implementation. In 1995 there were 144 govern-ment assisted networks covering more than 1 500 companies.

Moreover, in order to generate employment and to integrate Australia more strongly in the global economy, programmes are in place to encourage foreign direct investment. The *Investment Promotion and Facilitation Programme* (IPFP) oper-ates, at a limited overall budget, a number of representational offices abroad diffusing information about Australia as a place to invest. In recent years particular attention has been given to attracting regional headquarters of foreign companies which are planning to set them up in the Western Pacific rim. In addition to information and promotion the central government offers certain limited tax con-cessions to companies which start operating in Australia, in particular related to sales taxes on their office equipment and taxation of dividends from abroad. Noting that around half of the companies which invest in Australia claim that the IPFP has played "some" or "a major" role in their investment decisions, a recent report estimates that the programme induces an average net inward foreign investment of A\$ 230 million per year (Bureau of Industry Economics, 1996). On top of the Commonwealth efforts, state authorities have been particularly active in supporting investment into their area. The incentives used to persuade foreign companies include exemptions from payroll taxes and other forms of state taxa-tion for the years following the initial investment. According to a Queensland

Table 8.8. **Formal co-operation between companies in Australia**

	Per cent of firms co-operating
All firms	41
Industry	
Clothing and footwear	32
Engineering	41
IT&T	54
Science/medecine	48
Food	39
Exporters	
Exporter	54
Non-exporter	35
Size (employees)	
Micro	36
Small	44
Medium	43
Large	63
Technology	
Low	32
Medium	40
High	50
Performance	
High	50
Low	35
State	
New South Wales	40
Victoria	42
Queensland	37
Southern Australia	38
Western Australia	48

Source: Bureau of Industry Economics (1995).

estimate, tax concessions corresponding to up to A\$ 7 000 per employee per year for the first 3 to 4 years are involved. A recent report found that the states engage in competitive bidding for major investment which, while quite costly to the public purse, produce no net gains on the national level (Industry Commission, 1996).

Regional support. State governments and agencies are running numerous programmes to support new and small enterprises. It is difficult to get a comprehensive picture of these programmes, but they seem to be extremely dispersed and narrowly focused. One reason for this is that many services are provided jointly with the Commonwealth government. States' financial contributions are, however, typically very small; *e.g.*, *Victorian Small Business* has a yearly budget of A\$ 2 million.

The number of small firms using these support services seems to be low – less than 5 per cent according to the 1995 Business Longitudinal Study.

Inspired by the obvious success of such American high-tech environments as Silicon Valley which is seen to depend, partly, on their ability to draw on technological spin-offs from large nearby universities,[13] much attention has been given to establishing science and technology parks close to most of the larger tertiary education institutions. So far 16 such parks have been established and a further four are under construction, most of them funded either by state authorities or the universities themselves.[14] Thus far around A$ 100 million of public money have been invested in science and technology parks. However, while the impact of such parks is notoriously difficult to assess, the anecdotal evidence is that they have so far not generated many new high-tech companies – the only success story frequently cited being West Australia's science park in Perth. One of the main reasons for this seems to be unwillingness on the part of universities and other institutions to transfer the value of intellectual property to potential entrepreneurs among their staff. Another is that Australian academics are, reportedly, much less willing to engage in commercial activities than their American counterparts.

A review of support programmes. In 1996 the Minister for Industry, Science and Tourism announced a comprehensive Review of Business Programs, the purpose of which is to decide on the optimal mix of business programmes "to assist industry meet the challenges of an increasingly competitive global market". The outcome of this work, the so-called Mortimer Report, is currently much debated in Australia. The report found that the number of Commonwealth industry programmes is too large and too unfocused – and, to some extent, dictated by tradition rather than current relevance – so that businesses intended to benefit from them have to incur an unreasonable burden in terms of time and costs. Moreover, it concluded that the delivery of programmes was not efficient and that monitoring and follow-up on individual programmes was lacking. Its main recommendation was, therefore, that programmes should be fewer, have a large individual budget and be focused towards areas which are likely to improve the international position of the Australian business sector, namely: boosting investment; encouraging innovation; promoting exports; improving business competitiveness; and making for sustainable resource management. The most controversial suggestion from the Mortimer Report is the proposed establishment of a new agency "Invest Australia" intended to devise financial incentives to attract foreign direct investment. The formal justification for the proposal is twofold: i) other countries in the region tend to support foreign investment even more generously; and ii) many disincentives to investment in Australia seem to relate to the negative impact of higher taxes and stricter Government regulation. Therefore, it is argued, the Government should offer would-be investors offsetting compensation.

Concluding remarks

The overall finding of this chapter is that, while conditions for enhanced entrepreneurship have improved over the last decade, there have been only scattered signs of a strengthened entrepreneurial endeavour. These include emerging small companies which have built their success on export sales from an early stage and a strong performance of venture-capital-backed companies. The government has contributed to stimulating entrepreneurial spirit by exposing Australian companies to international competition, raising labour market flexibility, fostering the functioning of financial markets and stepping up efforts to encourage domestic competition. It has also tried to facilitate company creation and growth through various programmes, often in collaboration with the States. Problems remain, however. The costs of tax and regulatory compliance remain particularly onerous for small companies, intermediation of risk capital is still insufficient, and researchers are lacking receptiveness to commercialisation of their inventions some of which are world-class.

It is important to continue improving the climate favouring entrepreneurship through the on-going process of strengthening market mechanisms and reducing the burden of government regulation and taxation. In this context, it would be particularly beneficial to make further efforts to simplify the tax code, improve labour market flexibility, encourage product market competition and submit a large part of the public sector to market test.

As to specific public support schemes, the key recommendation of the recent *Mortimer Report* to limit their number is well taken. However, a policy of selectively supporting activities perceived as particularly important for external competitiveness is not well founded. Rather, a good policy should sharpen the current focus on dealing with market failures, compensating for the disadvantage of small scales and facilitating companies' effort to seize new opportunities. The suggested increase in subsidies to attract foreign companies to operate in Australia would be unwise, and so is competition among the States and Territories to attract companies by offering tax concessions and subsidies.

Notes

1. It should be noted that this comparison does not allow any inference to be made about the evolution over time of each of the enterprises.

2. The rule is: persons who have been directors of two companies which have both been placed in liquidation and defaulted on more than half their debts may be disqualified from working as a company director for a period of up to five years.

3. OECD (1990) estimates that the burden of compliance is, on average, four times heavier than average in small enterprises. This study notes that, according to surveys of small business in six industrialised countries, the burdens of compliance and regulation was the single most important factor discouraging economic activity.

4. ACCI Review (1996) lists compliance as an issue of particular concern to employers.

5. For an example, see Australian Taxation Office (1993).

6. Responding to the detailed proposals by a *Deregulation Task Force* of business leaders, the government issued the report "More Time for Business": Statement by the Prime Minister (1997).

7. Coopers and Lybrand (1997). There is an element of double counting in these figures. Of companies which expect to list, 53 per cent nominated the ASX as their sole choice of listing market, while a further 14 per cent nominated the ASX as one of two possible listing markets. In addition, 21 per cent of companies that nominated a listing market made NASDAQ their sole choice. It was a possible choice for a further 9 per cent of companies.

8. Prudential regulation requires banks to limit equity investments in non-financial businesses to an aggregate amount not exceeding 5 per cent of Tier 1 capital without prior reference to the Reserve Bank. Individual investments are generally subject to a limit of 0.25 per cent of Tier 1 capital. A ban on banks' investment in SME equity was lifted in 1995.

9. Some examples of a "mismatch" between supply and demand are quoted in the so-called Investment Readiness Study (Ernst & Young, 1997).

10. On the other hand, it may be argued that a high proportion of home-ownership and relatively low mortgage debt work in the opposite direction.

11. Entrepreneurs who choose to invite "business angels" to invest in their companies and accepted by the investors are likely to be those who are faced with a particularly favourable prospect.

12. Current spending is deductible at 125 per cent up front. Capital spending is deductible at 125 per cent over three years. The reduction in the tax concession to 125% was associated with an increase in non-tax based assistance for R&D. This reduction in the

level of the tax concession was designed to improve the efficiency of R&D assistance and produce fiscal savings.

13. For a discussion of the factors behind this success, see OECD (1997a).

14. Private science parks also exist, but they typically have a more narrow focus.

References

AUSTRALIAN CHAMBER OF COMMERCE AND INDUSTRY (ACCI) (1996),
"What business seeks for the next government of Australia – results of a national survey of Australian employers", ACCI *Review*, No. 18.

AUSTRALIAN BUSINESS CHAMBER (1996),
"Competition in the Finance Industry", A survey of the 506 manufacturers comparing conditions in 1996 with those in 1992.

AUSTRALIAN SECURITIES COMMISSION (ASC) (1994/95),
ACS *Digest*.

AUSTRALIAN SECURITIES COMMISSION (ASC) (1997),
Annual Report, 1996-97.

AUSTRALIAN TAXATION OFFICE (1993),
Small Business Cost of Compliance Project, University of Newcastle.

BICKERDYKE, I. and LATTIMORE, R. (1997),
"Reducing the regulatory burden: does firm size matter?", *Staff Research Paper*, Industry Commission.

BUREAU OF INDUSTRY ECONOMICS (1995),
"Beyond the firm. An assessment of business linkages and networks in Australia", *Research Report 67*.

BUREAU OF INDUSTRY ECONOMICS (1996),
"Evaluation of the Investment Promotion and Facilitation Program", report 96/4.

BUSINESS SKILLS SECTION (1997),
"Annual Post-arrival Survey Reports", Monitoring and Evaluation Unit.

COLINS, J. (1991),
Migrant Hands in a Distant Land, Sydney.

COOPERS & LYBRAND (1997),
The Economic Impact of Venture Capital.

DEBORAH WILSON CONSULTING SERVICES (1996),
"Impact of the Cost of Compliance with Government Regulations, Licences, Taxes and Charges on Small Businesses in Queensland", *Report to the Department of Tourism, Small Business and Industry*.

DEPARTMENT OF INDUSTRY, SCIENCE AND TOURISM (DIST) (1996),
Annual Review of Small Business 1996.

ERNST and YOUNG (1997),
"Investment Readiness Study", report for the Small Business Research Program.

FOREIGN AFFAIRS AND TRADE (1995),
Winning Enterprises. How Australia's Small and Medium Enterprises Compete in Global Markets.

HARTWELL, R.M. and LANE, J. (1992),
   Champions of Enterprise: Australian Entrepreneurship 1788-1990, Focus Books, Double Bay, NSW.

INDUSTRY COMMISSION (1996),
   Annual Report 1995-96, AGPS, Canberra.

LOGOTECH S.A. (1997),
   "Étude comparative internationale des dispositions légales et administratives pour la formation de petites et moyennes entreprises aux pays de l'Union européenne, les États-Unis et le Japon", EIMS Project 96/142.

McKINSEY AND COMPANY (1993a),
   Emerging Exporters. Australia's High Value-Added Manufacturing Exporters.

McKINSEY AND COMPANY (1993b),
   "Toward Successful Support for Australia's Small and Medium-sized Enterprises", report submitted to the CSIRO.

NATIONAL INVESTMENT COUNCIL (1995),
   "Financing Growth", report prepared by Marsden Jacob Associates.

OECD (1990),
   "Public Management and Private Enterprise: Administrative Responsiveness and the Needs of Small Firms", *Occasional Papers*, Public Management.

OECD (1993),
   The OECD Jobs Study, OECD publications, Paris.

OECD (1996a),
   OECD *Economic Surveys – Australia*, OECD publications, Paris.

OECD (1996b),
   Network of Enterprises and Local Development, OECD publications, Paris.

OECD (1997a),
   OECD *Economic Surveys – United States*, OECD publications, Paris.

OECD (1997b),
   Revenue Statistics, OECD publications, Paris.

PRODUCTIVITY COMMISSION (1997),
   "Informal Equity Investment", report for the Small Business Research Program.

REVESZ, J. and LATTIMORE, R. (1997),
   "Small Business Employment", *Staff Research Paper*, Industry Commission.

STATEMENT BY PRIME MINISTER (1997),
   "More Time for Business".

Chapter IX

The Netherlands

The Netherlands has a long and well-established enterprise culture and commercial orientation, with an exceptionally open economy as measured – *inter alia* – by export and import shares in GDP. Nevertheless, concern has been expressed within the Netherlands about the depth and vigour of entrepreneurial activity and the extent to which policies and programmes may be reoriented to achieve a better economic performance. This chapter examines some aspects of the state of entrepreneurial activity in the Netherlands, the institutional framework within which Dutch businesses operate and the programmes and policies of the Dutch government aimed at stimulating entrepreneurship.

A long tradition of entrepreneurship

Small businesses and entrepreneurship

A commonly used proxy for entrepreneurship is based on the operation of the small business sector. As in all countries, the large majority of enterprises in the Netherlands are relatively small: there are around 600 000 private enterprises and only around 700 of them employ more than 500 persons. According to this definition, in 1990 SMEs accounted for 57 per cent of total employment[1] and produced exactly 50 per cent of GDP (OECD, 1996a). Thus, an exclusive focus on SMEs would overlook the potential for dynamic and entrepreneurial activity in the rest of the economy. It is also often argued that overall, the small business sector must be entrepreneurial, because it generates most of the job growth in the economy. But measuring the contribution of small- and medium-sized enterprises to net job creation is fraught with conceptual and statistical difficulties,[2] and in any case many smaller enterprises are not new, nor particularly innovative or growth oriented, whereas large well-established firms can be highly innovative and entrepreneurial. Between 1989 and 1994, 975 000 new jobs were created in the business sector as a whole, compared with a total of 3 220 000 existing jobs at the beginning of the period (Bais *et al.*, 1997). At the same time 770 000 jobs were lost, resulting in a net increase of 205 000. Job creation was concentrated in starting SMEs or, more generally, in relatively few, fast-growing firms. On the one hand, starting firms with less than 100 employees (excluding subsidiaries) created 230 000 gross jobs between 1989 and 1994.[3] Nevertheless, most young firms do not grow any further after start-up: according to a survey among starters, only 17 per cent of these firms hired new employees within the first 2½ years of their existence (Van Dijken *et al.*, 1997). On the other hand, "fast-growing firms"[4] that existed throughout this period (representing only 8 per cent of total existing firms) accounted between them for 220 000 new jobs, of which a third was in SMEs. However, fast-growing firms (in terms of employment) in the Netherlands created comparatively fewer jobs than fast-growing firms in the United States (EIM, 1995).

Entrepreneurship and firm turnover rates

Another approach to the study of entrepreneurship emphasises firm start-ups and closures as an indicator of willingness to engage in risk taking activity and capacity to innovate, and as an indicator of the ease with which resources are able to move quickly from one activity to another. It is almost impossible to get a reliable cross country comparison of start up and closure rates, given large differences in institutional procedures. However, the "natality rate" – the number of new firms relative to the stock of existing firms – has grown steadily in the Netherlands from 6.7 per cent in 1987 to 8.6 per cent in 1993, although some of this growth is attributable to the particularly strong increase in new establishments created by existing enterprises (Figure 9.1).[5] Since 1994, the natality rate has stabilised. The total number of firms has risen by about 50 per cent in the period from 1987 to 1996, although the number of self-employed as a percentage of the labour force remains below the rates experienced in the early 1970s. By international standards, the Dutch birth rate is about average and the exit rate is relatively low. This low exit rate may be an indicator of low competitive pressures. Although firm exit rates have also moved up, new enterprises in the Netherlands also have one of the highest survival rates in Europe, with around 60 per cent still in operation after five years. And those that survive generally expand: from 1½ working persons on average at the outset to 3½ working persons after 6 to 7 years operation (Kleiweg & Nieuwenhuijsen, 1996). Nevertheless, although start-ups may be taken as an important indicator of a dynamic business environment, entrepreneurial behaviour within well-established companies can also play an important role. Indeed, analysis of growth rates of firms over the period 1989 to 1994 shows that 15 per cent of the fast-growing companies in the Netherlands were more than 50 years old (Table 9.1). This relatively modest business dynamism in the Netherlands may have a negative impact on productivity and innovation.

Figure 9.1. **Enterprise start-ups, new subsidiaries and exits in the Netherlands**

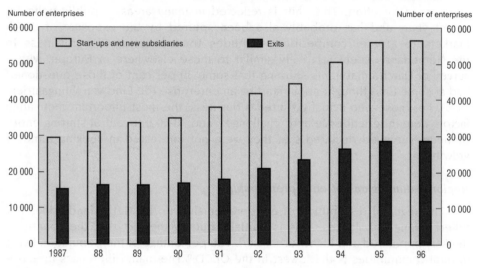

Source: Ministry of Economic Affairs.

Table 9.1. **Distribution of firms by employment growth characteristics and age**[1]

Employment growth	Age of the firms (per cent of total)				*Memorandum:* Number of firms
	5-9 years	10-19 years	20-49 years	Over 50 years	
Fast-growing	29	35	21	15	2 704
Normal-growing	24	39	22	14	10 714
Stable	20	39	26	15	2 881
Shrinking	20	35	26	19	7 117
Total	23	37	24	16	23 416

1.   Percentage of firms with more than 20 employees in 1994, only firms that existed both in 1989 and 1994 are included.
Source: Bangma and Verhoeven (1997).

The role of attitudes

There is an ongoing debate over whether cultural attitudes determine a society's legal and institutional framework or vice versa. It is however clear that if individualism, risk-taking or earning high returns are discouraged by the legal framework or by public policies, then less risk taking and innovation is likely to occur. Current social attitudes in the Netherlands seem to reflect some shift towards less reliance on social programmes and more emphasis on self-reliance and reward for effort. This shift is reflected in many areas of public policy in recent years and has probably also been spurred by the exposure of Dutch markets to greater competition. Attitudes towards going into business in the Netherlands seem relatively similar to those elsewhere in Europe, with a survey of Dutch inhabitants showing that some 30 per cent of those questioned had at some time thought about starting an enterprise (de Lind van Wijngaarden, 1995). For those who actually started a business, the most important motivating factors were independence and "challenge", and 30-40 per cent of starting entrepreneurs surveyed declared that they were not interested in seeking turnover growth.

Regional dimensions of entrepreneurship

The regional distribution of entrepreneurship in the Netherlands does not reflect strong imbalances. This is partially due to the fact that the country is densely populated and highly urbanised. The percentage of the population living in rural communities is the lowest in the OECD.[6] The main differences in entrepreneurship (as measured by firm turnover) can be observed between the less developed north/east as compared with the Randstad[7] area with a concentration of high value-added industries. Overall entrepreneurship measured by "birth rates" is relatively even among the larger provinces (Table 9.2). The most problematic territorial dimension of entrepreneurship and job creation in the Netherlands can rather be seen in increasingly spatially and ethnically concentrated socio-economic deprivation. The local social and economic environment

Table 9.2. **Enterprise birth and death rates in Dutch provinces**

Province	Birth rate		Death rate	
	1995	1996	1995	1996
Groningen	13.7	12.7	6.9	6.7
Friesland	10.1	9.3	3.6	4.1
Drenthe	10.6	9.8	5.0	5.2
Overijssel	11.0	10.5	6.1	6.4
Flevoland	17.4	15.5	8.3	7.4
Gelderland	10.7	9.6	5.3	5.0
Utrecht	11.9	11.3	5.8	5.5
North Holland	11.9	11.1	6.3	6.1
South Holland	11.7	11.2	6.3	5.7
Zeeland	8.7	8.2	5.4	4.7
North Brabant	11.3	10.6	5.6	5.4
Limburg	10.2	9.7	5.7	6.0

Source: Vereniging van Kamers van Koophandel (1997).

related to high unemployment rates in problem neighbourhoods such as for example Spangen (Rotterdam) or Den Haag Zuidwest (Kloosterman, 1996), both reflect and reinforce weak entrepreneurial dynamics in particular areas. Indeed, suitable space for entrepreneurial activity is very limited in these "urban renewal" areas and the infrastructure needed to attract such activities is lacking.

Factors affecting entrepreneurship

While it is difficult to pin down precise and robust indicators of the amount or degree of entrepreneurial activity taking place, it is nevertheless clear that entrepreneurship is significantly affected by the overall business environment and the prevailing web of regulations and other institutional factors. Removing impediments to entrepreneurial activity and fostering a more favourable business environment would therefore form an important part of government efforts to stimulate entrepreneurship. The rest of this section considers the main institutional factors that affect new businesses and act as constraints on business expansion or

Figure 9.2. **Main long-term constraints on business expansion**[1]

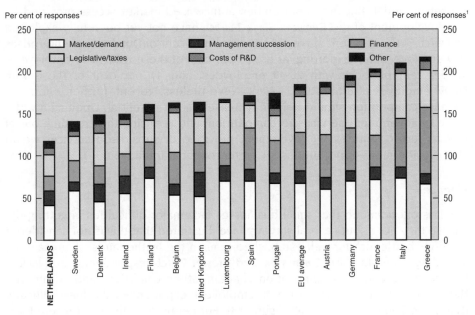

1. Sum of responses, given as percentage of respondents. Respondents were allowed to choose more than one constraint.
Source: Grant Thornton International Business Strategies, Ltd., 1997.

more generally on the ongoing allocation of resources to their most productive uses. Dutch businesses do not seem to consider themselves significantly constrained, at least relative to their counterparts in other European countries. A pertinent *European Business Survey* found that existing Dutch businesses felt less constrained in expanding business activities than enterprises anywhere else in Europe (Grant Thornton International Business Strategies Ltd., 1997) (Figure 9.2). Furthermore, the main long-term constraints most often cited by Dutch firms related to lack of demand and/or management succession issues. The biases inherent in this type of survey should, however, be noted: surveys of existing firms exclude those firms that constraints have already forced out of business and potential start-ups that never materialised because the hurdles were too great.

Markets and competition

Although 26 per cent of the European Business Survey respondents considered limited market demand a main long term constraint, and 14 per cent considered accessing new markets a main constraint, Dutch firms nevertheless seem less concerned about these constraints than respondents in other European countries. As noted earlier, the Netherlands exports a relatively high proportion of its output, and its well-developed trading expertise helps to tap and exploit market potential. But the opportunities of increased market access provided by the development of the *European Single Market*, have not yet been fully exploited by Dutch SMEs. A recent survey shows that 9 per cent of Dutch micro-enterprises (1-9 employees) are exporting, as are 23 per cent of those with 10-19 employees, 32 per cent of those with 20-49 employees, and 47 per cent of those with 50-99 employees (EIM/ERBO, 1996). Nevertheless, recent further efforts to increase competition should help to increase market potential. Opening a wider range of government services to competition, and reducing the crowding out of private sector ventures by government provided or subsidised services would also provide more opportunities for entrepreneurial initiatives.

Finance

It is often argued that small businesses face major difficulties in getting the finance they need, but several surveys have illustrated that this is not considered a serious bottleneck for well-established firms in the Netherlands.[8] For example, according to one *European Commission* study, fewer Dutch respondents rated lack of finance as a barrier to innovation than in other countries, and within the Netherlands, firms with less than 50 employees experienced the least difficulty (European Commission, 1995b) (Figure 9.3). Furthermore, in the most recent *European Business Survey*, only 18 per cent of respondents cited either the cost or the availability of finance as a main long term constraint, compared with 45 per cent in the European Union as a whole.[9] However, one very recent study has indicated

Figure 9.3. **Lack of finance as a perceived obstacle to innovation**

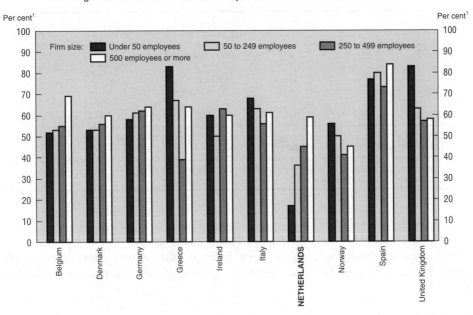

1. Percentage of enterprises that consider a lack of finance as a major obstacle to innovation.
Source: European Commission (1995*b*).

that young and particularly innovative new firms may respond differently to initial difficulties experienced in obtaining finance. Although they do not face larger difficulties than their counterparts in the United States, for example, the Dutch firms are more likely to respond by modifying the investment project, whereas American firms are more likely to continue searching for other sources of finance (Ministry of Economic Affairs, 1997). In a private sector survey of businesses' assessment of total capital costs, the Netherlands ranked second only to Denmark, equal to Japan and Germany and only marginally ahead of the United States (Ministry of Economic Affairs, 1997). Although long-term nominal interest rates were the same as in Germany and lower than in the United States on average during the period 1983 to 1994, estimated risk premia on equity, at 6.3 per cent, were relatively high in the Netherlands, although risk premia on debt were similar to those in other countries (Table 9.3). This may in part explain why Dutch firms rely to a relatively high degree on financing through retained earnings: aggregate corporate saving amounts to around 13½ per cent of GDP, which exceeds the private sector investment ratio (excluding dwellings). The tax regime

Table 9.3 **Risk premia on debt and equity in selected OECD countries**

	Risk premium on debt[1]	Risk premium on equity[2]
Netherlands	0.9	6.3
Belgium	1.8	6.1
Denmark	n.a.	4.7
Germany	0.6	2.9
Japan	n.a.	8.0
United States	n.a.	2.9

1. Calculated as the average difference between interest on commercial bonds and long-term interest rates on Government bonds. Data refer to the period 1991-95.
2. Calculated as the difference between average total return on the equity market (including capital gains) and nominal long-term interest rates. Data refer to the period 1970-94.
Source: Ministry of Economic Affairs (1997).

also favours internal financing, because with no imputation system, distributed earnings are taxed higher than retained earnings[10] and capital gains are not taxed.[11]

Venture capital

The formal venture capital market seems to be quite well developed in the Netherlands, and the amount of investments made, relative to GDP, is similar to those in the United States.[12] To some extent the relatively strong Dutch performance also reflects definitional differences, most notably concerning the inclusion of some debt instruments in the European data which are excluded from the US statistics. A closer look also reveals that the venture capital market in the Netherlands is investing a significantly smaller proportion of its funds in seed and start-up projects than is invested in similar stage projects in the United States (see Chapter 10, Table 10.2).

Anecdotal evidence points to a significant difference in attitudes towards control between American and European entrepreneurs. Venture capitalists generally want to exercise control over the companies in which they invest, and are willing to remove the founder-entrepreneur if they believe it would improve the performance of the company. While American entrepreneurs seem to accept this trade-off between making money from the investment and exercising control (OECD, 1997c), Dutch entrepreneurs seem less willing to accept the loss of management control that venture funding would entail. The cultural importance of keeping control, and the role of business in reflecting personal ideas and value systems, can be seen in the prevalence of family businesses in the Netherlands and the strong preference to keep the business within the family: almost 60 per cent of family businesses in the Netherlands are managed by second, third, or fourth generation family members (de Lind van Wijngaarden, 1996). In contrast, only around one-third of family businesses pass to the second generation in the United States (Upton, 1995).

One explanation for weak early-stage venture capital activity may be a lack of expertise in putting together packages or deals that make a proposal attractive to venture capitalists. To some extent this may simply be a lack of opportunity to develop the pertinent expertise due to the small number of deals put together.[13] A related conjecture is that the Netherlands suffers from a scale problem in evaluating projects. According to this argument, there is an insufficient number of projects available in the Netherlands to make it worthwhile for Venture Capitalists to invest in developing the required technical, sector-specific expertise. One response, developed by the *Technology Rating Foundation* with assistance from the Dutch authorities, is the technology certification scheme.[14] This scheme is designed to reduce the costs associated with evaluating high-tech projects by providing an evaluation using a network of experts. It is difficult to assess *whether in fact a scale problem exists in practice, especially in the context of the Single* European Market, and if it does, whether the technology certification scheme can really be effective in remedying it.

On the supply side, an exceptionally high proportion of venture capital in the Netherlands is coming from banks – two-thirds of all venture capital funding, compared with a European average of just over one-third and an insignificant amount in the United States.[15] This may also explain why venture capital funding in the Netherlands is concentrated in later stage investments rather than seed and start-up financing. The bank-related funds may be investing in these companies in part to complement and support their parent company's traditional banking business by investing in more longer-term relationships than would be possible with early stage investments with a higher failure rate[16] (OECD, 1996c). However, the emphasis on later stage investments may simply reflect greater caution in the Netherlands after the discouraging results of the last decade, where average returns from seed investment were negative[17] (McKinsey Global Institute, 1997). Another supply-side explanation is that venture capital companies tend to look for a larger deal size than is normal for early-stage investment (K+V Organisatie Adviesbureau bv and Entrepreneurial Holding bv, 1996).

Ease of exit from the investment is generally an important prerequisite for a well developed venture capital market. In the Netherlands, as in much of Europe, the single most important exit route for venture capital is via "trade sales" – sale of the company to another company. The number of trade sales increased from 50 in 1995 to 63 in 1996. But exit from venture capital investment through *initial public offerings* (IPOs) is also increasing, from 15 in 1995 to 47 in 1996. There are now four options for IPOs, through the *Nieuwe Markt Amsterdam* (NMAX), through EASDAQ, through listing on NASDAQ in the United States (an option that has been chosen by some fast growing European companies[18]) or through listing on the regular *Amsterdam Exchange*. On balance there does not seem to be a visible difficulty for Dutch Venture Capitalists to exit from their profitable investments.[19]

Informal investors

The Dutch informal investor market is estimated to be at least as large as the formal venture capital market.[20] Informal investors, often known as "angels", play an important role in providing not only funding but also important management skills. They are generally relatively young, almost half are 50 years or younger, and 64 per cent are still active entrepreneurs (K+V Organisatie Adviesbureau bv and Entrepreneurial Holding bv, 1996). On average they spend around 22 hours per month on "supervision" of their investment. Furthermore, half of the informal investors had founded their own successful businesses, giving them valuable experience about starting up. Informal investors stress the importance of building up a portfolio to spread the risk of failure, and three-quarters of informal investors co-invested with other investors, most often through syndicates.[21] Informal investors have in the past invested more heavily in the early stages of company development, with almost half the number of deals involving the pre-start or start-up phases.[22] However, despite estimated realised rates of return of around 17-20 per cent,[23] reported dissatisfaction with the rates of return on early stage funding is leading to a shift towards later investments. Anonymity and searching for opportunities through intermediaries seem to be important factors to informal investors. Main reasons for this seem to be a general reserve about personal wealth becoming known, and fear of either unwanted contacts or of being swamped by unsolicited investment proposals. Less than 10 per cent of informal investors contact entrepreneurs directly about investing in their business, with the remainder split more or less equally between those who actively approach intermediaries and those who take a "wait and see what comes along" attitude. Several private sector initiatives have been developed in the Netherlands to help entrepreneurs and angel investors to find each other. However, notwithstanding these networks, the biggest single constraint identified by informal investors is the perceived quality of the proposals coming forward (K+V Organisatie Adviesbureau bv and Entrepreneurial Holding bv, 1996). Nevertheless the same study indicates that there may be an additional Gld 10 billion of capital as yet untapped, in the form of supply of "angel investment".

Innovation

One important characteristic of entrepreneurship is innovation. Innovation can take place in processes (such as better marketing or stock management) or in the development of new products and services. One indicator of the degree of innovation might be the number of resident patent applications per head of population, the "inventiveness coefficient" (Table 9.4). On this basis, the Netherlands does not seem to perform well, with between 1 and 2 patents per 10 000 residents, compared with Australia, Finland, Germany, Sweden, Switzerland and the United States, which all have between 4 and 5 patents per 10 000 residents.[24] However, a study of innovating Dutch firms indicated a lack of confidence in protection offered by patents (Table 9.5), and experience suggests that smaller innovating firms are less likely to seek patent protection than larger firms[25] (Brouwer & Kleinknecht, 1997). Recent moves to streamline the patenting process and reduce the costs per patent from Gld 4 000 to Gld 1 000 should help. In contrast, the Netherlands has become one of the leading countries in buying foreign technologies, with spending on acquisition of licensed technology reaching 0.5 per cent of GDP in 1991 (OECD, 1996d).

As noted in last year's OECD *Economic surveys – Netherlands*, research carried out in Dutch public institutions is highly regarded, with the citations rate of Dutch scientific publications being second only to the United States. While the relationship between basic research and commercial ventures is sometimes minimal, further efforts to find ways of commercialising the results of academic work seem

Table 9.4. **Inventiveness coefficient**

Resident patent applications per 10 000 population

	Average 1981-94
Switzerland	5.53
Germany	4.94
Sweden	4.36
Australia	4.25
Finland	3.83
United Kingdom	3.46
United States	3.14
New Zealand	2.99
Austria	2.93
France	2.18
Denmark	2.16
Norway	2.15
Ireland	1.95
Netherlands	**1.47**
Italy[1]	1.38
Canada	0.93
Belgium	0.90
Spain	0.50
Portugal	0.09
Mexico[1]	0.06

1.   Average over the period 1992-94.
Source: OECD (1997a).

Table 9.5   **Protection of product innovations against imitators[1]**

Judgements by innovating firms about the effectiveness of various mechanisms

Mechanism of protection against imitators	Judgement about effectiveness (percentages)				
	Insignificant	Modest	Moderate	Very important	Crucial
Time lead on competitors	20.5	6.1	16.3	37.8	19.4
Keeping qualified people in the firm	17.1	5.5	21.6	39.6	16.1
Secrecy	33.2	13.3	20.8	18.9	13.8
Patent protection	47.0	14.9	12.6	15.1	10.3
Complexity of product or process design	47.6	11.8	19.5	15.1	6.0
Copyright and related laws	61.5	14.6	12.4	8.7	2.8
Certification, normalisation	47.4	16.5	17.6	14.9	3.6

1.   Number of observations: 1 008.
Source: CIS-Netherlands, 1992, in Brouwer and Kleinknecht (1997).

warranted. Efforts are being made to improve the linkages between academic research and the business sector, with new incentive structures in place to ensure that the work in research institutes is more demand-driven and that their perform-ance will be judged more on the marketability of their output (Ministry of Eco-nomic Affairs, 1995*b*). Providing more scope for scientific researchers to capture some of the financial benefits that would flow from future commercialisation of their work would encourage more market-oriented research, as would encouraging a more entrepreneurial orientation in science and engineering courses.

Taxation and regulation

Taxation and regulation can have important effects on entrepreneurship, although relatively few Dutch businesses in the *European Business Survey* consid-ered that they were a major long-term constraint, compared with their European counterparts. Statutory corporate tax rates in the Netherlands are in line with rates in most OECD countries, at 36 per cent for the first Gld 100 000 of taxable profits and 35 per cent for additional profits.[26] But statutory tax rates have gener-ally been shown to be a poor indicator of *marginal effective tax rates* (METRs) on corporate earnings, which matter more for investment decisions (Leibfritz *et al.*, 1997). Although METRs on corporate income for various sources of finance are not available for the Netherlands, it seems likely that significant variations in METRs and associated distortions are likely to be present, because the Dutch tax system favours investment in owner-occupied housing rather than in production, debt financing rather than equity financing, and retained earnings rather than new equity investment, because of double taxation of dividends and the absence of a capital gains tax. Average effective tax rates on capital in the Netherlands seem to be close to the middle of the range of OECD countries (Table 9.6). And OECD Secretariat simulations indicate that a reduction in corporate taxes equivalent to 1 per cent of GDP (financed by reductions in transfer payments) would increase GDP in the Netherlands by nearly 3 percentage points and employment by almost 1 percentage point (Leibfritz *et al.*, 1997).

Many very small businesses in the Netherlands are unincorporated and profits are therefore taxed as part of personal income of the owners. In principle, the tax treatment is designed to be neutral with respect to incorporation. But the complex interplay of different personal and corporate tax rates, rules for carry-forward/backward of losses[27] and treatment of expenses, mean that in practice, the tax liability is not neutral and depends on the level of profits earned, accord-

Table 9.6. **Average effective tax rates on capital and labour income**

	Capital[1]			Labour[2]		
	1965-75	1975-85	1985-94	1965-75	1975-85	1985-94
United States	0.42	0.42	0.40[3]	0.17	0.21	0.23[3]
Japan	0.23	0.35	0.44	0.12	0.17	0.21
Germany	0.21	0.29	0.26	0.29	0.35	0.37
France	0.17	0.25	0.25	0.29	0.37	0.43
Italy	..	0.22	0.28	..	0.28	0.32
United Kingdom	0.50	0.60	0.52	0.24	0.25	0.21
Canada	0.41	0.38	0.44	0.17	0.22	0.28
Australia	0.34	0.42	0.45	0.13	0.18	0.19
Austria	0.17	0.20	0.21	0.33	0.38	0.41
Belgium	0.26	0.35	0.33	0.31	0.37	0.40
Denmark	..	0.42	0.42	..	0.35	0.41
Finland	0.22	0.32	0.41	0.23	0.31	0.38
Greece	..	..	..	..	..	..
Netherlands	..	**0.30**	**0.31**	..	**0.43**	**0.46**
New Zealand	..	..	..	..	..	..
Norway	0.25	0.38	0.37	0.33	0.34	0.35
Portugal	..	..	0.15	..	..	0.21
Spain	..	0.12	0.19[3]	..	0.25	0.29[3]
Sweden	..	0.45	0.58	..	0.46	0.48
Switzerland	0.17	0.24	0.25[3]	0.19	0.26	0.26[3]

1. Average effective tax rate on capital defined as household income taxes paid on operating surplus of private unincorporated enterprises and on household property and entrepreneurial income; plus tax on income, profit and capital gains of corporations; plus recurrent taxes on immovable property; plus taxes on financial and capital transactions; all divided by total operating surplus of the economy.
2. Average effective tax rate on labour defined as household income tax paid on wages plus payroll or manpower taxes, divided by wages and salaries (including income of self-employed) plus employers' contributions to social security and to private pension schemes.
3. Figure for 1993.
Source: Leibfritz *et al.* (1997).

ing to estimates of the Ministry of Economic Affairs.[28] This makes it difficult for an entrepreneur to judge in advance which corporate form would suit him best.

There are a number of tax related issues that affect the "unofficial" equity market. A high profile has been given to the "Aunt Agatha" scheme, which has been in place since 1996 and is designed to encourage investment in start-up companies. Capital returns of up to Gld 5 000 under this scheme are tax exempt, as long as the investment is held for 8 years, while losses up to Gld 50 000[29] on loans under these schemes may be written off against income tax. Special tax provisions also apply to recognised venture capital funds that invest at least 70 per cent in start-up companies, allowing them to deduct losses once the value of a participation falls below original cost price. Not withstanding these special schemes designed to encourage start-ups, there are significant differences in the tax treatment of different saving instruments. These differences are most significant for the taxation of new equity, which favours debt rather than equity financing, and retained earnings rather than new equity. This may tend to lock funds into investment projects within the same companies rather than allowing funds to be allocated to higher return investments in other companies.[30]

Reducing the costs of compliance with taxation and regulation has become a major focus of attention in the Netherlands (for a summary of the history of efforts to reduce administrative burdens on business in the Netherlands, see OECD, 1997d). A number of efforts have been made to estimate the costs of compliance. The most recent and comprehensive study indicates costs associated with taxes and levies amounting to almost Gld 6.2 billion or 1 per cent of GDP, in 1993 (Table 9.7). Compliance with labour-related regulations amounted to another Gld 1.4 billion, while compliance with business-related regulations, including environmental regulation amounted to another Gld 1.7 billion. Preparation of annual accounts was surprisingly costly, amounting to Gld 3.8 billion, but much of these costs would probably be incurred anyway, even if not required by law. These cost estimates also do not take into account the value of cash-flow benefits, nor the reduction in profit taxes because of compliance costs. Both this study and earlier ones found that compliance costs were regressive, falling relatively more heavily on smaller enterprises than larger ones. Moreover, Dutch micro-entrepreneurs, self-employed and start-ups, suffer from non-harmonised and sometimes tight legal definitions of entrepreneurship, which hampers a further development of entrepreneurial activities. This is especially relevant in the tax and social security systems, where different criteria and definitions are used.

The present government has embarked on a concerted strategy to reduce the undesired economic side-effects of regulation, recognising that both compliance and the excess burden of regulation are damaging and discouraging to entrepreneurial activity. A number of simplifications to administrative regulations have been implemented as part of the programme "Towards Lower Administrative

Table 9.7. **Administrative burden on Dutch business, 1993**

Cost related to	Gld billion	% of total
Taxes and levies	**6.16**	**47.0**
Wage tax, social insurance contributions[1]	2.34	17.8
VAT, excise duties	1.94	14.8
Corporation/personal income tax, dividend tax	1.68	12.8
Municipal levies	0.20	1.5
Labour-related regulations	**1.41**	**10.8**
Sick leave, deployment of special groups	0.54	4.1
Employment contracts, worker participation	0.47	3.6
Working conditions	0.40	3.1
Business-related regulations	**5.54**	**42.3**
Annual accounts	3.83	29.2
Information supply to Central Bureau of Statistics	0.55	4.2
Import/export regulations, transport permits	0.33	2.5
Government supervision and inspections	0.32	2.4
Environmental legislation	0.30	2.3
Chamber of Commerce regulations/levies[2]	0.21	1.6
Total	**13.11**	**100.0**
(% of GDP)	2.0	

1. Including government supervision and audits.
2. Including regulations and levies of other public law business organisations.
Source: EIM, cited in OECD (1997*d*).

Costs". For example, simplifications to environmental legislation mean that some 60 000 retail, trade, hotel and catering businesses will no longer have to obtain licences that cost between Gld 2 000 and 15 000 and instead must simply comply with general rules and report to the local authority, at a cost of less than Gld 50. Another simplification is that the *Central Bureau of Statistics* will use electronic data from accountants instead of surveying 10 000 small firms, and "delivery and distribution points" (DDPs) have been established to provide a single collection point for all employee-related data. More broadly, the "business effects test" has been developed and is applied to assess the impact on businesses of draft legislation. Major efforts to reduce tax compliance costs are also being made, building on the work of the *Van Lunteren Committee*.[31]

Start-ups

Starting a company entails particular challenges. The *Establishment Law*, which covers approximately 50 per cent of all small and medium-sized firms, forbids the establishment of a new business without a proper licence. These licences are issued by the *Chamber of Commerce* and require that entrepreneurs starting a business meet minimum general, and sometimes profession-specific, qualifications (see OECD, 1993 for a more detailed description). Despite significant liberalisation of this law in 1996, reducing the establishment rules from 88 to 8, the law still presents a significant hurdle that can discourage start-ups. Because of concerns about the effect on start-ups, a review of the current law will be brought forward to 1998 (from 2001). Even where a licence is not required, obtaining loan finance is likely to be extremely difficult without the "seal of approval" of the local *Chamber of Commerce*. Setting up a limited liability company (Besloten Vennootschap bv) takes a minimum of three months and requires a minimum capital of Gld 40 000. Costs of setting up a BV are estimated at 2 500 to 4 000 guilder and include taxes levied at 1 per cent of capital (Logotech, 1997). A further discouragement to new firms is the costs of learning about their obligations when they hire workers. One-off costs for hiring the first new employee in the Netherlands were estimated at Gld 2 800 of which 80 per cent is costs associated with finding out about the employer obligations (Table 9.8). These costs are higher than in other OECD countries examined. Remaining labour market rigidities also make it difficult for new businesses to expand.

The unemployment risk and bankruptcy legislation in the Netherlands are also likely to discourage someone planning to start a business. The "typical" entrepreneur in the Netherlands (as in most other countries) is a person who has worked for a number of years, usually in two or three different jobs, and is around 35 to 40 years old. Given that only 60 per cent of start-ups survive the first five years, the typical entrepreneur faces a higher probability of unemployment than if he had remained with his former employers. Furthermore, if he becomes unemployed, he will have no unemployment insurance entitlement. And if the entrepreneur goes bankrupt, he is currently liable for his debts for the rest of his life,

Table 9.8.   **Estimated administrative expenses related to hiring employees**

| Country | Estimated expenses in Dutch guilders | | | |
| | First employee | | Subsequent employees | |
	One-time basis	First year	One-time basis	First year
Netherlands	2 800	3 300	150	210
Germany	1 800	2 800	100	250
United Kingdom	2 100	2 400	250	300
United States	1 900	2 100	200	300
Belgium	150	650	100	600
France	600	1 500	150	200
Denmark	500	1 300	100	130
Japan	900	1 200	150	200

Source: Hulshoff *et al.* (1997).

although a bill currently before parliament would reduce the pursuit of debts to a maximum of five years, but only if strict conditions are met. After the 5-year-period, a so-called *"natuurlijke verbinding* (standby-claim)"* will nevertheless remain, implying sustained liability. The personal costs of failure are very high and are likely to strongly discourage would-be entrepreneurs from taking the risk. And, unlike in the United States, a second chance is virtually impossible. Although it is difficult to quantify, cultural attitudes towards failure in the Netherlands almost certainly compound these effects.

Public programmes and policies

Job creation through the promotion of entrepreneurship has become a high priority in Dutch economic policy, as illustrated by the policy paper *"Jobs through Enterprise"* jointly published in June 1995 by the *Ministries of Economic Affairs, Social Affairs and Employment,* and *Finance.* The paper contains a wide range of policy proposals designed to generate more jobs by increasing the scope for entrepreneurship in general, and for the start-up and expansion of new businesses in particular. The proposals aim at providing both for a healthy general economic climate (fiscal and regulatory environment) and a number of specific measures to provide an extra *stimulus* to entrepreneurship.

In principle, the criterion for assessing policies and measures to promote entrepreneurship is simple: do the overall benefits outweigh the costs? But in practice this can be very difficult to determine, especially where policies aim at improving economic outcomes indirectly and are expected to have a complex range of effects over a long period, for example where efforts are made to improve the entrepreneurial orientation of the education system or where economic and social development objectives are combined in one programme. It is also difficult to assess the overall effectiveness of "entrepreneurial policies" when they have developed as a mix of policy initiatives taken over the years, rather than designed as part of an overall strategy. And some of these policies may represent "second-best solutions", as measures designed to offset the distortions or shortcomings of the overall institutional framework for business discussed above.

Yet the difficulties of making accurate cost-benefit analyses are not a valid excuse for public inaction: ongoing programme evaluation is important and can lead to more cost-effective measures. For example, an important public intervention in the Netherlands has been the provision of "first line advice" and counselling for start-ups, on the assumption that without government intervention, the market would not provide these services adequately. Such advice can be critical for giving entrepreneurs a first orientation in matters relevant to starting a business as well as dealing with a somewhat opaque administrative environment.

However in the early 1990s, evaluations showed that the way these activities were carried out was not satisfactory. It was unclear to entrepreneurs what services were offered, and advice given was not well adapted to needs. Responding to this finding, the government started pilot projects, the so-called "Enterprise Houses", in which services of the local Chamber of Commerce, the IMK (Institutes for Small and Medium-sized Enterprises) and the ICs (Innovations Centres) were redesigned and integrated at the local level. This new approach was judged more cost-effective in an evaluation in 1996, and as a result will be applied nationally from the beginning of 1998.

Beyond the ongoing need for programme evaluation, this example shows that the promotion of entrepreneurship needs to involve a wide range of actors, coming from both a national and local level. Institutions concerned may be public, semi-public or private. The challenge to policy makers is to join these different actors in effective partnerships. Experience in OECD countries suggests that achieving this integration of resources through top-down intervention by the central government alone is difficult (OECD, 1996a). There is a need for both top-down and bottom up policy intervention. The Dutch Ministry of Economic Affairs is following this dual approach and is seeing itself increasingly as a facilitator of initiatives undertaken by a multitude of actors.

Another important area of entrepreneurship promotion in the Netherlands is built on the interaction between social and economic policies. Integration of the two policy areas can improve their effectiveness. Therefore governments increasingly seek to substitute passive income support policies by helping people to help themselves, for example through the promotion of self-employment. An essential question is whether society as a whole gains by providing special targeted support, other than that developed for normal business entrepreneurs, to specific groups like the unemployed, ethnic minorities, etc. The Netherlands is in fact developing such special programmes, which are extending the frontiers of traditional entrepreneurship policies. Three regional pilot projects were set up in 1996 to focus services more closely on the needs of unemployed who want to re-enter the labour market as entrepreneurs. Following the same idea, the social security system facilitates self-employment by freeing those unemployed from job-search duties up to one and a half years. Loans up to Gld 40 000 are also available to this target group.[32] Moreover a national expertise centre is being set up to promote regional counselling services to would-be entrepreneurs pertaining to specific ethnic groups. An evaluation of these programmes is presently underway and should help to improve programme design.

Entrepreneurial culture has increasingly gained attention as a potential object of policy intervention. It shapes people's willingness to take initiative and, in the long run, also influences how the institutional setting supports entrepreneurship. The question is whether government has any effective levers to

Box 9.1.   **Selected policies for entrepreneurship promotion
in the Netherlands**

R&D promotion

A major part of public assistance to small business is spent on R&D subsidies, based on the assumption that there exist considerable externalities, so that without government intervention there would be under-investment in R&D. Such under-spending can be more significant among small firms, as empirical research indicates that on average these businesses are reluctant to invest in basic and pre-competitive R&D because of the high financial costs and long lead times before a marketable product can be developed. The WBSO (*Act to promote* R&D) grants a tax reduction on labour cost of R&D staff.[1] The total budget of WBSO in 1996 was Gld 561 million, of which 60 per cent were given to enterprises with less than 250 employees. There is another programme focusing separately on research and development only, which in 1996 allocated Gld 22 million to research grants and Gld 38.5 to development loans,[2] respectively. There are no estimates at present on what the overall effects of these subsidies on enterprise growth, innovation or job creation are.[3] The emphasis in technology policy has shifted to promoting technological co-operation and the emergence of innovative clusters and networks of businesses and research institutes. The Dutch government wishes to both deepen and expand cluster policy in the coming years as a new dimension in industrial policy. A recent policy letter outlined three roles in government's fulfilment of its tasks in the field of innovative clustering: the role of creating favourable and stable conditions to enable businesses to increase their competitiveness (framework policy); the role of identifying and stimulating innovative clustering by providing strategic information and by matching supply and demand (broker policies); and its role as a demanding customer when providing public services (procurement policy).

Financial assistance for entrepreneurship

Another sizeable measure to promote entrepreneurship in the Netherlands is the SME *Credit Guarantees Decree* (BBMKB). The scheme aims at giving guarantees to banks which make loans to new, small and medium-sized businesses with difficult access to bank credit under normal banking conditions, due to a lack of adequate collateral. Research in some European countries has shown that granting public credits or guarantees for bank credits can contribute to inhibiting the development of the more entrepreneurial market for external equity (informal equity investors or venture capital) (Kaufmann & Kokalj, 1996). Moreover such programmes might strengthen the culture of debt rather than developing an equity culture. An entrepreneur who can obtain subsidised debt finance without offering collateral has in most cases no interest to obtain finance from outside equity investors as these expect much higher rates of return compared with market interest rates and usually want to exercise some degree of control.

However, one-third of the guarantees go to start-ups with an average loan size of Gld 105 000, an amount which should not be competition for the private equity market, according to research on the average size of both informal investors' and venture

(continued on next page)

(continued)

capital investments in the Netherlands (K+V Organisatie Adviesbureau bv and Entrepreneurial Holding bv, 1996). Also, the average size of guaranteed loans for non start-ups of Gld 225 000 does not seem to be in the range of external equity financing. Yet the maximum of the SME *Credit Guarantees Decree* loan is set at Gld 2 million, an amount of interest to the private equity market as well. The risk of hindering the development of a private equity market might be higher still for the *Special Financing Security Fund Scheme* which normally guarantees amounts between Gld 2 million and Gld 50 million. Nevertheless, as the costs of the Decree are low, about 12 million guilders a year, compared with the outstanding guarantees of about Gld 825 million a year (projects rarely fail), it is debatable whether the projects under guarantee are really risky projects, and whether the Decree effectively puts more risk capital into the market-place.

In order to promote the market for informal capital the government created a special tax allowance for investment in starting enterprises, the so-called "Aunt Agatha" scheme. Within this scheme losses of up to Gld 50 000 can be written off against income tax. In addition Gld 5 000 in interest received on loans to enterprises is tax-exempt for eight years. This scheme was at first intended to activate family capital. Now plans are under discussion to enlarge the scheme to the whole range of informal investors, including intermediated informal funds. Such schemes to promote the capital market beyond the traditional financial intermediaries can contribute to a more entrepreneurial climate. Yet again it needs to be ensured that such measures do not privilege debt at the expense of equity capital.

Local enterprise promotion

The Netherlands has a well-established system of information and advisory services for small and medium-sized enterprises. This system is aimed at stimulating innovation. The Dutch approach is to implement and partly finance these services at the local and regional level. Moreover a number of non-governmental institutions are involved in order to be close to the practical concerns of businesses (*Chamber of Commerce, institutes for Small and Medium-sized Enterprises, Innovation Centres*, etc.). The annual budget of the network will be about Gld 60 million in the coming years. A related new programme is aimed at assisting new and expanding enterprises with a coach who provides relevant advice and information.

Another interesting approach to entrepreneurship promotion at the local level has been the development of science parks in the Netherlands. A considerable number of enterprises in these parks are spin-offs from university research and start-ups or relocated firms coming from nearby areas (EIM/International, 1995). The resulting local concentration of enterprises is intended to influence their innovative capabilities. Some of the parks seek to improve the entrepreneurial environment through a range of local services. For example the *Technical University of Twente* has developed a network of support, including a business incubator, a programme for start-ups, a programme to stimulate technology transfer, and a network of high-tech enterprises around its *Business and Science Park* (Table 9.9).

(continued on next page)

(*continued*)

Table 9.9. **Science parks in the Netherlands**

Location	Year started	Area (Ha)	Number of establishments	Number of jobs (August 1994)	Jobs per establishment (August 1993)
Nijmegen	1989	1.5	25	100	4.0
Wageningen	1989	5.5	39	400	10.0
Amsterdam	1991	20.0	20	150	7.5
Leyden	1984	30.0	25	640	25.6
Enschede (Twente)	1981	18.5	106	1 115	10.5
Groningen	1988	6.0	51	460	9.0
Delft	1992	30.0	15	27	1.8

Source: Bartels and Wolff (1993).

Regional policy is an area which has a considerable influence on the entrepreneurial environment in a number of OECD countries. Instruments used in the Netherlands are investment grants, regional development corporations, regional programmes, the EFRD (*European Fund for Regional Development*) and the business environment instrument. These resources amounted to about Gld 380 million yearly in the first half of the nineties. A large part of these funds nevertheless is aimed at rather large projects as for example new large industrial premises, modern office parks for international companies or the construction of high speed railroad lines, etc. The contribution of these regional policy tools to entrepreneurship development appears therefore to be rather limited in the case of the Netherlands.

1. The R&D rebate amounts to 40 per cent for the first Gld 150 000 of total labour cost for R&D staff and 12.5 per cent in excess of this amount. Special deductions also exist for self-employed spending more than 625 hours a year on R&D.
2. Non repayable in the case of project failure.
3. Although a number of evaluations have been undertaken, no clear findings on the impact of measures could be reached. This is mainly due to problems related to measuring the complex potential impacts of the programmes (OECD, 1997*b*).

facilitate the transition to a more entrepreneurial society. Education could be such a critical lever, as the government traditionally has a strong role in this area. A recent survey showed that until now Dutch students have shown little interest in starting their own business (Universum, 1997). Dutch universities and professional schools have started to offer courses on entrepreneurship, for example a four year course on small business at the *Hoger Economisch en Administratief Onderwijs* (HEAO) in Harlem. Yet often the coverage of such programmes appears to be limited to a small fraction of the population. Broader approaches including changes at lower education levels could boost entrepreneurial spirit more pervasively. To this end the Ministry of Economic Affairs is partly funding projects where students can start so-called mini-enterprises within the framework of the Mini Onderneming foundation.

Though such measures have a considerable time lag before results are visible, their potential influence appears to be non-negligible. At the same time these initiatives should not divert attention from the question whether there is a need for a more general overhaul of the education system to better contribute to entrepreneurship and job creation. Private educational institutions in the US have had a critical influence on the development of entrepreneurship both on a local and national level (OECD, 1997 c). More experimentation with increasing private sector involvement in the education system could provide insight on how to make the whole Dutch education system more entrepreneurial.

How does the overall policy mix in the Netherlands contribute to entrepreneurship? The Dutch are following a strategy that combines efforts to improve the general institutional environment with specific measures targeted on new and growing enterprises. Improving the general business environment should help entrepreneurial activity to flourish, although quantifying the relationship is difficult. Targeting specific measures on new and growing enterprises can be expected to do more to promote entrepreneurship and generate less deadweight losses than if subsidies were given to all small and medium-sized enterprises. Yet there is need for ongoing evaluation to ensure the most appropriate allocation of government resources even amongst targeted programmes. Some of the spending choices are not self-evident to the outside observer, and no studies have been undertaken on the relative costs and benefits of all the different programmes to identify those which offer the best value for money. Furthermore, the present emphasis on promoting high-technology may be misplaced, since evidence in the United States and elsewhere shows that entrepreneurship, innovation and job creation do not exclusively emanate from SMEs in high-tech areas, but occur also in low-tech sectors such as retailing and other services. Therefore, an entrepreneurship promotion policy focusing on particular sectors or high technology can miss out important areas for innovation and job creation.

Notes

1. Micro-enterprises (0-9 employees) and small enterprises (10-99 employees) accounted for 22 per cent of employment each, while medium-sized enterprises (100-499 employees) accounted for the remaining 13 per cent.

2. For a discussion of some of these difficulties and a careful assessment of the data for the Netherlands, see Kleiweg and Nieuwenhuijsen (1996).

3. However, about 20 per cent of starters and new subsidiaries close within 1½ years and about 50 per cent of them before 5 years.

4. "Fast-growing firms" are firms that existed over the whole period 1990-1994 and showed relatively high employment growth. The classification depends on the size of the firm: a firm with 10 employees is called "fast-growing" if employment increases by more than 13 per cent while for firms with 10 000 employees, 4 per cent employment growth is sufficient. According to this definition, fast-growing firms make up 8 per cent of all existing firms.

5. Between 1987 and 1993, the number of new enterprises created by "new" entrepreneurs grew by around 6 per cent per year on average, while new establishments created by existing enterprises grew on average by 14.5 per cent per year (de Lind van Wijngaarden, 1995).

6. Rural communities are defined as those communities with population density below 150 inhabitants/km^2 (see OECD 1996b).

7. Metropolitan area in the western part of the Netherlands.

8. To some extent, this may reflect the BBMKB scheme described under programmes and policies below.

9. Even in the short term, availability and/or cost of finance was a main constraint for only 18 per cent of respondents, compared with an EU average of 52 per cent (see Grant Thornton International Business Strategies Ltd, 1997).

10. The difference between the level of taxation on retained and distributed profits was 32 per cent in 1991.

11. See OECD (1996d) for a more detailed discussion of these issues.

12. Some commentators attribute the development of the venture capital industry in the Netherlands in part to the favourable tax regime during the 1980s (EVCA, 1997).

13. This has been reported as a problem for informal investors, where there is limited experience of how to "close the deal" (K+V Organisatie Adviesbureau bv and Entrepreneurial Holding bv, 1996). It may also reflect a legal framework that is insufficiently flexible to allow innovative arrangements to be developed. On one analysis, countries which followed the civil law tradition, including the Netherlands, provided weak investor protection and as a result, had under-developed venture

       capital markets compared with countries with a common law approach (La Porta *et al.*, 1997).

14. This scheme is described in detail in OECD (1996c).

15. Unlike in the United States, where institutional investors, particularly pension funds, are now the major sources of venture capital funding, pension funds and insurance companies together provided less than 20 per cent of venture capital raised in the Netherlands.

16. This is in marked contrast to the venture capital investment strategies adopted in the United States, where venture capitalists expect that only one in ten investments will be highly successful, but the returns on that venture will more than offset the failures. Another two or three projects out of 10 will generate a modest return, and the remaining 60-70 per cent of projects will be failures. In the Netherlands, only around 30 per cent of total investments fail completely.

17. Although including all types of venture capital investments, realised returns on venture capital portfolios over 1986 to 1994 were estimated to average 12 per cent (K+V Organisatie Adviesbureau bv and Entrepreneurial Holding bv, 1996).

18. The main appeal of listing on NASDAQ seems to be the increased liquidity and higher profile of that market, compared with European markets.

19. Informal investors also attach a low weighting to limited exit opportunities when considering problems in the investment process (see K+V Organisatie Adviesbureau bv and Entrepreneurial Holding bv, 1996).

20. International comparisons are difficult, but in the United States the informal investor market is estimated to be at least twice the size of the formal venture capital market.

21. Roughly half of these syndicates are formed on an ad-hoc basis and the rest comprise more or less permanent membership.

22. Although 16 per cent of all deals are "turn-arounds" – financing of existing businesses in trouble – to assist them in reorganisation to restore profitability.

23. Assuming the average informal investment is held for five to six years before being realised (K+V Organisatie Adviesbureau bv and Entrepreneurial Holding bv, 1996).

24. It should be noted, however, that patent legislation differs between countries, and patent statistics can therefore only be taken as a broad indicator of innovation. The methodological issues are discussed in OECD (1994).

25. A recent unpublished study by the Ministry of Economic Affairs found that in one sample of inventors, only one in every four inventions was actually patented.

26. From the beginning of 1998, all corporate profits will be taxed at 35 per cent.

27. Under corporate tax, losses can be carried backwards for 3 years and forwards indefinitely, whereas under income tax, such carry backwards and forwards of losses are not generally permitted. For investors this difference in tax treatment matters, because investment losses are not generally deductible. It has been argued that this discourages informal investment, especially because even when the business has failed, the investment cannot be written off for tax purposes until the winding up procedures have been completed, which may be a long time after the actual losses have been incurred.

28. For profits of less than Gld 100 000, an enterprise will be taxed more if incorporated than if unincorporated. For profits more than Gld 150 000 the tax liability will be lower if incorporated.

29. In comparison, more than half of all Dutch start-ups start with less than Gld 25 000 (de Lind van Wijngaarden, 1995).

30. This bias is compounded by the imposition of a capital tax levy of 1 per cent on companies' new equity issues.

31. The *Van Lunteren Committee*, comprising specialists from government and business, was set up in Autumn 1994 by the *State Secretary of Finance* and was charged with presenting proposals for reducing administrative costs within the tax administration (OECD, 1997*d*).

32. The interest rate for these loans is 7 per cent.

References

BAIS, J., BANGMA, K.L. and VERHOEVEN, W.H.J. (1997),
"Het beland van bedrijfstypen voor de werkgelegenheidsontwikkeling", EIM/
Economisch beleid, Zoetermeer.

BANGMA, K., VAN NOORT, E. and VERHOEVEN, W.H.J. (1997),
Creation and loss of jobs in the Netherlands, EIM/Small Business Research and Consultancy,
Zoetermeer.

BARTELS, C.P.A. and WOLFF, J.W.A. (1993),
"Science Parken in Nederland", Economisch Statistische Berichten, 10 November.

BROUWER, E. and KLEINKNECHT, A. (1997),
"Innovative output and a firm's propensity to patent: an exploration of the CIS micro
data", in Into Innovation Determinants and Indicators, Erik Brouwer, ed.

DE LIND VAN WIJNGAARDEN, K.I. (1995),
Start-ups in the Netherlands, EIM/Small Business Research and Consultancy, Zoetermeer.

DE LIND VAN WIJNGAARDEN, K.I. (1996),
The State of Small Business in the Netherlands 1996, EIM Small Business Research and
Consultancy, Zoetermeer.

EIM/INTERNATIONAL (1995),
The State of Small Business in the Netherlands 1995, Zoetermeer.

EIM (1997),
Oplevend Ondernemerschap in Nederland, Zoetermeer.

EUROPEAN COMMISSION (1995a),
"Technical note: The Commission Services' method for cyclical adjustment of government budget balances", European Economy 60, Brussels.

EUROPEAN COMMISSION (1995b),
Green Paper on Innovation, Bulletin of the European Union, Supplement 5/95, Brussels.

EVCA (1997),
A Survey of Venture Capital and Private Equity in Europe, 1997 Yearbook, Belgium.

GRANT THORNTON INTERNATIONAL BUSINESS STRATEGIES Ltd (1997),
European Business Survey of Small to Medium-sized Businesses Spring 1997, United Kingdom.

HULSHOFF, H.E., NIJSEN, A.F.M. and VISEE, H.C. (1997),
"Administratieve lasten in dienst nemen werknemers", OSA-werkdocument W156,
The Hague.

KAUFMANN, F. and KOKALJ, L. (1996),
Risikokapitalmärkten für mittelständische Unternehmen, Schriften zur Mittelstandsforschung,
Bonn, p. 104.

K+V ORGANISATIE ADVIESBUREAU BV and ENTREPRENEURIAL HOLDING BV (1996),
The Role of Informal Investors in the Dutch Venture Capital Market, Arnhem.

KLEIWEG, A. and NIEUWENHUIJSEN, H. (1996),
Job Creation by Size Class: Measurement and Empirical Investigation, Research Report 9604/E EIM Small Business Research and Consultancy and Central Bureau of Statistics.

KLOOSTERMAN, R.C. (1996),
"Migration in the Netherlands and the emerging post-industrial social divide in urban areas", paper prepared at the European Research Centre on Migration and Ethnic Relations, Utrecht and presented to the OECD Experts Meeting on "the Integration of Immigrants in Cities".

LA PORTA, R., LOPEZ-DE-SILANES, F., SHLEIFER, A. and VISHNY, R.W. (1997),
Legal Determinants of External Finance, NBER Working Paper 5879, Cambridge, Massachusetts.

LEIBFRITZ, W., THORNTON, J. and BIBBEE, A. (1997),
"Taxation and economic performance", *Economics Department Working Papers* No. 176, OECD, Paris.

LOGOTECH S.A. (1997),
"Étude comparative internationale des dispositions légales et administratives pour la formation de petites et moyennes entreprises aux pays de l'Union européenne, les États-Unis et le Japon", EIMS project, 96/142, Athens.

McKINSEY GLOBAL INSTITUTE (1997),
Boosting Dutch Economic Performance, Amsterdam.

MINISTRY OF ECONOMIC AFFAIRS (1995a),
Benchmarking the Netherlands, The Hague.

MINISTRY OF ECONOMIC AFFAIRS (1995b),
Knowledge in Action, The Hague.

MINISTRY OF ECONOMIC AFFAIRS (1997),
1997 Benchmarking the Netherlands; Prepared for the future, The Hague.

OECD (1993),
OECD *Economic Surveys – the Netherlands*, OECD Publications, Paris.

OECD (1994),
The OECD Jobs Study: Facts, Analysis and Strategies, OECD Publications, Paris.

OECD (1996a),
SMEs: Employment, Innovation and Growth, the Washington Workshop, OECD Publications, Paris.

OECD (1996b),
Territorial Indicators of Employment, Focusing on Rural Development, OECD Publications, Paris.

OECD (1996c),
"Venture capital in OECD countries", *Financial Market Trends*, No 63, February.

OECD (1996d),
OECD *Economic Surveys – the Netherlands*, OECD Publications, Paris.

OECD (1996e),
"Social expenditure statistics of OECD Member countries", *Labour Market and Social Policy Occasional Papers*, No. 17, Paris.

OECD (1997a),
    Main Science and Technology Indicators, No. 1997.1, OECD Publications, Paris.
OECD (1997b),
    Evaluation of Industrial R&D Support in the Netherlands, Conference on Policy Evaluation in Innovation and Technology, OECD Publications, Paris.
OECD (1997c),
    Economic Survey of the United States, OECD Publications, Paris.
OECD (1997d),
    Best Practices for Small and Medium-Sized Enterprises, OECD Publications, Paris.
UNIVERSUM (1997),
    "Examining students' attitudes", report prepared for the Ministry of Economic Affairs.
UPTON, N. (1995),
    "Family Owned Businesses", in Brophy, D. (ed.), The Age of Enterprise: Prospects for Small Business and Entrepreneurship in the Twenty First Century, SBA, Washington, D.C.
VAN DIJKEN, K., PRINCE, Y.M. and VERHOEVEN, W. (1995),
    Waarin een klein land groot kan zijn; Een internationale vergelijking van middelgrote bedrijven, EIM, Zoetermeer.
VENTURE ONE (1997),
    National Venture Capital Association 1996 Annual Report, San Francisco.
VERENIGING VAN KAMERS VAN KOOPHANDEL (1997),
    "Bedrijvendynamiek 1996", Woerden.

Chapter X

Spain

Against the background of the recent improvements that have been made in Spain's economic policy framework and its overall economic performance, intensified entrepreneurial activity could play an important supporting role. This chapter examines some aspects of the state of entrepreneurial activity in Spain, the institutional framework within which Spanish businesses operate and the programmes and policies of the Spanish Government aimed at stimulating different aspects of entrepreneurship.

The state of entrepreneurship

Small businesses and entrepreneurship

Entrepreneurship is often associated with the activity of SMEs, although a well-functioning and dynamic economy is likely to be associated with entrepreneurial behaviour in large as well as small firms. As in many other countries, Spanish SMEs have been a major source of employment creation in recent years. Spain has around 2.7 million enterprises, and 55 per cent of them are one-person businesses, a much higher proportion than elsewhere in Europe. Spain also has a very high proportion of very small enterprises or micro enterprises (with one to nine employees), compared with the rest of Europe, let alone the United States and Japan. These differences are most apparent in the services sector, especially trade, hotels and restaurants. For example, in Spain 45 per cent of employees in the trade, hotels and restaurants sector are employed in very small firms and another 28 per cent in small firms (with 10-49 employees). In Europe, only Italy and Portugal have a higher proportion of employment in very small enterprises in this sector.[1] In the United States, in contrast, almost half of the work force of the sector is employed in 6 500 very large enterprises (500 or more employees – Eurostat, 1995). And in the Spanish transport sector, more than three-quarters of businesses are one person operations, in striking contrast to other OECD countries. To some extent these statistics may reflect a more extensive use of subcontracting arrangements, so as to circumvent tight job protection measures. However, the higher proportion of micro enterprises in some of these sectors where larger enterprises have tended to develop in many other countries and where some economies of scale and/or scope might be expected to exist, may be a signal that some barriers to expansion exist.

Entrepreneurship and firm turnover rates

One approach to the study of entrepreneurship emphasises firm start-ups and closures as an indicator of willingness to engage in risk taking activity and capacity to innovate, and as an indicator of the ease with which resources are able to move quickly from one activity to another. The reported enterprise birth rate – the number of new firm registrations relative to the stock of existing firms – is estimated to be around 4 to 5 per cent in Spain, which is lower than other European countries. However the definitions used for firm births vary considerably from one country to another, making international comparisons very difficult. To facilitate cross country comparisons, the European Observatory for SMEs has produced estimates of birth rates, according to "harmonised" definitions. On these estimates, the firm start-up rate is one of the highest in Europe, although it also has the widest margin of uncertainty attached to it.[2] Given the uncertainties attached to the harmonised statistics and also the possibility that the unadjusted statistics may significantly understate the degree of turbulence,[3] the existing data on firm start-up rates do not provide a reliable indicator of the degree of entrepreneurship in the Spanish economy. However, one possible interpretation of the differences between the birth-rates could be that opening a one-person business is less difficult than opening a larger one.

Regional dimensions of entrepreneurship

Indicators of the regional distribution of entrepreneurship show significant differences as in other OECD countries. In the period 1990-92 unadjusted start up rates exceeded 8 per cent in the regions of Madrid and Murcia and were below 5 per cent in regions such as Castilla-La Mancha, Canarias, Estremadura and Galicia (IMPI, 1996). However geographical variations would be more relevant and significant at sub-regional level as most industrial firms and related business services are concentrated within industrial districts or so-called "local productive systems". More than 140 such clusters of firms have been identified (Celada, 1991). They are located in all regions, including within the main metropolitan areas, urban-industrial centres of intermediate size as well as in smaller urban nuclei with a strong local artisan or industrial tradition. They are heavily concentrated in Cataluña (23 clusters), the Valencia Region (23 clusters) and

Andalucía (29 clusters). They are specialised in a variety of industries, ranging from software in Sabadell (Cataluña), machine tools (Bajo Deba) and aeronautical components (South Madrid) to toys (Ibi), ceramics (Castellon) and furniture (Urola). These industrial districts are an important source of industrial production and exports. Their strength is largely derived from a geographical concentration of specialised, flexible and co-operating firms, which permits them to take advantage of externalities and the minimisation of transaction costs.

According to one research study on a sample of firms (one from each of 23 selected local systems), a distinction should be made between two types of clusters. On the one hand, clusters of competing yet also co-operating small and medium size enterprises which develop complementary production activities often related to local resources. On the other hand, there are systems organised around a large and vertically-integrated firm which subcontract and outsource a large range of activities to smaller and highly flexible firms. The survey listed the positive externalities gained by both forms of collaboration. These comprised the following: First, the existence of a well skilled, locally mobile and flexible labour force. Second, the practice of exchanging orders so as to smooth fluctuations in demand. Third, the rapid diffusion of incremental and adaptive innovation through informal communication, imitation and rivalry. Fourth, the use of common bodies for accounting, raw material procurement and product distribution and, in some cases, the joint acquisition of shared equipment (Costa Campi *et al.*, 1993). These attributes of clusters allow firms to operate in a more dynamic and entrepreneurial fashion.

Factors affecting entrepreneurship

Despite the strong macroeconomic performance and a number of recent structural reforms, the Spanish economy has not yet fully overcome the strong corporatist philosophy and heavy regulation of economic activity from its past. Even after recent reforms, the overall business environment and the prevailing web of regulations and other institutional factors combine to generate what could be significant impediments to entrepreneurial activity. These features of the institutional framework could discourage risk-taking, either in establishing new ventures but more likely in the expansion of existing activities, and limit the scope for developing flexible and innovative working arrangements. Removing impediments to entrepreneurial activity and fostering a more favourable business environment should therefore form an important part of government efforts to stimulate growth. The rest of this section considers the main institutional factors that affect new businesses and/or act as constraints on expansion.

Product markets and competition

Competition in product markets can be expected to stimulate entrepreneurship, especially because innovation of processes or products can be rewarded by greater market share and increased returns. The *European Single Market*, by providing greater scope for competition from imports and opening up new markets, has played a positive role in stimulating entrepreneurial activity in Spain. However, competition in Spain has traditionally been severely limited in many sectors of the economy, especially at the level of major enterprises where the public sector has dominated as well as for some services normally provided by smaller and medium sized enterprises (especially those providing professional services).

The *Tribunal for the Defence of Competition* has made recommendations in a number of service sectors of the economy, where it has found effective competition lacking. Since several of their recommendations have recently been implemented, the identified shortcoming may have played a significant role in constraining entrepreneurship only in the past. For example, professional services were subject to a compulsory minimum fee structure and other constraints until 1996, and until 1996, funeral services were operating as local monopolies in a number of municipalities. However, some areas of road transport still need further liberalisation, including the removal of the quota system limiting the number of vehicles for discretionary passenger services and heavy freight vehicles. The rules governing installation and maintenance services were also found to be complex by the *Tribunal* and thus deleterious to competition. The *Tribunal* has also made recommendations in the areas of commercial distribution, petrol distribution, retail banking, ports, pharmacies, and the film industry. Acknowledging the recent progress in many areas, further action seems necessary to promote product market competition, including from foreign sources which can contribute know-how in production and trading.

Opening or closing a business

Setting up a new business in Spain appears to be a more cumbersome process than in other European countries. Irrespective of an entrepreneur's choice to incorporate, all new enterprises must undertake approximately 13 to 14 general steps prior to starting a business, and some additional steps apply in specific sector.[4] Moreover, incorporation involves a minimum of five additional steps (only 12 per cent of enterprises are incorporated).[5] On average, each step requires four separate pieces of documentation, and involves a minimum of six different agencies, with the total time required to fulfil these legal requirements estimated to be between 19 and 28 weeks. In contrast, it takes around half a day to establish a new enterprise in the United States.

Closing a business is also a complicated and expensive process in Spain, especially because of the labour regulations. These make it difficult to reduce the workforce for economic reasons despite recent legislative attempts in this regard, which raises losses sustained when an uneconomic business does close (see below). Furthermore, only about one quarter of businesses that go bankrupt is covered by limited liability (ENSR, 1995), so that the cost to the owner of an unsuccessful business can be very high. This is likely to discourage people from taking the risk. An *Inter-Ministerial Commission* is currently reviewing the trade-off between the rights and obligations of debtors and creditors, in recognition of the adverse effects that current bankruptcy legislation has on risk-taking, and entre-preneurship more generally, while also taking into account the effect that reduced creditor protection may have for credit costs.

Finance

Obtaining finance has been difficult and costly for many Spanish businesses. As recently as late 1997, 43 per cent of Spanish firms surveyed in the *European Business Survey* cited the cost of finance as a main short-term constraint on expansion, while 32 per cent cited it as a long term constraint (Figure 10.1). Difficult access to bank finance could be related to the high interest rates that existed in

Figure 10.1. **Cost of finance as a constraint on entrepreneurship**

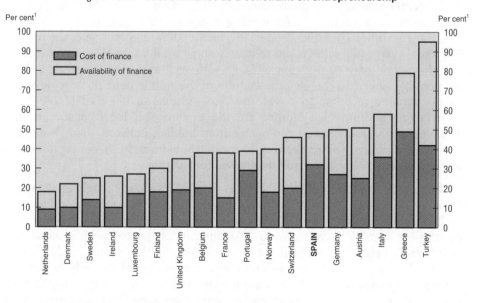

1. Sum of responses, given as percentage of respondents. Respondents were allowed to choose more than one constraint.
Source: Grant Thornton International Business Strategies Ltd., 1997.

Spain until 1996-1997, and, perhaps more importantly, to credit rationing by banks which have traditionally focused their activities on better-established and larger enterprises. Among smaller and medium sized Spanish enterprises, only 47 per cent of those surveyed felt that they had sufficient access to finance to be able to carry out their plans over the next three years, compared with a European average of 55 per cent. At the other extreme, in Denmark and the Netherlands, around 70 per cent of such enterprises felt confident about their access to finance (Grant Thornton, 1996).[6]

Venture Capital

Venture capital is typically viewed as an important source of finance for potentially fast growing companies and therefore plays an important role in a dynamic and entrepreneurial economy. The Spanish venture capital market remains relatively under-developed and to some extent still reflects a government dominated origin.[7] Despite the recent development of private providers, even as recently as in 1996, government agencies provided almost 20 per cent of new venture capital raised in Spain, compared with less than 3 per cent in Europe as a whole. Banks were the largest private sector provider, supplying 37 per cent of new venture capital raised in Spain, compared with 27 per cent for Europe generally.

In contrast, institutional investors (mainly insurance funds and pension funds) provided virtually no such funding in Spain, while playing a much larger role in many other countries, especially in the United States and the United Kingdom. In part, this reflects the relatively small total financial assets of institutional investors (only 40 per cent of GDP), with such investors' relatively limited size possibly linked to the generous nature of the public pension scheme which has discouraged recourse to private pension systems in the past (Table 10.1). Other factors limiting such funding are the existence of legal constraints that effectively prohibit insurance companies from holding unlisted shares[8] and private pension funds' (which were only established from 1987) concentration of their investments almost entirely in government paper.

Very little venture capital funding is flowing into early stage investments (Table 10.2). Instead, Spanish venture capitalists are far more active in financing expansion, and unlike other European countries, institutional buy-outs and replacement capital do not absorb a significant amount of venture capital in Spain.[9] As Government involvement in venture capital has diminished, the percentage of early stage deals has fallen from 80 per cent in 1986 to only 26 per cent in 1996. Notwithstanding the increasing emphasis on later stage investments, which would generally be considered less risky than early stage investments, an analysis of 75 completed disinvestments showed that less than 10 per cent generated an annualised rate of return of more than 25 per cent. Another 30 to

Table 10.1. **Financial assets of institutional investors**

Per cent of GDP

	Insurance companies	Pension funds	Investment companies	Other	Total
United States	40.7	59.8	39.2	31.1	170.8
United Kingdom	71.8	68.8	21.7	0.0	162.3
Netherlands	52.5	88.7	17.2	0.0	158.4
Sweden	52.4	2.4	22.2	37.8	114.8
Canada	29.3	39.5	19.1	0.0	87.9
Japan	38.3	0.0	9.8	29.3	77.4
Australia	35.2	28.7	9.3	2.7	75.9
France	37.8	0.0	37.5	0.0	75.3
Denmark	45.6	17.5	3.7	0.0	66.8
Korea	23.4	3.1	31.2	0.0	57.7
Finland	12.4	0.0	0.9	36.7	50.0
Germany	28.1	2.7	15.3	0.0	46.1
Norway	31.3	6.4	4.9	0.0	42.6
Spain	**17.8**	**2.1**	**18.4**	**0.0**	**38.3**
Portugal	9.7	8.8	16.4	0.4	35.3
Austria	20.1	1.0	14.1	0.0	35.2
Greece	2.5	10.9	9.6	0.0	23.0
Italy	9.2	0.4	7.4	0.0	17.0
Hungary	3.3	0.1	1.1	0.0	4.5

Source: OECD (1997*b*).

35 per cent generated returns of between 0 and 25 per cent while the remaining disinvestments were loss making. While losses are to be expected, what seems to be missing are the spectacular successes associated with venture capital investment in other countries, such as the United States.

Venture capital investment may be constrained by exit difficulties, which have been cited as a problem in Spain (Marti Pellon, 1997). Most successful venture capital disinvestments have been realised through management buy-backs, and only 5 *initial public offerings* (IPOs) arising from venture-capital backed investments took place in 1996 (although a number of successful non-venture-capital backed IPOs also took place). Perhaps reflecting administrative difficulties, several of these IPOs took place in the UK and US markets, rather than in Spain itself. Although there exist several second-tier markets operating in Spain, none of them seem to be particularly attractive to such companies. The recent introduction of the electronic trading system *mercado continuo*, could provide further opportunities for smaller companies to make IPOs.

Informal investors, known as "angels" have played a significant role in a number of other OECD countries in providing equity finance together with general guidance and/or specific business skills, especially to starting businesses.[10] Many

ble 10.2.   **Venture capital in Europe and the United States, 1996**

Total investments, excluding institutional buy-outs

	Investments made, in million ECU	Number of deals	Investments made, as a per cent of GDP	Seed and start-up investment as a per cent of total investment
United States	7 892.4	1 502	0.13	34.8
Total Europe	3 744.7	4 081	0.05	11.8
United Kingdom	840.4	1 014	0.09	4.9
France	746.4	1 000	0.06	13.0
Germany	564.0	708	0.03	16.8
Netherlands	408.0	248	0.13	22.6
Italy	356.0	174	0.04	12.7
Sweden	236.3	158	0.12	2.3
Spain	**181.2**	**152**	**0.04**	**6.5**
Belgium	105.8	153	0.05	19.2
Norway	82.2	150	0.07	6.9
Switzerland	55.6	21	0.02	9.6
Ireland	35.5	62	0.07	8.5
Finland	35.1	101	0.03	25.9
Denmark	34.0	38	0.02	6.8
Greece	32.0	23	0.03	19.5
Portugal	30.5	71	0.04	3.8
Austria	1.0	4	0.00	25.8
Iceland	1.0	4	0.02	0.0

Source: EVCA (1997), and Venture One (1997).

such "angels" in other OECD countries have themselves been successful in business and want to invest their funds and expertise in new ventures. The very nature of this type of finance makes it hard to measure and no data are available for Spain. But the evidence from other countries suggests that there is a virtuous circle with angel investment: the more successful entrepreneurs that exist, the more potential angels there will be. In Spain, the strong presence of family businesses would almost certainly be linked to intra-family informal investment which may be a significant and particularly flexible and less costly source of finance, especially for young and small businesses.

Taxation

Overall taxation is low in Spain, and the average effective tax rate on capital is estimated at 19 per cent in 1993, compared with an unweighted OECD average of around 35 per cent (Table 10.3). However, while there are in principle few

Table 10.3. **Average effective tax rates**

	Capital[1]			Labour[2]		
	1965-75	1975-85	1985-94	1965-75	1975-85	1985-94
United States	0.42	0.42	0.40[3]	0.17	0.21	0.23[3]
Japan	0.23	0.35	0.44	0.12	0.17	0.21
Germany	0.21	0.29	0.26	0.29	0.35	0.37
France	0.17	0.25	0.25	0.29	0.37	0.43
Italy	..	0.22	0.28	..	0.28	0.32
United Kingdom	0.50	0.60	0.52	0.24	0.25	0.21
Canada	0.41	0.38	0.44	0.17	0.22	0.28
Australia	0.34	0.42	0.45	0.13	0.18	0.19
Austria	0.17	0.20	0.21	0.33	0.38	0.41
Belgium	0.26	0.35	0.33	0.31	0.37	0.40
Denmark	..	0.42	0.42	..	0.35	0.41
Finland	0.22	0.32	0.41	0.23	0.31	0.38
Netherlands	..	0.30	0.31	..	0.43	0.46
Norway	0.25	0.38	0.37	0.33	0.34	0.35
Portugal	..	..	0.15	..	..	0.21
Spain	..	**0.12**	**0.19**[3]	..	**0.25**	**0.29**[3]
Sweden	..	0.45	0.58	..	0.46	0.48
Switzerland	0.17	0.24	0.25[3]	0.19	0.26	0.26[3]

1. Average effective tax rate on capital defined as household income taxes paid on operating surplus of private unincorporated enterprises and on household property and entrepreneurial income; plus tax on income, profit and capital gains of corporations.
2. Average effective tax rate on labour defined as household income tax paid on wages plus payroll or manpower taxes, divided by wages and salaries (including income of self-employed) plus employers' contributions to social security and to private pension.
3. Figure for 1993.
Source: Leibfritz *et al.* (1997).

differences in the treatment of incorporated and unincorporated businesses, in practice the differences can be significant. Most importantly, personal income tax rates are progressive, from 25 to 56 per cent, with the highest tax rate applying from 182.4 per cent of the average income, compared with a flat corporate tax rate of 35 per cent. However, since 1992, small unincorporated businesses in Spain can avoid the higher personal income tax rates by choosing "standard forfaitaire flat rate" taxation in exchange for simplified accounting requirements.[11] Moreover, personal corporate taxation contains a plethora of tax deductions applying to SMEs. The simplification of capital gains taxation in 1997, which made it into a flat rate of 20 per cent should encourage investment in SMEs.[12]

There are two specific tax provisions, however, that could deter entrepreneurship for incorporated enterprises. First, the treatment of losses is relatively strict under Spanish regulations. Losses can be carried forward and offset against future profits for only five years, compared with the United States and the Netherlands, for example, where losses can be carried forward for 15 years and indefinitely, respectively.[13] These limits penalise start-ups, in particular as these may sometimes make losses for several years before breaking even and then moving into profit. Second a tax of 1 per cent on all new equity capital issued adds to the costs of incorporation or expansion and could be another deterrent. This tax also discourages the use of equity options as a way of sharing the risk with employees.

Labour markets

Labour markets could be more important in deterring entrepreneurial activity in Spain than in other countries. In Spain, the labour market remains relatively inflexible, despite recent developments. Employment protection legislation is among the strictest in the OECD, and has led to the widespread use of fixed-term contracts which are not subject to high dismissal costs. Thus, fixed-term contracts provide opportunities for greater flexibility and are particularly used by smaller firms. If the much lower prevalence of fixed-term contracts in larger firms reflects the need for more stable employment relationships as a means for firm development, then the dual labour market may be evidence of constraints to firms' ability to grow beyond a small size. Another obstacle to firm expansion could be collective agreements which also apply more frequently to larger firms and establish rigid job demarcation of the tasks and responsibilities that can be carried out by different employees. Of course the cost of restructuring for well-established larger firms is also high, discouraging these firms from becoming more entrepreneurial. One possible impact of these labour market rigidities could be to push activity into the informal sector, although by its very nature it is difficult to estimate the extent to which this has taken place.

High unemployment in Spain may also have two particular implications for entrepreneurship. The profile of the typical entrepreneur in other countries is someone aged 35 to 45 with significant experience gained by working two or three years in medium or large enterprises. This typical entrepreneur generally starts a business that builds on that experience. However, adding to the risk that a new business will not survive, there is a risk in Spain of staying unemployed after the termination of an entrepreneurial venture. Combined with comprehensive protection for workers who have permanent contracts, and the significant insurance and security this entails, a potential entrepreneur could be discouraged. High youth unemployment may exacerbate the situation, because the formative years of experience would be harder to gain, and time previously spent in unemployment would be likely to further discourage someone from subsequently quitting a good job.

Administrative and compliance burden

An examination of the ongoing regulatory and administrative requirements on Spanish businesses would suggest that the administrative burden is high. Surprisingly, however, when surveyed in 1996, established small and medium-sized enterprises in Spain reported fewer constraints due to regulation and associated administrative burden than in any other European country (Figure 10.2). There are two possible explanations for this: first, there is an inherent self-selection bias in the survey, because only existing firms are surveyed and these have learnt to deal adequately with these constraints. The lengthy process of starting a business, outlined earlier, may have discouraged firms unable to deal effectively with administrative requirements from ever starting up. The other possible explanation is that enforcement is weak, so compliance is not considered important by firms.

Evidence, albeit partial, suggests that the legal framework for business, as in other countries, could be improved. However, the overall judicial system has been rated as less efficient than in many OECD countries (Figure 10.3) and the

Figure 10.2. **Regulation and administrative burdens**

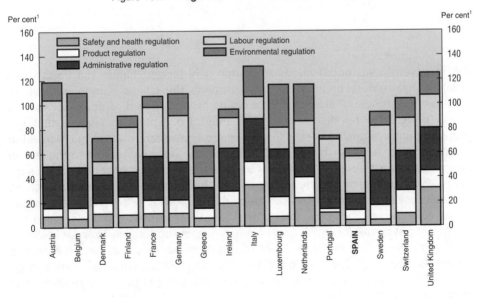

1. Sum of responses, given as percentage of respondents. Respondents were allowed to choose more than one constraint.
Source: Grant Thornton International Business Strategies Ltd., 1997.

Figure 10.3. **Efficiency of judicial systems**[1]

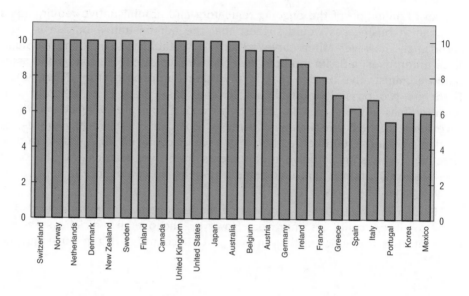

1. Each item is scaled from zero to ten, with the higher score indicated higher confidence in the system.
Source: La Porta, *et al.*, 1996.

risk of government modifications to contracts is judged higher (La Porta *et al.*, 1996). If legal enforcement of contracts through the courts is more difficult to obtain, entrepreneurial activity that depends on drawing up contracts for sharing of risk is likely to be discouraged. This may also explain to some extent the preponderance of micro enterprises, which are less reliant on legally enforceable contracts.[14] On the other hand, small firms are relatively vulnerable to the lack of protection against abusive provisions in contracts,[15] breach of contract by a supplier (where one such occurrence may force the business into bankruptcy), and the high cost of enforcing a contract through the judicial system. One illustration of the relative weakness of small versus large enterprises can be seen in the pattern of payments for invoices. Spain has one of the longest average payment periods in the OECD (73 days), half of the firms never charge interest on late payments, and small Spanish enterprises are the most punctual payers in Europe while large Spanish enterprises on average have longer payment periods than anywhere else in Europe.

One specific aspect of the administrative burden which may particularly discourage entrepreneurial activity is the administration of land development.

The obstacles to land development have resulted in an artificial scarcity of land and high land prices. Developers face a long and involved administrative process to get the necessary permission, and significant costs. Such restrictions on land development may be particularly inhibiting to larger-scale entrepreneurial activity and business expansion and may go part of the way towards explaining why Spain's retail service sector may not be fully exploiting apparent economies of scale and/or scope.

Innovation

Entrepreneurship is closely linked to the development of new products and processes, although not necessarily high-technology intensive. Not all innovations arise from formal research and development and a significant proportion of Spanish production has been in sectors where formal R&D is anyway less significant (for example, tourism). But Spain has among the lowest ratios of R&D expenditure to GDP and researchers to 10 000 people in the OECD,[16] and a smaller proportion of these researchers are working in enterprises (Table 10.4), which suggests that Spain's capacity for generating or adapting new ideas is more limited in this narrow sense than in many other OECD countries. Reinforcing this view, the inventiveness coefficient (resident patent applications per head of population) is lower in Spain than in many other OECD countries and fewer Spanish patent applications per head of population were registered with the *European Patent Office* in 1996 than for almost any other European country (Table 10.5). Although direct data on the overall amount of innovation taking place are difficult to obtain, in manufacturing only 11 per cent of firms were recorded as having developed or introduced innovations in products or processes during the period 1992 to 1994 (*National Statistical Institute*). Around 80 per cent of manufacturing SMEs have no R&D activities and only 9 per cent have financed internal R&D projects.

Some industrial districts provide good examples of strong interaction between firms, and in a few cases (such as Valencia,) between a technological centre (IMPIVA) and enterprises. The research mentioned above (Costa Campi *et al.*, 1993) shows that 80 per cent of firms surveyed within these selected districts have introduced product innovation and 70 per cent have introduced process innovation during the last three years, mostly through co-operation with more advanced local firms or through sub-contracting and association. More than 80 per cent of the technical information acquired by the enterprises comes from the local market, through the informal interchange of knowledge between entrepreneurs, technicians and workers. In addition, half of these firms have established formal agreements in the R&D field. Such innovation and close linkages have created more opportunities for start-ups.

There are a number of explanations for the relatively mediocre innovation performance in Spain. One panel of 75 experts concluded that main factors

Table 10.4. **Researchers by sector of employment**[1]

	Business enterprise	Government	Higher Education	Total researchers per 10 000 labour force
	Percentage			
United States[2]	79	6	13	74
Japan	70	6	22	81
Germany[2]	56	15	29	58
France	45	18	35	59
Italy	37	18	45	33
United Kingdom[3]	57	10	29	51
Canada[2]	46	10	43	52
Australia[3]	26	15	57	64
Austria[2]	55	7	38	34
Belgium[4]	48	4	46	43
Czech Republic	41	36	23	26
Denmark[2]	43	22	34	47
Finland[2]	36	23	40	61
Greece[2]	16	24	59	20
Hungary	28	34	39	28
Iceland	34	39	25	58
Ireland	40	5	52	52
Mexico	10	31	58	5
Netherlands	38	22	38	48
New Zealand[2]	24	27	49	37
Norway[2]	48	20	32	69
Poland	22	23	55	28
Portugal[5]	8	24	46	16
Spain	**23**	**16**	**60**	**30**
Sweden[2]	52	8	40	68
Switzerland[6]	54	4	43	46
Turkey	14	12	74	7

1. Data for researchers by sector refer to 1995 unless otherwise noted. Data for number of researchers refer to 1994 unless otherwise noted.
2. Data refer to 1993.
3. Data refer to 1994.
4. Data refer to 1991.
5. Data for number of researchers refers to 1992.
6. Data for researchers by sector refer to 1991; data for number of researchers refer to 1992.
Source: OECD (1997c).

impeding innovation included culture (87 per cent of experts), and the lack of financial and human resources for innovation (82 per cent), followed by the poor ability of public research institutions to promote technological development, and deficient public finance institutions to finance innovation (Fundación COTEC, 1997b). And in a survey of enterprises, finance and lack of know-how were consid-

Table 10.5. **Inventiveness coefficient**[1]

Resident patent applications per 10 000 population

Switzerland	4.7
Australia	4.7
Sweden	4.6
Germany	4.6
Finland	4.6
United States	4.1
New Zealand	3.6
United Kingdom	3.2
Austria	2.5
Denmark	2.5
Norway	2.4
Ireland	2.3
France	2.2
Luxembourg	1.4
Netherlands	1.2
Canada	0.9
Belgium	0.9
Iceland	0.8
Spain	**0.6**
Portugal	0.1
Turkey	0.0

1. Data refer to 1994.
Source: OECD (1997c).

ered the most significant obstacles to innovation in Spain. But for each of the possible barriers to innovation, a higher percentage of Spanish firms found them very important than was the case with other European enterprises (Figure 10.4). Protection of intellectual property does not seem to feature as an issue, although little research on the effectiveness of patent protection in Spain is available.

Management skills and the role of the education system

Robust development and expansion of enterprises require strong management skills. Though the degree to which these are obtained from secondary education is an issue, amongst very small enterprises only one third of owners/ managers has completed secondary education, and even for firms with more than 50 employees, some 20 per cent of managers have not completed secondary education. More importantly, management training efforts are not only limited but they are highly concentrated in some industrial regions and cities and need not only to be spread more widely but also intensified, according to FORCEM. Supporting the importance of an open economy, in some export-oriented indus-

Figure 10.4. **Barriers to innovation**

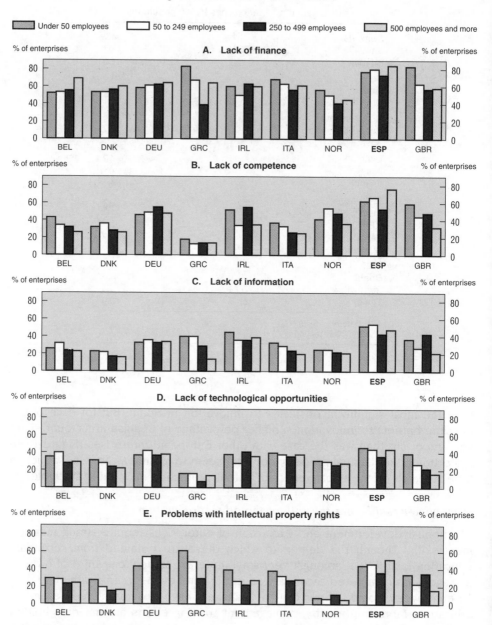

Source: European Commission (1995).

trial districts there are signs that management skills have improved with EU membership due to structural changes related to a new competitive environment and the pressure to innovate. Improvements in business training have been actively supported by employers' organisations, chambers and the network of technological institutes, often located close to these districts. But universities seem particularly inactive in this field and do not seem to be much involved in promoting a new entrepreneurial spirit and management skills (except for the few business schools and those institutions involved in relevant European programmes).

Public programmes and policies

Policies for SMEs

The Spanish government earlier this year announced a new strategy for SMEs (and by extension, the promotion of entrepreneurship). This strategy has five main planks: institutional change, administrative simplification, taxation issues, enterprise promotion and economic promotion. The institutional changes, primarily a shift of responsibilities for SME policy from the Ministry of Industry to the Ministry of Economy, reflects a broadening of SME policies from their earlier focus on the manufacturing sector and a recognition of the importance of linking policies in this area with the broader economic framework.

Administrative simplification is recognised as an ongoing process, but two particular channels have been set up to facilitate the process. The first is the establishment of a Working Group on SME policies under the Government Commission for Economic Affairs, to take stock of measures affecting SMEs, examine ways of getting simplified and better co-ordinated administrative procedures and develop a common policy for study of SMEs. The second is the establishment of the Observatory of SMEs to provide a permanent dialogue with SMEs and a vehicle for identifying problems and solutions. Information on firms, technology and markets, as well as promoting co-operation between firms (as a means to improve competitiveness, transfer of technology and access to export markets), are also new priorities. An "information area" has been set up (with around 250 information requests a month) and the design of a national network – based on few regional bodies that already exist – has been planned.

An Inter-Ministerial Commission has recently reported on a number of tax issues and a number of changes were announced in the 1998 budget. For SMEs, corporate tax will apply at the rate of 30 per cent instead of 35 per cent on the first 15 million pesetas of profit. The rate will also apply to equity increases arising from the sale of assets related to the company's activities. The limits for calculating tax according to the standard flat rate method have been raised to

Ptas 100 million and the forfaitaire system will be integrated into the standard flat rate method without requiring increased accounting obligations.

Innovation

Both national and regional governments have taken a number of initiatives in order to improve diffusion and transfer of innovation to firms, with significant funding also coming from the EU. The initiatives include information, training and advice on product design[17] as well as technological development projects.[18] In addition, the 12 technological parks which have been set up during the last decade host 400 high technology, small and medium-sized firms. A large amount of public money (EU in particular, as well as national and regional) has been allocated in the past to financing industrial land development, with very mixed – and diverging – appreciation of their impacts and benefits. In 1995, half of the Ptas 5.7 billions budget was allocated to the funding of projects to establish enterprise support agencies or structures[19] and more than a quarter to "industrial product development" projects submitted by firms.[20] At the regional level, publicly-funded networks of around 230 enterprise agencies supporting innovation have been set up and especially among these, a network of regional technology agencies which, in addition to technological advice, provide a large range of services such as information and training as well as testing, certification and standardisation.

Only a few national and regional innovation programmes have been assessed, and these according to quite narrow criteria. For example, an evaluation of the *Programme on product design* shows that such support increased employment in around half of the firms concerned and export capacity by around 30 per cent. And the evaluation of the Madrid regional government *support scheme to technological innovation, Programa de Modernizacion Industrial* (PMI), showed that two thirds of participating enterprises increased their sales and improved the quality of their products.[21] However, the *programme* had a poor impact on the level of training and skills of employees (Fonfria Mesa, 1996). These results are not surprising for firms (not least because they may reflect selection bias), but they give no indication of the economy-wide impact nor whether these schemes provided value for money.

Entrepreneurial development programme

An important new support programme on *"entrepreneurial development"*, with several different objectives and targeted on SMEs, has been launched for the years 1997-1999 with 50 per cent co-financing by EU funds (and up to 70 per cent in developing areas).[22] This programme puts more emphasis on information and advice (intangible supports). The Ptas 13 billion budget for 1997 includes several sub-programmes: co-operation among firms; information; support to design and innovation; financing support (mostly guarantees) and aids to supporting business institutions and services (the so-called intermediary organisations). An additional aim is to rationalise, better co-ordinate and integrate the large range of dispersed support provided to firms by central and regional governments, including EU funding.

Concluding remarks

An assessment of the extent to which entrepreneurial activity is actually occurring in Spain is not altogether straightforward as it relies on imperfect indicators, which may be unable to detect some of the more entrepreneurial aspects of the Spanish economy. Nevertheless, there are signs that entrepreneurial activity could be strengthened through efforts to improve the institutional framework within which economic activity takes place. Major efforts have already been made over recent years to improve the institutional framework and these efforts have been rewarded with the recent strong performance of SMEs. But some aspects still require further reform especially in addressing the rigidities that discourage firm expansion. In particular, further efforts to increase labour market flexibility and improve product market competition would provide more scope for entrepreneurial activity. Making it easier to start up and close a business would also be positive steps. Improvements in the range and quality of data and further research and analysis of different aspects of entrepreneurship in Spain would also help the authorities to better determine the most effective combination of policy settings for entrepreneurship.

Notes

1. Sectoral data is not available for Greece.

2. The main adjustment for Spain is the inclusion of the self-employed in the harmonised estimates.

3. Turbulence would include data on firm closure rates. Very little is known about the true firm closure rates (i.e., the percentage of firms which cease trading each year) and the only study of firm survival rates suggested a survival rate of 70 per cent after the first three years (ENSR, 1995). Because of the arithmetic link between start-up, closure and survival rates, such a high survival rate could only be consistent with a low start-up rate.

4. These steps are set out in detail on the website of the Ministry of Economics, http:// www.mcx.es/pyme/.

5. The percentage of businesses that are incorporated varies from almost 10 per cent in the United States and Germany to just under 50 per cent in Japan and the Netherlands (OECD, 1994c).

6. Of responding firms, 19 per cent had 1-10 employees, 36 per cent had 11-25 employees and 20 per cent had 26 to 50 employees.

7. Venture capital in Spain was originally developed as a government tool for allocating money for regional development. Reflecting these origins in 1986, 18 out of the 22 venture capital investment bodies were primarily funded by central or regional governments.

8. The lifting of similar restrictions in the United States in the early 1970s led to a major inflow of funds into venture capital (see OECD, 1997a). Overall, Spanish institutional investors held only 6 per cent of their portfolios in (listed) shares in 1996.

9. Most venture capital is being invested in industrial products and services, agriculture/ fishing, leisure and other non-financial services (but not transportation) (Marti Pellon, 1997)

10. In the United States, for example, such investment capital is estimated to be at least twice as important as formal venture capital and in the Netherlands and Australia it is estimated to be around the same size as the formal market (OECD, 1997b).

11. The forfaitaire system (taxation based on observable physical characteristics) can be chosen by unincorporated businesses with less than two staff and turnover less than Ptas 7.9 million. The standard flat rate applies to unincorporated businesses with less than 12 staff and turnover less than Ptas 50 million. Under the standard flat rate, unincorporated businesses can deduct wages and a flat rate to cover general expenses (which varies between sectors).

12. Previously, capital gains tax applied to investments, where the assets had been held for at least one year, and the capital gains paid were reduced for each subsequent year that the assets are held, although they were indexed to inflation.

13. Losses can also be carried backwards for up to 3 years in the United States and the Netherlands.

14. It is often argued that micro-enterprises rely to a significant extent on factors such as reputation and local networking for enforcing contracts, rather than relying on recourse through the judicial process.

15. Under Spanish civil law, protection against abusive contract provisions for businesses relies on the provisions embodied in the 100 year old civil code.

16. More than half of these R&D activities are located within the regions of Madrid (40 per cent) and Cataluña (27 per cent).

17. The *Sociedad para el Desarrollo del Diseño y la Innovacion* (DDI), whose aim is to improve the quality, the image, the design and the competitiveness of products, has financed around 1 000 projects since its creation in 1992.

18. The *Plan de Actuacion Technologico Industrial* managed by the *Ministry of Industry* supported 637 projects in 1995 at a cost of Ptas 11.6 billion and the *Centro para el Desarollo Technologico* co-financed 271 technological development projects in 1995.

19. Projects were funded up to 75 per cent.

20. Projects were funded up to 50 per cent.

21. While a similar proportion improved their relations with their clients; the subsidy/investment ratio was 1 to 6.7; the proportion of participating firms which regard their commercial position as "better than their competitors" increased from 16 to 38 per cent while firms that consider they have been able to improve their technological position have risen from 5 to 36 per cent.

22. EU Objective 1 structural funds.

References

CELADA, F. (1991),
"Los sistemas productivos locales de caracter industrial", Area y Sistema, Madrid.

COSTA CAMPI, M.T. et al. (1993),
"Cooperation entre empresas y systemas productivas locales en España", IMPI, Ministry of Industry, Madrid.

ENSR (1995),
"The European Observatory for SMEs", Third Annual Report.

EUROPEAN COMMISSION (1995),
Green Paper on Innovation, Bulletin of the European Union, Supplement 5/95, Brussels.

EUROSTAT (1995),
"Enterprises in Europe", Fourth Report, Luxemburg.

EUROPEAN VENTURE CAPITAL ASSOCIATION (EVCA) (1997),
A survey of venture capital and private equity in Europe, 1997 Yearbook, Zaventen, Belgium.

FONFRIA MESA, A. (1996),
"Factores organisativos en el desarollo tecnologico de las PYMES", Economia Industrial, No. 310, 1996/IV, p. 163.

FUNDACIÓN COTEC (1997a),
"Informe COTEC, Tecnologia y innovation en España", Chapter VI, Madrid.

FUNDACIÓN COTEC (1997b),
"Documento para el debate sobre el Sistema de Innovacion", Libro verde, Madrid.

GRANT THORNTHON INTERNATIONAL BUSINESS STRATEGIES Ltd. (1996),
European Business Survey, May, United Kingdom.

IMPI (1996),
"La pequena y mediana empresa en España 1995", Informe annual, Madrid.

LA PORTA, R. LOPEZ-DE-SILANE, F., SHLEIFER, A. and ROBERT, W. (1996),
"Law and Finance", NBER Working Paper, 5661.

LEIBFRITZ, W., THORNTON, J. and BIBBEE, A. (1997),
"Taxation and economic performance", Economics Department Working Papers No. 176, OECD, Paris.

LOGOTECH, S.A. (1997),
"Étude comparative internationale des dispositions légales et administratives pour la formation de petites et moyennes entreprises aux pays de l'Union Européenne, les États-Unis et le Japon", EIMS Project, 96/142, Athens.

MARTI PELLON, J. (1997),
"El capital Inversinon en España: Estudiois y Monografias", Editorial Civitas, Madrid.

OECD (1994*a*),
  The OECD *Jobs Study*, OECD Publications, Paris.

OECD (1994*b*),
  Taxation and Small Business, OECD Publications, Paris.

OECD (1996),
  Economic Survey of Spain, OECD Publications, Paris.

OECD (1997*a*),
  OECD *Economic Surveys – United States*, OECD Publications, Paris.

OECD (1997*b*),
  Institutional Investor Statistical Yearbook, OECD Publications, Paris.

OECD (1997*c*),
  Main Science and Technology indicators, OECD Publications, Paris.

TRIBUNAL FOR THE DEFENCE OF COMPETITION (1995),
  Competition in Spain: Appraisal of Progress to Date and Some New Recommendations 1995, Madrid.

VENTURE ONE (1997),
  1996 Annual Report, National venture capital association, San Francisco.

Chapter XI

Sweden

The macroeconomic crisis from 1990 to 1992 brought massive labour-shedding in the large industrial conglomerates, which have been the traditional focus of Swedish business sector policies, and even though this sector is now growing, this stimulates productivity growth rather than employment growth. The policy focus has therefore shifted toward entrepreneurship and small and medium-sized enterprises, both as a source of future jobs and as a way to ensure a more dynamic and quickly-adjusting enterprise sector. This chapter attempts to present some of the factors influencing the entrepreneurial climate in the Swedish economy, with special regard to those affecting the establishment and growth of small and new enterprises.

The state of entrepreneurship

At its most general, entrepreneurship can be defined as the dynamic process of identifying economic opportunities and acting upon them by developing, producing and selling goods and services. Dynamism is not necessarily related to size, since the force of competition should ensure that firms are growing and shrinking throughout the size distribution scale. But from a historical perspective they appear to be related in Sweden where an unusually large share of the business sector's employment is attributable to large enterprises. In the Swedish case the business sector is dominated by large industrial conglomerates with roots in the resource-based industries, most of which were major players well before the Second World War (one outstanding exception is described in Box 11.1). And whereas some of these conglomerates have shown considerable ability to renew and innovate – Ericsson and Electrolux being frequently quoted examples – it is not obvious that their success can be emulated by others. Rather, the perceived inability of small enterprises to grow beyond medium-size has at

Table 11.1.   **Share of employment in selected sectors by enterprise size**

	Size of enterprise	Share of sector employment						
		Sweden	Germany	France	United Kingdom	Netherlands	Denmark	EU average
Manufacturing	< 20	14	10	11	15	15	20	18
	20 to 99	16	14	20	17	27	26	17
	100 to 499	20	19	21	16	26	30	20
	500 +	50	57	48	52	32	24	45
Construction	< 20	37	50	41	64	33	59	57
	20 to 99	19	28	28	12	38	21	21
	100 to 499	10	13	13	11	20	10	12
	500 +	34	9	18	13	9	10	10
Trade, restaurants and hotels	< 20	43	52	44	40	45	54	59
	20 to 99	21	19	25	20	21	19	17
	100 to 499	14	11	12	27	13	12	12
	500 +	22	18	19	13	21	15	12
Business services	< 20	48	44	24	31	26	49	41
	20 to 99	19	15	19	14	18	21	13
	100 to 499	17	15	17	11	24	12	14
	500 +	16	26	40	44	32	18	32

Source: Submission from the European Observatory for Small and Medium-sized Enterprises.

times been highlighted as an indicator of serious impediments to entrepreneurship in the Swedish economy, lowering the growth potential of the economy.

Actually, the share of manufacturing employment found in large enterprises is only slightly above average in Sweden (Table 11.1), but Sweden has an unusually large share of manufacturing in the business sector. Only in a few non-manufacturing sectors – construction and retail sales in particular – is there a significant tendency toward comparatively few small enterprises. The overall importance of large companies in the Swedish labour market and job creation thus relates more to its relatively large manufacturing sector in international comparison than to concentration within individual sectors. However, the share of self-employment in the Swedish labour force is internationally low; only during the last recession has it approached the levels prevailing in other North European countries.

Job creation and destruction: does size matter?

In Sweden, as elsewhere, net enterprise creation has contributed almost as much to net job creation as the expansion of existing enterprises (OECD, 1995),

Box 11.1.   **IKEA: a recent example of Swedish entrepreneurship**

One of the relatively few outstanding examples of entrepreneurship in Sweden after the Second World War is the success of IKEA, which at the same time drives home the point that a company does not have to be in the "high-tech" category to be both fast-growing and profitable.

IKEA was established during the war by 17 year old Ingvar Kamprad in rural Småland. The region has no industrial tradition and very little contact with the traditional clusters of Swedish industry, but it is characterised by a high share of craftsmen and traders in the population and by a large propensity toward self-employment. The company started mail-order sales shortly after the war, but did not enter into its later business selling self-designed wooden furniture through its own outlets until 1955. The company's business idea has remained broadly unchanged ever since: make quality furniture available to a larger group of people through the lowering of prices. The prices have been kept low by a policy of: *i)* sale in large-surface outlets; *ii)* an element of do-it-yourself on the part of the purchaser; and *iii)* sub-contracting most of the production, more recently to low-cost countries.

The initial expansion focused on setting up outlets in the neighbouring countries, but the Danish EU entry in 1973 led IKEA to move its administrative headquarters to Copenhagen. This became the start of a period of rapid international expansion (Table 11.2). By 1996, the company's annual turnover came close to 3 per cent of Sweden's GDP.

Table 11.2.   **Company characteristics – IKEA**

	Outlets	Countries	Employment	Turnover ($ million)
1954	1	1	15	0.5
1964	2	2	250	15
1974	10	5	1 500	139
1984	66	17	8 300	837
1996	136	28	33 400	5 709

Source: Facts and Figures 95/96 – IKEA.

The founder still controls the company, but formal ownership has passed to a Netherlands-based family foundation in order to reduce some of the effects of Swedish taxation. However, the tax treatment of personally-owned companies has reportedly induced the family to consider leaving Sweden altogether.

particularly in the years before the recession. The considerable increase in labour shedding in the early 1990s seems primarily to have been related to the contraction of enterprises, whereas net job creation from new enterprises held up during the early stage of the recovery. Jobs associated with new enterprises also tend to last for a comparatively long time, as almost 70 per cent of new enterprises still exist after three years, and an internationally high 60 per cent survive after five years (EFER, 1996).[1] However, the average employment in these enterprises after ten years is fewer than three persons (including the owner), with very few employing more than ten persons and around half employing no additional personnel. It should also be noted that around one-third of these start-ups are unemployed persons benefiting from the government's support schemes for self-employment.

Despite the limited size of new enterprises, job creation in existing companies is usually related to their expansion. The 1995 OECD *Economic Survey of Sweden* showed that during the past decade, the net contribution of large establishments to Swedish net job creation was negative, the largest positive contribution coming from establishments with fewer than 20 employees. Studies based on data for the period 1985 to 1989, in which overall job creation was high, find that small single-establishment firms account for more than 60 per cent of net private sector job creation, while accounting for around 30 per cent of private sector employment (Davidsson, 1995 and OECD, 1997). Moreover, gross job creation and losses were both much higher in the small and medium-sized segment than in larger companies, indicating a more dynamic process. Finally, confirming an international trend toward increasing globalisation, small and medium-sized enterprises currently account for around one third of total exports – and around 20 per cent when the exports by subsidiaries of larger companies are excluded.

The role of the service sector

One possible explanation for the importance of new and small companies in job creation would be the increasing importance of the service sector: around 60 per cent of the net employment contribution of small firms occurred in trade, household services and construction. Data on net new enterprise creation, in terms of the number of companies, seem to confirm this trend. The total number of service companies remained broadly unchanged even at the depth of the recession in 1992, whereas the industrial sector shrank significantly. Over the past four years taken as a whole, the number of enterprises in manufacturing and construction has been broadly unchanged, whereas the service sector expanded considerably. The growth was particularly pronounced in such parts of the service sector as business services – which may, partly, reflect outsourcing of certain services from industrial enterprises to smaller subcontractors – and, most significantly, personal and social services (Table 11.3).

Fast-growing enterprises

A recent Swedish study demonstrates that fast-growing companies (FGCs), defined as limited companies which have more than doubled their turnover over

Table 11.3. **New enterprises and bankruptcies by sector in Sweden**

	1994		1995		1996		Average 1992 to 1996	
	New enterprises	Bank-ruptcies	New enterprises	Bank-ruptcies	New enterprises	Bank-ruptcies	New enterprises	Bank-ruptcies
	Per cent of all enterprises within group							
Industries	5.9	3.8	5.6	2.9	5.2	2.6	4.9	4.2
of which:								
Manufacturing	5.5	3.2	5.2	2.6	5.0	2.4	4.5	3.9
Construction	6.3	4.4	6.0	3.2	5.3	2.8	5.1	4.5
Services	8.4	3.4	7.9	2.8	7.7	2.9	7.2	3.7
of which:								
Trade, restaurants and hotels	6.7	4.4	6.2	3.6	6.0	3.6	5.8	4.8
Transportation	5.6	3.0	5.3	2.3	4.4	2.4	4.7	3.2
Finance and consultancy	10.7	2.8	10.3	2.4	9.9	2.8	9.7	3.2
Personal and social services	12.2	1.5	10.4	1.3	10.3	1.0	9.2	2.0
Total	7.8	3.6	7.4	2.8	7.1	2.6	6.7	3.8

Source: SCB.

the period 1992 to 1996, tend to be concentrated among small and medium-sized firms (Blixt, 1997[2]). Half of all fast-growers were found to be enterprises with fewer than 20 employees, and small enterprises with particularly high turnover were the fastest growers. However, reflecting the dominant share of very small companies with a low turnover among Swedish enterprises, only one half per cent of all enterprises with fewer than 20 employees were fast-growing. Only 7 per cent of all larger enterprises (more than 200 employees) were fast-growing, but these accounted for the largest absolute job creation among the fast-growers.

Particularly fast-growing European enterprises – generally concentrating on developing new products and technologies – are usually dependent on exports as a source of growth. Swedish enterprises are no exception. As for the sectoral distribution of fast-growing companies, two broadly-defined sectors stand out. Owing to the export boost over the reference period – but also reflecting rising export prices due to currency depreciation – the export-oriented parts of the manufacturing sector (electronics, mechanical and transport equipment) recorded a large share of fast growers (Figure 11.1). Also the service sector, and particularly business-related services, recorded a share of fast-growing firms significantly above average. While clearly related to the rapid growth in industry, this also

Figure 11.1. **Fast-growing companies in selected sectors in Sweden[1]**

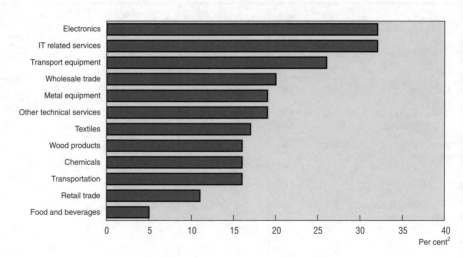

1. Companies with an average annual growth in turnover exceeding 25 per cent from 1992 to 1995.
2. Per cent of all companies in selected sector.
Source: NUTEK (1996*b*).

seems to reflect the increasing importance of services in the Swedish economy. A final observation to be drawn from this study is that, irrespective of size classes, fast growing enterprises tend to be somewhat younger than average.

The regional dimension

Swedish public debate often tends to focus on differences in business performance across regions, a common perception being that geographically-disadvantaged counties in the north and the middle of the country are performing worse than the south and the large urban centres. In recent years there has been a certain tendency for the latter parts of the country to have a higher gross enterprise creation, but the differences in net enterprise and job creation in recent years are not compelling. A recent study finds that gross enterprise creation relative to working-age population from 1990 to 1993 was somewhat above the national average in Stockholm and the south west of the country, but several of the regions presumed to be less well-performing held up strongly in this comparison. There is, however, a tendency for enterprise creation to cement traditional differences in the structure of the business sector: gross enterprise creation in the manufacturing sectors was particularly pronounced in the counties with a strong reliance on traditional industries (north and centre), where regional clusters in forestry, metal processing and machinery and electronics industry persist. Moreover, since these industries taken as a whole have reduced their employment, it is reasonable to assume that this enterprise creation was, at least partly, connected with the downscaling and outsourcing of existing activities. Most of the creation of service-sector enterprises, on the other hand, took place in the larger urban areas.

The regional distribution of fast-growing enterprises has been remarkably even. Although on the whole the large urban centres recorded a slightly higher share of fast growing enterprises, the difference is not significant, and only a couple of geographically-isolated counties seem to be significantly below the national average.

Implications

Summing up, new enterprises play a crucial role in net job creation, and fast-growing companies tend to be concentrated in the SME sector. Rapid employment growth in a subset of new enterprises combined with downsizing in larger and maturing companies should be seen as an inherent feature in a well-functioning market economy. However, the large majority of SMEs show no tendency to grow and can consequently not be considered as particularly entrepreneurial, nor important for new employment creation. Given the importance of both net and gross enterprise creation for net and gross job creation as well as for the dynamism of the product and service markets, it is safe to conclude that reducing the number of obstacles to enterprise creation and growth is a way to promote entrepreneurship and thereby increasing overall incomes and, most likely, employment.

Incentives and impediments to enterprise start-up

The first question to arise is whether incentives to create enterprises – and for existing enterprises to grow – are sufficiently strong in Sweden. According to surveys of enterprises started in 1995, around one-fourth of the entrepreneurs were motivated by a desire to avoid unemployment, one fourth by a wish to work independently and another fourth by a desire for self-realisation. Only 16 per cent perceived entrepreneurship primarily as a way of earning more money. Moreover, more than 40 per cent of the existing small and medium-sized companies reported that they either did not see any possibility to grow, or that they saw a possibility but did not wish to seize it. Of those who did not want to grow, more than half cited either a preference for leisure over possible gains, or too low an expected return on expansion relative to risk.

The welfare state and entrepreneurship

The egalitarian principles embedded in the Swedish social model have resulted in high marginal personal tax rates, which have almost certainly restrained the development of the business sector. Notwithstanding significant lowering of the rates in the 1990-91 tax reform, Sweden has retained one of the higher marginal tax rates in the OECD area. While income taxation is broadly neutral *vis-à-vis* the growth decisions of a going concern, the decision to start an enterprise or undertake specific risky projects is influenced by weighting the default risk (ultimately bankruptcy) against expected after-tax gains, encompassing not only the effect of tax rates but also of provisions allowing losses to be carried forward or set against other types of income. In 1996, loss-offset provisions for Swedish unincorporated enterprises were improved as capital losses from new establishments were allowed to be offset against labour income. In the absence of complete loss-offset provisions, a country maintaining high marginal tax rates is likely to have less business start-ups and a lower share of self-employed persons.

The *"solidaristic wage policy"* is also likely to have disadvantaged new enterprises insofar as it has led to a compressed wage structure. According to recent cross-country studies, larger and older companies pay significantly higher wages. In most European countries, a wage level of around 15 to 20 per cent below national averages is normal in small enterprises, and in the United States the difference is around 40 per cent.[3] In Sweden, a recent study found a differential of 7 per cent, almost all of which could be attributed to differences in skill levels and seniority of employees in small and larger enterprises (Albæk, *et al.*, 1996). While an equalisation of wages across skills and seniority levels may contribute to a more efficient static resource allocation, there may be a dynamic loss of efficiency stemming from the compressed wage structure in Sweden to the extent that lower wages are necessary to retain profitability during the start-up phase of enterprises.

Moreover, high taxes and an equal wage distribution, together with an extensive public pension system, have contributed to internationally low household savings, and shifted savings away from financial wealth toward tax-favoured schemes such as housing investment and private pension schemes.[4] Recent figures show that Swedish household net financial assets (including private pension savings) are an estimated 80 per cent of GDP, compared with 140 per cent in Germany, 200 per cent in the United Kingdom and 275 per cent in the United States. Since most capital in the earlier stages of an investment is provided either by the entrepreneur himself or persons close to him, low household wealth may reduce the capital available for enterprise start-ups. The possibility of quantitative rationing in the demand for start-up capital is underpinned by a recent survey-based study which found that households reaping large windfall gains have a significantly higher probability of starting an own enterprise (Lindh &

Figure 11.2. **Tax wedges and the service sector**[1]

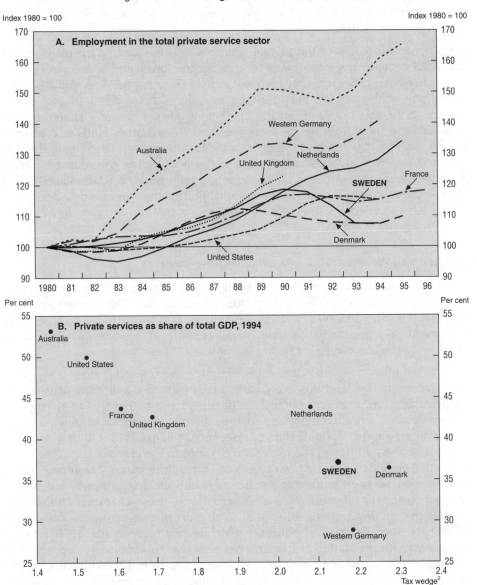

1. The private service sector includes wholesale and retail trade, restaurants, hotels, transport, communication, finance, insurance, real estate, business services.
2. Total labour cost relative to purchasing power of take-home wage for an average production worker.`
Source: OECD, 1997*c*; OECD, 1996; OECD, 1997*b*.

Ohlsson, 1996[5]). Another recent empirical study concludes that the compression of wealth differentials has had a negative impact on the rate of enterprise starts (Lindh & Ohlsson, 1998).

The development of the private service sector has been particularly disadvantaged because wage compression, high income taxes and high indirect taxes have raised the difference between the cost of personal services and the take-home pay of the service provider (the so-called "tax wedge") to one of the highest in the OECD area (Figure 11.2). This has almost certainly shifted household demand away from personal services and toward other kinds of consumption. It has also discouraged the development of economic activities in the service sectors which are close substitutes to the households' own domestic effort (cooking, cleaning, gardening, etc.), where new enterprises can be established at a low entry cost and where few formal qualifications are required. Indeed, this sector has recorded considerable net enterprise creation in many other OECD countries.

Start-up and closure: rules and administrative burdens

Slow or expensive procedures in connection with the establishment of a new enterprise can also lower the start-up rate. In Sweden, however, there seem to be only limited problems of this kind. The number of administrative requirements and the delays appear to be below the international averages, and the costs involved are negligible (see Chapter 3, Table 3.1).

On the other hand, the rules for bankruptcy and otherwise closing an enterprise are restrictive, and this is arguably a factor which significantly discourages entrepreneurship. Concerns about limiting abuse and outright fraud are indeed legitimate ones, since if left unchecked, they distort competitive conditions facing entrepreneurs and undermine the tax base. The challenge is to combat abuse and fraud, if necessary through the relevant provisions in the criminal code, while not restricting genuine risk-taking, which can often result in failure.[6] Moreover, there is a trade-off between protecting creditors and encouraging entrepreneurs. In the Swedish case, the absence of a discharge clause (see Chapter 8, Table 8.3) implies that an unsuccessful attempt at setting up an own enterprise can, in the worst case, lead to financial obligations for the rest of one's life. (This may be contrasted with the United States experience where "a good try" is encouraged, and where many successful entrepreneurs have one or two bankruptcies behind them before they succeed.) A further tightening of the bankruptcy rules is currently under consideration. According to a proposal from an expert commission, persons involved in three corporate bankruptcies within ten years and persons still liable for tax debt exceeding SKr 217 000 (approximately US$27 000) from bankrupt companies will be legally barred from starting a new enterprise during a period of three to ten years. In seeking to strike a proper balance between controlling abuse and fraud and avoiding the creation of barriers to entrepreneurship, it would seem important to ensure that the criteria used do not discriminate against genuine entrepreneurial dynamism.

Impediments to enterprise expansion

Among those companies which wanted to grow, the major obstacles have varied over time, factors such as weak demand and scarcity of labour showing strong cyclical variation. Small companies (up to 20 employees) list lack of venture capital and labour market legislation as equally important obstacles to growth, with a tendency for high-tech sectors to focus somewhat more strongly on capital (Figure 11.3). On the other hand, surveys including somewhat larger enterprises (up to 50 employees) conclude that labour market restrictions are by far the most important obstacle (Industriförbundet, 1996[7]).

Disadvantages of small scale? Financing, training and R&D

Small enterprises may be disadvantaged in comparison with larger ones in three ways (the three so-called "gaps"): availability of finance; training of staff

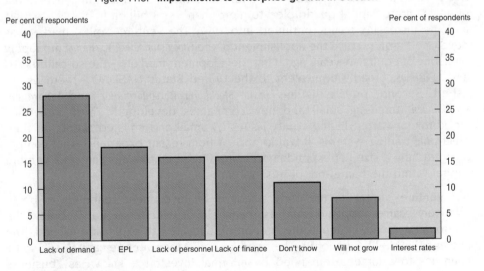

Figure 11.3. **Impediments to enterprise growth in Sweden**[1]

1. Based on a survey of 1 807 enterprises with less than 20 employees.
Source: LRF Konsult, 1997.

("human capital investment") and development and use of new technology (Swedish Government, 1996[8]). As for finance, it is often claimed that small businesses are disadvantaged in the ability to raise loan capital relative to larger competitors due to information asymmetry and larger risk. Banks, unable to correctly assess the credit risk involved, charge excessive interest rates or decline credit altogether. In this case, small and new enterprises could obtain cheaper financing via injections of equity capital which allow investors to cover the high default risk against the expected share of the profits of successful enterprises.

There is some past evidence of a financing gap, where the subset of small companies which intended to undertake innovative activity perceived a lack of venture capital as a hindrance (Deiaco, 1992). Indeed, following the banking crisis, which particularly affected the financial system around 1992, bank lending was scarce in the Swedish economy and this disproportionally affected companies which were either weakly capitalised or attempting to grow fast. More recently, surveys have not pointed to any widespread lack of finance, and the 1997 *Economic Survey of Sweden* found no evidence of bank lending rates to small businesses which were higher than justified by default risks.

However, high-risk enterprise start-ups and expansion may more appropriately be financed through equity capital than borrowed funds. As for venture capital there may have been a problem in the past, but it would appear that the supply of venture capital is now rapidly increasing. Indeed, a recent cross-country comparison shows that Sweden has the fourth largest venture capital stock (relative to GDP) in Europe (Figure 11.4, panel A). Furthermore, the annual investment of new venture capital quadrupled to more than SKr 3 billion from 1995 to 1996 and the increasing trend continued into 1997. The venture capital market has developed rapidly since the abolishment of the *Stockholm Stock Exchange* monopoly on listing of equity six years ago. First, development markets – the so-called OTC and O-*listings*, broadly equivalent to the United States NASDAQ – were established. Second, private listings (*e.g.*, Stockholm Börsinformation and Innovation-*smarknaden*) targeting small and new companies developed. Third, individual stockbrokers started listing equity issues by small and unlisted clients on their electronic trading systems. It would appear from recent experience that companies reaching a size corresponding to some fifteen employees can seek venture capital within the framework of this system.

Venture capital for the early stages of an investment continues to be in relatively scarce supply, insofar as the share of venture capital is below the European average, although the proportion allocated to expansion exceeds the average (Figure 11.4, panel B). The need for early-stage venture capital is in some countries to a large extent filled by informal investors – known as "business angels" – who closely monitor, or even work with, the entrepreneur. While there are no formal studies of such investors in Sweden, the presumption used to be

Figure 11.4. **Venture capital**

Per cent

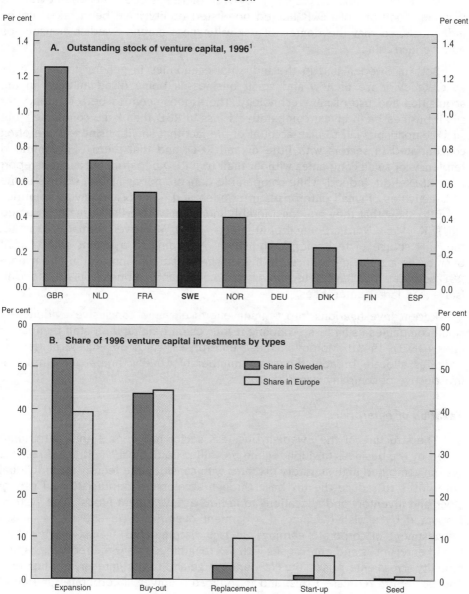

1. Stock as a per cent of GDP.
Source: OECD (1996).

that they are rather limited in number, reflecting *inter alia* the scarcity of household wealth mentioned above. Recently, however, there has been anecdotal evidence that large portions of newly-floated non-listed equity have been taken up by individuals, so that the degree of risk-willingness among Swedish households may be increasing.

Both in Sweden and in the industrial economies in general there is little concrete evidence of new and small businesses being disadvantaged in the acquisition and use of new technology. There does seem to be a tendency for small businesses to invest comparatively less in R&D than large companies, but such comparisons fail to take account of the fact that small businesses are often concentrated in sectors with little overall R&D, and that there is a confirmed tendency for small companies without their own R&D department to under-report their R&D effort. Indeed, while comparable data are not available, studies of the R&D activities of small enterprises in Sweden and other Scandinavian countries seem to show that they are considerably more innovative than usually assumed (NUTEK, 1996a; Nordic Council of Ministers, 1995). Moreover, formal R&D is not the only source of technology acquisition. According to a recent study, small businesses acquire a significantly higher share of their "innovation" from non-R&D sources – purchase of technology and consultancy, hiring of outside specialists – than larger enterprises.

Recent investigations into training efforts elicit no conclusive evidence of small companies using less economic resources on training their staff than larger ones (OECD, 1998a). Moreover, those enterprises which do engage in training activities allocate broadly the same number of working hours per employee irrespective of company size.

Taxation of enterprises

The structure of the Swedish business sector has been significantly influenced by the business taxation regime prevailing up to the 1990/91 *tax reform*. This system combined high statutory tax rates with considerable leeway for individual enterprises to reduce the tax base through accelerated depreciation of capital stock and inventory and allocations to in-house "investment funds". The system, motivated by a wish to smooth investment over the cycle and to encourage reinvestment of corporate earnings, in fact discriminated against newly-established enterprises and enterprises with few tangible assets while reducing capital mobility across enterprises, thus favouring large and capital-intensive industries.[9] The tax reform redressed this, and introduced a universal corporate tax rate of 30 per cent which was lowered to 28 per cent in 1994. This general taxation of business earnings applies equally to incorporated and non-incorporated enterprises, thereby implying a more equal treatment of small and large enterprises – albeit at the cost of a considerably more burdensome tax compliance.

The tax reform also diminished the tax-distortions between different forms of enterprise financing, most notably by reducing the prohibitively high marginal tax rate on new share issues in companies owned by households. A temporary abolition of double taxation of dividends in 1994 contributed further to this (Table 11.4). The reintroduction of double taxation of dividends in 1995 can be considered as impeding the supply of risk capital, affecting not the larger enterprises with internationally-traded shares but listed and unlisted enterprises which rely on domestic equity finance. While a partial exemption for unlisted businesses was re-introduced with effect from 1997, the present rules still imply disincentives to grow and to become listed. More generally, it may be noted that the high effective taxes facing households as investors, especially as purveyors of equity capital, have contributed to a long-term decline in households' participation in the equity market. For small and growing enterprises, this may historically have had particularly adverse effects on the supply of risk capital as a direct placement market failed to emerge.

Further adverse effects of the corporate tax code on enterprise growth may emanate, paradoxically, from the desire to provide some relief for particularly small companies. Enterprise wage bills below SKr 850 000 (the wage costs of three to four employees) face a lower social security contribution than those above that level, increasing the costs for a further expansion. The complexity of

Table 11.4. **Effective marginal tax rates in Sweden**

Real pre-tax of return 10 per cent at actual inflation rates

	Debt	New share issues	Retained earnings
1980			
Households	58.2	136.6	51.9
Tax exempt institutions	−83.4	−11.6	11.2
Insurance companies	−54.9	38.4	28.7
1994			
Households	32.0/27.0 [1]	28.3/18.3 [1]	36.5/26.5 [1]
Tax exempt institutions	−14.9	21.8	21.8
Insurance companies	0.7	32.3	33.8
1995			
Households	32.0/27.0 [1]	67.7/57.7 [1]	48.0/38.0 [1]
Tax exempt institutions	−3.5	25.7	25.7
Insurance companies	21.0	53.3	50.4

Note: All calculations are based on the actual asset composition in manufacturing.
1. Excluding wealth tax. Wealth tax on unlisted shares was abolished in 1993.
Source: Henrekson, M. (1996), Företagandets villkor.

tax rules stems also from efforts to prevent tax arbitrage between wage and capital income, resulting from the large discrepancy between internationally-competitive capital income taxes at 28 to 30 per cent and wage income taxes close to 60 per cent. For active owners of closely-held companies,[10] earnings less than 5 per cent of a benchmark – calculated as the capital invested corrected for certain wage payments[11] – are exempt from the tax on capital income and are only taxed at the corporate level (28 per cent); income from 5 to 12 per cent of the benchmark is taxed at both the corporate and the personal level (giving an overall tax burden of approximately 50 per cent). However, income exceeding 12 per cent of the benchmark is taxed at the high marginal tax rate applying to wage income which together with the corporate tax on the underlying income results in an overall tax burden approaching 70 per cent. While tax arbitrage may be prevented, the complexity of the system may discourage entrepreneurs and involve relatively high administrative costs for small enterprises.

The personal wealth taxation may create some advantages for small businesses, compared with larger enterprises. According to recent changes in the tax code, all equity listed on the OTC *and the* O-*lists* of the stock market, along with equity unlisted altogether, is considered as working capital. Such working capital is untaxed, whereas ownership of publicly-listed equity (equity appearing on the so-called A-*list*) is taxed. In order to avoid disincentives to public listing in the future, main owners of companies moving from the OTC *and* O-*lists* to the A-*list* will retain their exemption from wealth taxes.

The labour market

Labour market legislation is listed by many employers as one of the main impediments to enterprise growth. Regulations which raise the costs of laying off labour inevitably discourage companies from hiring and thereby affect job creation in general, but there are reasons to believe that small and medium-sized businesses are particularly affected. For example, to the extent *employment protection legislation* (EPL) discourages lay-offs of staff ill-suited for their current work assignments, companies with a limited number of workplaces are in a disadvantageous position compared with larger enterprises, who can redeploy and use natural wastage to adapt. The *Jobs Study Follow Up* in the 1997 OECD *Economic Survey of Sweden* concluded that the EPL in Sweden was not just more restrictive than the average in Europe, and considerably more so than in the United States, but that the rules guiding the order of dismissal and re-hiring of employees discriminated against small and – particularly – medium-sized employers.[12]

Finally, it has been argued that the payroll taxes are excessive and that they are one major reason for sluggish growth of Swedish enterprises (Swedish Employers' Confederation and Federation of Swedish Industries, 1996). However, while high total labour costs definitely discourage hiring, most studies indicate that the long-run incidence of payroll taxes falls on the wage earner rather than on the employer. The implication of this is that lower payroll taxes – while they might have some positive short-term impact – would eventually result in higher wages rather than more jobs. On the other hand, improving labour market flexibility to allow smoother adjustment of wages to demand and supply in the labour market would indeed help improve the entrepreneurial climate.

Market factors

Weak competition impedes the creation and growth of new enterprises, insofar as it gives incumbent companies an advantageous market position. Therefore, a strict and rigorously enforced competition law is favourable to entrepreneurship. Swedish competition laws were tightened in 1993, notably to encompass the *"prohibition principles"* prevailing in the EU area, which must be considered an improvement in the framework for small and new enterprises. Some problem areas remain, notably in the service sector, which has performed less well as a creator of new jobs than in most other countries. Cartelisation remains a problem, *inter alia* in transport services, and the market for professional services remains strongly regulated.

As a particularly important example, the retailing sector has recorded no increase in employment over the last two decades, compared with a yearly growth of around 1 per cent in most European countries, and 1.5 to 2 per cent in North America. While this is partly linked to slower growth in private consumption and restrictive opening-hour legislation which was lifted only in 1989, it also reflects an internationally very concentrated retail sector. For example, three food retailers continue to cover close to 70 per cent of the total market (Table 11.5). While this oligopolistic power is not actively encouraged by the authorities, there is some evidence of local authorities using their control of the zoning rules to discourage changes to the traditional pattern of retail outlets.

Whereas the central government's involvement and ownership in the business sector remains modest, local authorities' business activities can be seen as an impediment to the development of the private business sector in some areas. At the beginning of 1994 local governments had control (a minimum 50 per cent equity stake) of close to 1 500 companies with nearly 50 000 employees and an annual turnover of SKr 115 billion (8 per cent of GDP), the strongest involvement being in housing and utilities. Swedish rules allow government providers to compete with private providers, and although the competition authorities have the right to intervene in the case of dumping and predatory pricing practices the burden of proof still falls on the private sector operator. But this creates problems of ensuring that prices offered by government entities actually cover all costs, especially capital and rental costs. Overall, the provision of a wide range of free or

Table 11.5. **Characteristics of the distribution sector in selected European countries**

	Retail outlets per 100 000 inhabitants			Concentration	
	Total	Supermarkets[1]	Hypermarkets[2]	1995 market share of the three top food retailers	Share of sole proprietorship
Sweden	**940**	**23.5**	**0.8**	**68**	**29.8**
Germany	850	12.1	1.4	40	81.5
France	970	12.6	1.9	38	71.8
Italy	1 710	7.4	0.3	17	90.4
United Kingdom	810	3.4	1.3	49	n.a.
Spain	1 340	19.1	0.6	26	92.0
Netherlands	800	13.8	0.3	57	70.1
Belgium	1 410	19.8	1.0	61	74.5
Denmark	1 000	17.3	0.3	50[3]	76.6
Norway	920	31.0	0.7	86	18.0
Finland	770	20.6	1.5	83	41.9

1. Supermarkets are defined as covering between 400 and 2 499 square metres.
2. Hypermarkets cover 2 500 square metres and more.
3. Top two retailers only.
Source: OECD Secretariat.

subsidised services which are operated by private companies in most OECD countries – the municipal laundry services are a frequently quoted example – have discouraged the development of those private service sectors which have been among the most rapidly-growing elements in the US and UK labour markets. As a result of the focus on the actual and potential distortions of competitive conditions in this field, the government has decided to establish a council which will review and monitor the competitive inter-relationship between public and private producers, with a mandate to formulate general rules as well as analysing specific complaints.

Public programmes and policies

Swedish economic policy has traditionally worked to consolidate and promote the expansion of large enterprises. In the past, *competition policy* focused on promoting economies of scale, while the *tax system, capital market regulations* and the *foreign direct investment regime* combined to favour large capital-intensive enterprises. In addition, a tendency for secondary and tertiary education systems to focus on meeting the needs of large industry and public administration helped to create a *"wage-earner culture"* where risk-taking and entrepreneurship were not actively encouraged. Starting in the early 1990s, financial markets and tax policy

Box 11.2. **Swedish government programmes for assisting new enterprises and SMEs**

Swedish enterprises have access to EU schemes aimed at promoting business sector growth, of which several can be said to be of particular relevance to smaller firms. For example, the BRE and BC-Net *programmes* and the *Enterprise* initiative facilitate the search for business partners in other European countries; the *Europartenariat* aims at promoting business links with less favoured regions; the SME *Initiative* supports SME investment in improvement of production and organisation; the *Framework Programme for Research and Technical Development* aims at co-ordinating and supporting research in different areas; and the CRAFT *programme* encourages networking between enterprises facing common technical need.

Furthermore, the following national programmes are in force:

- *Start-up and information.* The ALMI *Business Partner* company, which is owned by the government, and 22 regional development companies owned by county councils, offer consultation, financing and information to persons planning to start a new business. The initial consultation is free of charge, later services are offered in return for a fee. The *National Board for Industrial and Technical Development* (NUTEK) operates a special telephone service with information and advice for new-starters. Moreover, these two entities provide SMEs in general with legal, technical and commercial advice related to product development, financial solutions, marketing and patent issues.
- *Financing.* ALMI *Business Partner provides* new firms with soft loans with a maturity of six to twelve years, covering up to 30 per cent of the total capital requirements. Generally these loans are interest-free and not amortised during the first two years. Moreover, credit guarantees can be granted. For existing enterprises investing in equipment or engaging in product and process development, loans and credit guarantees for a period up to eight years are given. NUTEK finances technical innovation at an early stage, before any product has been introduced on the market. Support is provided as loans, capital against royalty or project guarantees to a maximum of 50 per cent of the cost of the project. The *Swedish Industrial Development Fund* manages the following programmes in favour of smaller enterprises: *i)* loans for specific projects (maximum 50 per cent of total costs); *ii)* capital against royalty (maximum 50 per cent); *iii)* credit guarantees (maximum 80 per cent of the loan); and *iv)* venture capital in exchange for shares or convertible loans. The *Innovation Centre* supports the early stages of the innovation process, such as technical and commercial licenses.
- *Trade promotion.* The *Swedish Trade Council* (joint initiative of the government and private enterprises) promotes exports through information, advice, arranging trade fairs and joint marketing. Special priority is given to SMEs. The *Swedish Export Credits Guarantee Board* provides credit insurance to enterprises and banks in relation to exports and investment in other countries. The premium for the guarantee varies with the estimated risk, but an element of subsidy is included. The *Swedish Export Credit Corporation* (partly government-owned) provides medium and long-term export credits. Market-based interest rates are charged throughout the credit period.
- *Women and minority groups.* ALMI *Business Partner* has a special scheme for loans to enterprises wholly owned by women. These loans, which can be granted for

(continued on next page)

(continued)

both start-ups and existing enterprises, generally have a term of ten years including a grace period of one to three years, and a one to two year interest-free period. NUTEK finances several programmes in favour of female-owned enterprises: *i)* female business advisors in many regions; *ii)* training, information and networks for women entrepreneurs; *iii)* support to R&D by female entrepreneurs; *iv)* conferences for female entrepreneurs; and *v)* scholarships.

---

have become more neutral with respect to enterprise size, but small enterprises rarely expand into larger ones. Over the years several policies and targeted programmes aimed at nurturing small enterprise growth have therefore been put in place. The main areas covered relate to investment, exports, technology, R&D, management and education, consultancies and environment issues – albeit at a comparatively limited budgetary cost. In all there exist 140 types of subsidies with an additional 110 available from the EU. Some of the most important of these are listed in Box 11.2.

In addition to policies pursued at the national level, regional authorities and, particularly, municipalities have been active in support of the local business community – and have given this area increasing attention in the face of growing labour market imbalances. The kind of assistance offered varies significantly across regions. In areas dominated by "knowledge intensive" parts of the business sector (the three main urban centres and certain areas around major education centres) the municipalities' efforts are concentrated on fostering contacts and facilitating the exchange of information among existing enterprises. In areas dominated by "basic industries" (the northern parts of the country and the rural southeast) half of all municipalities are involved in developing new business activities together with local enterprises. In addition to the formal programmes for business development, local authorities reportedly use their influence on labour market programmes and their control over primary and secondary education – where far larger budgetary amounts are involved – to create a favourable climate for local enterprises.

A new policy orientation?

Since the recession of the early 1990s, which particularly hit regions and segments of the labour market which had become dependent on a few dominant enterprises, some additional reorientation of Swedish industrial policies have been under consideration. The government's programme for promoting growth and reducing unemployment by half by year 2000 singles out policies to promote entrepreneurship and SMEs as a field of action. A catalogue of measures intended to exploit entrepreneurial potential and further level the playing field between small and large enterprises has been adopted, easing the tax burden and the labour market rigidities for new and small businesses. In particular, the government has taken the position that small and medium-sized knowledge-intensive enterprises are likely to be the main source of private sector growth and employment creation in the near future. Policies relying on the diffusion of technology and networking in local areas thus play a prominent role. The main elements relating to the business sector are summarised in Box 11.3.

One element of the action plan which is still under consideration is the tentative devolution of some business-sector related policies to the regional and local authorities. The political debate has focused on whether local authorities should have a freer hand in reallocating the state-financed unemployment compensation toward job creation in enterprises and the public sector. The 1997 and 1998 experiment with extending the subsidised employment in the local authorities (the "Kalmar model"), is seen by some discussants as a test model for "active" use of the labour market funds in local areas.

Box 11.3. **The Swedish government's programme for growth and employment**

Development, renewal and growth for enterprises: (three year programme)

- Increase the diffusion of knowledge and technology by *i)* improving contacts between locally based tertiary education institutions and small and medium-sized enterprises; *ii)* encouraging the transfer of technology from large to small companies through the, largely self-financed, *Industrial Development Centres*; *iii)* increasing the supply of technologically skilled labour through the establishment of *Science Centres*; and *iv)* supporting the development of environmentally oriented technologies and industries.
- Make enterprise start-up and growth easier through *i)* a 5 per cent reduction in employers' social contributions up to a (low) limit; *ii)* some easing of *EPL*, in particular improved access to temporary employment and a right to deviate from certain dismissal rules by local agreement; *iii)* an exemption from double taxation of parts of the dividends from unlisted equity; and *iv)* some increase in the amount self-employed persons can earn subject only to corporate tax rates.
- A strengthened role for the regions, including in particular increased co-operation of local authorities among themselves and with the business sector, and the devolution of some central government tasks to the regional and local level. Concrete measures include SKr 500 million (in addition to existing programmes) to locally administered labour-market related programmes for self employment and a programme to promote tourism.

Concluding remarks

To the extent that entrepreneurship is a function of the cultural and educational features of Swedish society and that are embedded in the nature of the Swedish welfare state, the shortcomings analysed above cannot be easily redressed without conflicting with other policy objectives. However, economic factors seem to have exerted a negative impact on the entrepreneurial climate in general, and on the start-up and growth of small enterprises in particular, and these could be addressed at a low direct cost. Progress has already been made in removing some of the biases in favour of large enterprises stemming from the taxation, corporate finance and regulatory systems. However, a recent OECD study found that policies to encourage the growth of smaller enterprises tend to be focused more toward investment, R&D and goods exports and are thus more effective within the manufacturing sector than in the service sector (OECD, 1997a). More fundamentally, while the proliferation of schemes to support small businesses may be seen as a way of correcting the negative effects of previous policies which favoured large Swedish enterprises, such support can only play a limited role with respect to the impediments arising from other sources, in particular restrictive labour market regulations, a tax code which may still discourage investment in both human capital and technological diffusion and a public procurement process which is weighted against private-service provision.

To deal with these problems, new initiatives are needed in the following areas:

- *Labour market legislation*, and particularly employment protection legislation, limits enterprise growth and job creation and should be critically reviewed. To the extent that it creates special problems for new and small businesses, such companies could, as a second best, be granted statutory exemptions from parts of such legislation;
- If the *marginal tax on labour income* could be lowered towards that of capital income, less emphasis would have to be put on closing off windows for tax arbitrage; as a consequence, the tax code could be simplified. The *tax code* could be made more neutral, *inter alia* with respect to enterprises' decisions to expand and innovate and to seek a stock-exchange listing;
- While entry costs are modest, exit costs seem prohibitively high. The concern to limit the abuse of corporate bankruptcy may be a valid one, but the penalties involved in a personal bankruptcy are such that they discourage entrepreneurial activity;
- The efforts to improve companies' market access should be continued. The strictest possible enforcement of competition laws on the domestic market environment will, in particular, benefit small and new enterprises. This should include fair and equal competition with government entities providing market-produced goods and services.

With respect to state support for diffusion of information and technology, it is important that these be promoted through generic programmes:

- Where support services for newly-established enterprises are provided it is important to ensure that such activities do not conflict with work which is done – or could equally well be done – by private business consultants, lawyers, accountants and venture capitalists;
- Public authorities can facilitate the diffusion of information among enterprises: for example small enterprises faced with a particular problem are often unaware of the solutions at hand. Also, networking toward technological development or marketing can sometimes be facilitated though outside participation.

In addition to the national policy measures and support schemes, a case could be made for increased local authority involvement in nurturing an entrepreneurial climate. Due to their closeness to the local markets, regional authorities and municipalities may be well placed to diagnose and solve specific problems. However, local authority involvement is necessarily circumscribed by their own budget constraints and should be subject to mechanisms which assure transparency, and a standard of quality in design which ensures that competitive forces are not inhibited.

This chapter has found little evidence that small and new enterprises suffer any systematic disadvantage of scale – except possibly in the financing of the earliest stage of an investment, where it is not obvious that the government should play any direct role. The introduction of further support schemes for selected parts of the business sector thus does not seem advisable. The number of specific programmes is already large, and it should be borne in mind that the proliferation of current schemes risks creating bureaucratic conflicts and information problems and diverting enterprises' attention from entrepreneurial activity toward rent-seeking. Broader structural policy reform is necessary for the improvement of the institutional and regulatory environment. The most important role for public authorities remains the provision of a stable macroeconomic situation, a neutral system of taxation, a well-functioning labour market and a competitive business sector environment.

Notes

1. For an overview, see OECD (1994) and ENSR (1995).

2. This study includes only companies active during the whole period 1991/92 to 1994/95 with a turnover in the last year of at least SKr 25 million. Companies growing through mergers and acquisitions are disregarded.

3. These figures are, however, not corrected for sectoral influences.

4. Of these, pension savings cannot be used for setting up an own enterprise, whereas housing capital may be used as collateral for loans.

5. Lindh and Ohlsson, using data from the early 1980s, study the effect of winning large sums in the national lottery on the propensity to start an own enterprise.

6. It should be noted that government-run schemes which guarantee wage claims outstanding in case of bankruptcy also enter into this legislative sphere insofar as they may affect employees' surveillance of financial developments of their enterprises.

7. Older surveys quoted in OECD (1995) also concluded that lack of capital was not among the major obstacles to enterprise growth.

8. *Regeringens proposition* 1995/96:222 explicitly refers to these gaps.

9. The possibility of transferring the ownership of enterprises to tax-exempt institutions continues to favour large enterprises over new and small enterprises, insofar as a larger share of the latter's earnings are necessary for the subsistence of the owner(s).

10. A closely held company is defined as a company owned by "few" persons (usually fewer than ten), and where persons employed by the company hold more than 70 per cent of the equity.

11. The formula is: invested capital plus the total wage cost minus salaries to active partners minus SKr 363 000.

12. The Swedish EPL imposes rules on: notice periods at dismissal; the reason for dismissal; trial employment; and the order in which employees may be dismissed and re-hired. The law stipulates that in the case of labour shedding the last person hired must be the first person laid off, and that in the case of re-hiring any person laid off within the last nine months must be the first person re-hired. Some easing has been put in place recently. Moreover, Sweden has one of the shortest legislated maximum trial periods in Europe.

References

ALBÆK, K. et al. (1996),
"Employer Size-Wage Effects in the Nordic Countries", working Paper 96-03, Center for Labour Market and Social Research, Aarhus.

BLIXT, L. (1997),
"Tillväxtföretag i Sverige – stora som små och från norr till söder", Teknikpolitiska analyser, Arbetsrapport, NUTEK.

DAVIDSSON, P. (1995),
"SMEs and Job Creation in Sweden", paper presented at the OECD High-Level Workshop "SMEs: Employment, Innovation and Growth", in Washington, D.C., United States.

DEIACO, E. (1992),
"New Views on Innovative Activity and Technological Performance. The Swedish Innovation Survey", OECD STI Review, No. 11.

EFER (1996),
Europe's 500 Dynamic Entrepreneurs. The Job Creators, Brussels.

EUROPEAN NETWORK FOR SME RESEARCH (ENSR) (1995),
Third Annual Report, EIM Small Business Research and Consultancy, the Netherlands..

HENREKSON, M (1996),
Företagandets villkor.

INDUSTRIFÖRBUNDET (1996),
"Tillväxthinder för småföretag. Södra Norrland", Rapport no. 2, Nyindustrialiseringsprojektet.

LINDH, T. and OHLSSON, H. (1996),
"Self-Employment and Windfall Gains: Evidence from the Swedish Lottery", The Economic Journal, Vol. 106.

LINDH, T. and OHLSSON, H. (1998),
"Self-Employment and Wealth Inequality", Review of Income and Wealth, March.

LRF KONSULT (1997),
Småföretagsbarometern, Föreningsbanken, Företagarnas Riksorganisation, Fall.

NORDIC COUNCIL OF MINISTERS (1995),
"Forskningsnära företag i Norden – forskning och utveckling 1993", TemaNord 1995:575.

NUTEK (1996a),
Forsknings- och utvecklingsverksamhet inom forskningsnära och teknikerintensiva småföretag 1993, Stockholm.

NUTEK (1996b),
Tillväxtforetag I Sverige, Stockholm.

OECD (1994),
Employment Outlook, OECD Publications, Paris.

OECD (1995),
OECD Economic Surveys – Sweden, OECD Publications, Paris.

OECD (1996),
The Tax/Benefit Position of Production Workers, OECD Publications, Paris.

OECD (1997a),
OECD Economic Surveys – Sweden, OECD Publications, Paris.

OECD (1997b),
Revenue Statistics, 1965/1996, OECD Publications, Paris.

OECD (1997c),
National Accounts, OECD Publications, Paris.

OECD (1998a),
OECD Economic Surveys – Sweden, OECD Publications, Paris.

OECD (1998b),
OECD Economic Surveys – Australia, OECD Publications, Paris.

SWEDISH GOVERNMENT (1996),
"Vissa åtgärder för att halvera arbetslösheten till år 2000, ändrade anslag för budgetåret 1995/96, finansiering m.m.", Regeringens proposition 1995/96:222, Stockholm.

SWEDISH EMPLOYERS' CONFEDERATION and FEDERATION OF SWEDISH INDUSTRIES (1996),
Abolish government aid to companies in exchange for lower payroll taxes.

Chapter XII

The United States

The OECD *Jobs Study* (OECD, 1994*a*) showed that the US labour market has performed well relative to other OECD countries. Employment growth has been very strong and unemployment has shown little tendency to rise over the long term. The *Jobs Study*, as well as this work, has argued that entrepreneurship is one of the keys to a buoyant economy capable of adjusting to economic developments and structural change. Not only can entrepreneurship contribute to job creation, it may contribute to real income gains and greater flexibility in the job market. The US economy appears to be strongly entrepreneurial: many new firms enter the market every year, many US firms are among the most innovative in their industry, and setting up one's own business is perceived as a life-style choice. This chapter attempts to explain why the entrepreneurial phenomenon is so pervasive in the United States. The chapter first documents various aspects of entrepreneurial activity, discusses the factors behind it and concludes with policy implications.

The pervasiveness of entrepreneurship

A common proxy for entrepreneurship is the small business sector. It is clear that small firms in the United States make up the bulk of enterprises: over 98 per cent of firms are Small and Medium-Sized Enterprises (SMEs, *i.e.*, employ fewer than 500 workers) and employ half of the workforce. Furthermore, the claim has been made that small businesses contribute disproportionately to job creation, although this is hotly debated.[1] However, referring to the small business sector as a proxy for entrepreneurship may be misleading since many small businesses are not particularly innovative or risk-taking.

Despite the attention focused on small firms, many larger firms behave in an entrepreneurial and dynamic manner. Furthermore, larger firms play a significant role in the economy: in the United States, firms with 500 or more employees account for 52 per cent of GDP and 46 per cent of private sector employment

(OECD, 1996a). Indeed, in the United States, large firms (over 500 employees) account for a high share of employment compared with most other OECD countries, suggesting either that firm size is not necessarily a good proxy for entrepreneurial activity or, instead, that it is relatively easy for US firms to start small, prosper and become large firms. This latter point suggests that indicators based on the performance of *"gazelles"* or fast-growing firms, may provide a better proxy for the degree of entrepreneurial activity. These firms appear to account for a disproportionate fraction of net job growth in the US economy.[2] Furthermore, and contrary to popular perception, only around one-third of these gazelles are "high-tech" companies. Fast-growing firms can be found across a wide range of activities (for example, *Wal-Mart, Starbucks, Office Depot, Federal Express,* Amazon Bookstore) and their success often comes from innovative approaches to marketing, organisation or distribution. Franchising has also provided a way for firms to grow quickly and good ideas to be exploited, while sharing the risks and reducing the capital the firm would otherwise require to finance expansion.

Yet another proxy measure for entrepreneurship is the pace at which firms are starting up and closing down. This notion of turbulence attempts to capture the dynamic nature of entrepreneurial activity and has the advantage of not relying on definitions of firms' size, age, or growth. Unfortunately the nature of most business start-ups and close-downs makes them difficult to measure accurately. The SBA, for example, uses three different proxies for new business formation for the United States: the total number of tax returns filed, the number of new employer identification numbers issued by the *Department of Labor* and the Dun and Bradstreet new business incorporation series. Using the measure constructed from *Department of Labor* data, some 8 to 900 000 firms are created each year, 16.4 per cent of the total number of firms on average each year, and some 7 to 800 000 firms terminate their activities, at an average termination rate of 14.3 per cent (Figure 12.1.). However, relatively few of these closures – some 5 to 10 per cent – are business failures, involving losses to creditors (Dennis, 1995). Another indicator of turbulence is firm survival rate. The United States has a lower firm survival rate than most countries, with only around 60 per cent of new firms still operating three years later, indicating a high degree of turbulence.

It is often argued that low firm survival rates lead to lower job stability, which may, in turn, lead to firms investing less in job training. Despite low firm survival rates in the United States, overall job turnover does not seem to be markedly higher than other countries, as shown in Table 12.1. Job turnover, due to firm births or firm terminations, does appear to be relatively high, but this is offset by lower rates of job turnover in existing firms. And while the average and median job tenure statistics are lower for the United States than most countries, the percentage of the work-force who have held their present job for five years or less is not significantly higher in the United States than in several other OECD countries (Figure 12.2).

Figure 12.1. **Firm creation and termination rates in the United States**
Per cent of total firm population

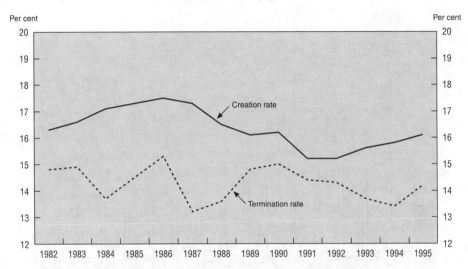

Source: Small Business Administration (1996).

Table 12.1. **Job gains and losses**
Average annual rates as a percentage of total employment

		Gross job gains from		Gross job losses from		Turnover
		Openings	Expansions	Closures	Contractions	
United States	1984-88	**8.9**	**4.3**	**7.2**	**2.9**	**23.2**
	1989-91	7.4	5.1	7.6	3.5	23.7
Canada	1983-89	3.2	11.7	2.8	7.3	25.0
	1989-91	3.4	10.0	3.7	12.8	29.9
France	1984-89	7.3	6.6	6.9	5.9	26.7
	1989-92	6.9	6.8	7.1	6.8	27.6
Germany	1983-90	2.5	6.5	1.9	5.6	16.5
Italy	1984-89	4.1	8.6	3.6	7.0	23.3
Sweden	1985-89	7.3	8.8	5.2	8.1	29.4
	1989-92	5.6	7.0	4.9	11.3	28.7
United Kingdom	1987-89	2.7	6.3	3.3	1.9	14.1
	1989-91	1.9	6.1	3.4	3.0	14.4

Source: OECD, 1994d.

Figure 12.2. **Distribution of employment by employer tenure**

Per cent of total employment

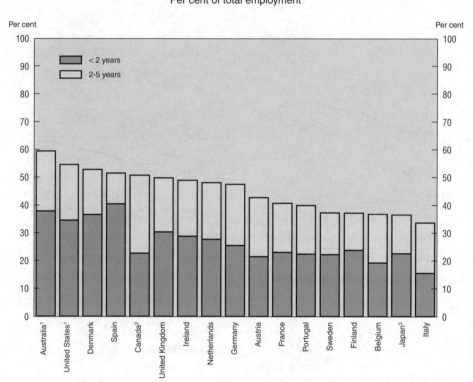

1. 1996.
2. Data shown refer to duration groups under 1 year and 1 to 5 years.
3. Data shown refer to duration groups 2 years or under and 3 to 4 years.
Source: OECD (1997).

The regional dimension. Analysis across states and cities shows that those with higher job loss and lower firm survival rates are among the most prosperous economically (Birch *et al.*, 1997) suggesting that turbulence is an important feature of economic growth. Other proxies of entrepreneurship also have regional dimensions. Significant differences were found in the prevalence of nascent entrepreneurs, with higher levels in the West and North East, and lower levels in the North Central region and the South (Reynolds, 1997).[3] In an earlier study (Reynolds & Storey, 1993), start-up rates across regions (defined as travel-to-work areas) varied between 2.4 and 114 start-ups per 10 000 persons per year.

Why is entrepreneurship more prevalent in some regions than in others? There is no clear explanation, but some variables appear particularly important. The close proximity of universities and skilled labour pools are likely to generate entrepreneurship by providing new ideas and a labour force which needs relatively little training to adapt (Birch *et al.*, 1996). This research also pointed to other determinants such as the proximity of a major, preferably international, airport and the perception that the area is "a nice place to live". Empirical work (Reynolds, 1995) has found that several variables are statistically relevant in explaining the variation across regions of firm birth; regional economic diversity, population growth, greater personal wealth, presence of mid-career adults, low unemployment and greater flexibility of employment relationships (as proxied by the absence of unions and the presence of right-to-work laws).

Clustering. To some extent, the regionalisation of entrepreneurial activity may also reflect the phenomenon of "clustering" – the apparent tendency of firms in the same line, or closely related lines, of business to be geographically concentrated. Silicon Valley in California is currently the most prominent cluster of computer-related entrepreneurial firms (Table 12.2). Other clusters are found in industries as varied as financial services in New York, entertainment in Los Angeles, and carpet manufacturing in Dalton, Georgia. Clustering is thought to arise from aggregation economies, since concentrations of firms create larger markets for specialised labour and intermediate inputs and generate informational spillovers – the ability to stay abreast of the latest industry developments. These advantages of geographical concentration can be of particular benefit to smaller firms which, because of their size, often cannot provide specialised training or maintain in-house services such as R&D or marketing.

However, it is not clear why some regions have more enterprise clusters than others. Clusters may develop naturally because of intrinsic advantages found in a region, including natural resources such as mines or port facilities. For example, firms in the steel industry are often established close to energy supplies and good transportation networks. Or some regions may provide more fertile ground for enterprise development because of the presence of an enterprise culture or a more favourable institutional framework. Silicon Valley's origin can be traced to an enterprising individual, a Stanford University professor, who established the *Palo Alto Research Centre*, which pioneered the development of computer technologies. The size of clusters is limited by the size of the market, which may in turn be limited to the national market if there are barriers to international trade. Thus, there is some evidence suggesting that the United States is more cluster-intensive than Europe because the US market is larger than national European markets, which are still segmented as a result of different tax regimes, regulations, and policies which favour national products ("national champions") (Krugman, 1991).

Table 12.2. **High-tech establishments and employment, Silicon Valley and Route 128**

	Establishments			Employment		
	SV	128	SV/128	SV	128	SV/128
1959	109	268	0.4	17 376	61 409	0.3
1975	831	840	1.0	116 671	98 952	1.2
1990	3 231	2 168	1.5	267 531	150 576	1.8
1992	4 063	2 513	1.6	249 259	140 643	1.8

Note: The type of high-tech establishments are: computing and office equipment, communications equipment, electronic components, guided missiles, space vehicles, instruments and software and data processing.
Source: Saxenian (1994).

The benefits of clusters may be cumulative in that once a cluster has developed, its advantage increases with the size of the cluster: success breeds success. As a result, established clusters may be difficult to challenge and should therefore tend to be stable and long-lived. However, while a cluster can be stable over long periods of time, it would appear that these cumulative advantages are not altogether decisive, and the position of an entrenched cluster can be successfully challenged. Examples of this abound: steel in both Europe and the United States, certain types of computer chip-making in the United States and Japan, automakers in the United States, cameras in Germany, textiles in many industrial countries. Therefore, as production becomes standardised over time, localisation within an industry can tend to fade away. There appears to be a cycle in which emergent new industries initially flourish in localised industrial districts, then disperse as they mature. Nevertheless, some clusters have proven very resilient, able to adapt to new technologies and new demands and remain at the cutting edge of their industry. Silicon Valley is one example, and others can be found in Italy (the fashion industries of Emilia-Romagna) and in Spain (the leather industries of Valencia). It has been suggested that the vitality of Silicon Valley arises from its decentralised and co-operative industrial system (Saxenian, 1994) (Box 6.1).

A combination of factors encouraging entrepreneurship

Culture. The United States is often described as having a strong entrepreneurial "culture". The focus on a free-market economy, a relatively small role for government and the social importance attached to self-reliance have made entrepreneurship a respectable, indeed admired, attribute. A national poll of adult Americans showed that over 90 per cent would approve of their child going into business for himself or herself (Jackson, 1986). However, there was somewhat less enthusiasm shown by owners who had started their businesses three years previously: only 54 per cent of them would approve (Cooper *et al.*, 1990). A more recent survey (Reynolds, 1997) estimates that almost a quarter of households is either starting a business, owns a business or is informally investing in someone else's business. There also appears to be no stigma attached to failure and failure is not automatically assumed to be the owner's fault. Evidence suggests that many entrepreneurs have failed in the past: in one study of bankruptcy more than one-third of the entrepreneurs had owned another business before starting the bankrupt business (Small Business Administration, 1996). The strong pro-entrepreneurial culture has helped to shape institutional characteristics of the US economy that facilitate business start-ups, reward firms based on their economic efficiency and allow rapid, low-cost exit for entrepreneurs who succeed, fail or simply want to move on to a new venture.

Ease of firm creation and closure.[4] It is relatively simple to create a firm in the United States. Compared with other countries, relatively few procedures must be carried out before and after the registration, and the registration process is not very time-consuming. Entrepreneurs can make use of private firms which undertake registration on their behalf and, in this manner, a business entity can be created by telephone or by fax and at low cost. Enterprise creation in the United States also involves fewer regulations; in some European countries craft-related activities from bakers to hairdressers to dispensing opticians require specific qualifications such as an apprenticeship or specific post-apprentice experience, which can take several years to acquire (Meager, 1993).

Just as legislation exists to regulate firm creation, bankruptcy legislation regulates firm termination, or exit. The US system offers the individual bankrupt a "clean slate" by way of discharge: the entrepreneur loses his assets to his creditors but cannot be pursued for any remaining claims which have not been met. While this approach has some disadvantages, it does allow for considerable flexibility and may help to reduce any stigma attached to business failure. In other countries, by contrast, legislation places more emphasis on creditor protection and, in some cases, the absence of discharge clauses means that failed entrepreneurs can be pursued for several years, a situation which is not conducive to risk-taking activity.

Availability of risk capital. A striking aspect of the US entrepreneurial environment is the ample availability of risk capital and generally well-functioning market mechanisms for allocating this efficiently across a wide range of size, risk and return configurations. Small-scale start-ups are typically financed through own funds and loans of various forms,[5] which are generally not difficult to obtain. It is sometimes argued that credit rationing by banks reflects a market imperfection that can be especially severe for small, innovative and risky ventures.[6] In fact, when surveyed, small businesses on average rank obtaining long-term or short-term loans as only 63rd and 64th respectively on the list of difficulties they face (Dennis, 1996a). In any case, equity financing may provide a more appropriate mechanism for managing risk and return for high risk ventures.

What distinguishes the United States from the rest of the world in terms of financing entrepreneurial ventures is the availability of equity capital. The development of the private equity market which provides third-party finance to enterprises not quoted on a stock exchange and the second-tier stockmarket which provides exit opportunities for the suppliers of private equity are especially relevant for new and/or fast growing companies.

The private equity market has been the fastest growing market for corporate finance over the last 15 years or so.[7] In recent years the amount of professionally-managed private equity capital outstanding exceeded US$100 billion, of which 30 per cent is venture capital. Much of the non-venture private equity managed by partnerships has been used to provide funds for the expansion of medium-sized private firms, leveraged buy-outs and investments in firms in financial distress.

Since the early 1980s venture capital gained importance as a source of funding for innovative new ventures. The stock of venture capital outstanding is currently running at about US$30 billion, 80 per cent of which is managed by partnerships and the rest by subsidiaries of financial and industrial corporations.[8] In 1996, about 37 per cent of new venture investment was directed to early-stage companies (so-called seed and start-ups), compared with 12 per cent in Europe (Venture One, 1997, and European Venture Capital Association, 1997). Striking differences are also found in the sectorial distribution of venture capital investment. Technology-based firms in the United States and Canada are able to attract more funding than similar firms in other OECD countries. In 1994, 65 per cent of US venture capital disbursements went to technology-based firms, compared with only 15 per cent in Europe (OECD, 1996b). Geographically, venture capital investment is concentrated in California and Massachusetts (see Chapter 4, Table 4.2). Even so, it is noteworthy that about half of the new venture capital in 1996 was invested elsewhere.

An important factor in the development of venture capital was the revision of rules governing investment by pension funds under the *Employment Retirement Income Security Act* (ERISA) in the late 1970s, which allowed them to undertake higher-risk investment, including venture capital operations. As a result, pension funds have become the largest source of venture capital funding in the United States, accounting for close to half of the funding in 1996. In contrast, pension funds in Europe play a smaller role (contributing about a quarter of funds) while banks and insurance companies are the primary sources of private equity.[9]

The governance structure in the venture capital industry has also contributed to its success. Venture capitalists ensure that the interests of the third-party investors (*e.g.*, pension funds) are well served by the manager of the companies in which they invest. The contractual relationship between venture capitalists as general partners and the investors as limited partners is clearly defined.[10] Many of the venture capitalists have the technical expertise required in high-tech environments. They also recruit staff, explore various marketing possibilities and do not hesitate to replace the founder-CEOs if they consider it would improve the firm's performance.[11] Venture capitalists monitor closely the companies in which they invest and participate actively in their management so as to maximise the probability of their commercial success. The need for close monitoring has required venture capitalists to invest in companies located in close proximity.[12] However, this has been changing with the development of syndication and networking. Thus, in 1996, even California-based venture capitalists directed 42 per cent of their total investments towards companies located elsewhere, even though California and Massachusetts remained major recipient states (Table 12.3).

The success of the venture-capital markets has also been reinforced by the easy access to exit mechanisms by which venture capitalists can "cash-in" their mature investments. These include private transactions, such as trade sales and private placements,[13] and *initial public offerings* (IPOs) on the securities markets. In addition to their direct role as exit vehicles, IPOs serve as benchmarks for pricing of private transactions. IPOs have been facilitated by the NASDAQ, the best known of the second-tier markets, which was created in 1971 as a nation-wide market for trades in young, innovative companies. Second-tier markets provide them easier access to public securities markets through less stringent admission requirements and lower admission and continuing costs than those for first-tier

Table 12.3. **Geographical preferences of venture capital firms, 1996**

Home state of venture capitalists	Where they invested Percentage of their total investments			
	Home state	California	Massachusetts	All other states
California	58.0	58.0	4.7	37.3
Massachusetts	30.0	17.2	30.0	52.8
New York	9.4	28.7	14.7	44.5
Connecticut	14.7	26.0	12.7	46.6
Minnesota	21.3	33.4	12.3	33.0

Source: Coopers & Lybrand, 1996.

markets. The success of NASDAQ has been substantial, and it serves as a bench-mark for all other second-tier markets. In 1994, there were a total of 4 902 compa-nies quoted, compared with 2 570 on the *New York Stock Exchange* (NYSE). Many companies which could be listed on the NYSE, such as Microsoft, Intel, MCI and Apple Computer have chosen to remain on NASDAQ rather than move to a first-tier market. A number of participants in the European venture capital market see the poor performance of the second-tier markets created in the 1980s to be a major hindrance to the full development of the European venture capital indus-try, and renewed attempts are being made (European-wide EASDAQ, France's *Second Marché*, Italy's METIM and the United Kingdom's AIM) to create viable second-tier markets.[14]

Small Business Investment Companies (SBICs) are SBA-licensed venture capital firms which account for 10 to 15 per cent of venture capital investment. SBICs are allowed to match their investments with SBA loans and enjoy certain tax benefits but in exchange are subject to certain limits on the size of the companies in which they invest as well as on taking controlling interests. SBICs managed to channel record amounts of equity financing to small, fast-growing companies back in the 1960s but also suffered from the poor quality of managers.[15] Having been increasingly dominated by venture capital partnerships, SBICs are currently in large part subsidiaries of financial and industrial corporations. SBICs typically invest in smaller deals than do partnerships, and their presence is important in those states where there is a significant potential for promising new firms but availability of venture capital is low. SBICs therefore play a complementary role to venture capital partnerships.

Business angels are yet another source of equity finance for start-ups and their subsequent expansion. Angel capital is not an organised source of finance, and reliable statistics are scarce. But it is thought to be at least twice the size of the venture capital pool, though individual deals are much smaller. The angel capital market is fragmented and localised, and the market segmentation is exacerbated by barriers created by state securities legislation. In the absence of organised intermediaries the match-making process is difficult: potential angels hesitate to publicise their willingness to invest, and entrepreneurs are not keen on revealing what they believe to be innovative ideas (Dennis, 1996*b*). In these circumstances, the SBA has taken the initiative to create the *Angel Capital Electronic Network* (ACE-Net). This is a nation-wide Internet listing of small innovative compa-nies with the access restricted to angels. In setting up the ACE-Net, *State Securities Administrators* agreed to remove restrictions on inter-state trading of unregistered stocks of those companies which are on the ACE-Net, a step which in its own right is crucial to the further development of angel capital markets.

Availability of advice. Just as the venture-backed companies benefit from the advisory role of venture capitalists, most other companies benefit from the well-developed business advisory service industry in the United States. The industry comprises management consultants, accountants, business lawyers and a whole range of government and non-profit bodies which cater to the needs of small business and start-ups. At the federal level alone there are 1 000 *Small Business Development Centres* in 50 states which offer training and counselling services as well as help small companies access various federal support programmes. Offices which provide similar services exist at the state, county and city levels and also in the private sector, such as *chambers of commerce and industry*, many of which target specific groups such as women and African Americans. Thus, one survey showed that the State of Wisconsin has at least 400 different programmes providing some 700 kinds of services (Center for the Study of Employment, 1993). However, knowledge of these programmes among the general population was low.

Patent protection. One element of advice that entrepreneurs find particularly useful concerns patent protection. In the United States, the cost of patent application is lower than in Europe and small businesses benefit from a 50 per cent discount on patent fees. It has been estimated that the cost of obtaining European patent protection is three times that in the United States in terms of patent office fees and representation expenses and is about ten times on the average including other related costs such as translation expenses. On the other hand, the high cost of litigation and uncertainty stemming largely from the application of the first-to-invent rule is a problem for smaller firms in the United States. A typical lawsuit on infringement costs between US$25 000 and US$200 000, and larger ones could cost US$1 million, well beyond the level with which small firms can cope effectively.

Taxation and the regulatory burden. Entrepreneurs in the United States benefit from a relatively low overall tax burden. Moreover, because of a generous carry-forward and backward of losses some 40 per cent of companies have no taxable profits. However, American entrepreneurs cite the tax burden and the complexity of the tax system among the most severe problems they face (Dennis, 1996a), a common complaint across OECD countries. This problem has been alleviated to some extent by tax reforms during the last decade that have generally lowered top marginal tax rates. For example, cuts in central government corporate income tax rates since the mid-eighties have averaged around 10 percentage points (OECD, 1991). Nevertheless, marginal effective corporate tax rates have increased since the 1980s from 14.4 per cent in 1980 to 24 per cent in 1990 and vary considerably across industries, asset types, financing sources and ownership (Jorgenson & Landau, 1993) (Table 12.4). But when combined with taxation on corporate earnings at the personal level, effective rates have been reduced to around 19 per cent, which is lower than in other major countries, except for the United Kingdom (see Chapter 3, Table 3.3).

Table 12.4. **Marginal effective corporate tax rates in the United States, 1980-90**

In per cent

	1980	1985	1990
Asset			
Machinery	−12.0	−18.6	18.5
Buildings	19.1	12.2	25.3
Inventories	28.5	28.7	26.3
Industry			
Manufacturing	33.8	27.5	34.0
Other industry	13.7	−16.7	11.0
Commerce	15.5	9.2	21.8
Source of finance			
Debt	−49.2	−55.5	−14.7
New share issues	47.1	43.0	44.1
Retained earnings	45.6	42.1	43.7
Owner			
Households	15.8	9.5	23.6
Tax-exempt institutions	9.1	2.4	19.3
Insurance companies	26.3	25.1	40.9
Overall tax rate	14.4	9.2	24.0

Source: Jorgenson and Landau (1993).

Although the tax burden remains a concern, attention has turned to focus on the compliance burden posed by reporting requirements and the complexity of the system. Research by the SBA has concluded that, in 1992, the average annual cost of regulation, paperwork and tax compliance amounted to US$5 000 per employee in firms with fewer than 500 employees and US$3 400 per employee in larger firms.[16] Even though it was found that firms, when surveyed, agreed that they would have had to collect much of the required information for other purposes, or found the information useful (GAO, 1996), the tax system's ambiguity, frequent changes, expiration clauses and layers of federal and state regulation remain the main sources of the high compliance burden on businesses.

The US tax code is fairly neutral with respect to the choice of legal form of a business with, in particular, the possibility of using S taxation (available to companies with fewer than 35 shareholders and that meet other conditions) which offers almost full elimination of double taxation (taxation of both corporate income and distributed profits) (OECD, 1994*b*). This view is supported by a survey by the NFIB in 1996, which found that choice of legal form was not related to tax issues.

The level of the *capital gains tax* rate (CGT) could have an important effect on the private equity market. While the large percentage of private equity capital provided by pension funds is tax-exempt (OECD, 1996c), the funds provided by other investors (venture capitalists, private investors, entrepreneurs) are not. The maximum CGT rate was cut from 49,5 per cent to 28 per cent in 1978, to 20 per cent in 1981 and raised again to 28 per cent as part of the 1986 tax reform. The rate was cut in 1993 to 20 per cent for new investment in small companies (less than US$50 million in assets) with a minimum holding period of five years. It is difficult to determine the impact of these tax changes on the supply of private equity because of structural and cyclical changes in the economy which occurred at the same time. Further changes to CGT were made in the *Taxpayer Relief Act* 1997. Rates on assets held for longer than 18 months will be lowered significantly.

Flexible labour markets. Widely observed features of the US labour market, such as high degrees of flexibility and mobility, assist the process of entrepreneurial activity. Little formal regulation of labour contracts and light-handed employment protection legislation facilitate the adjustment of labour inputs associated with high rates of turbulence. Moreover, decentralised wage formation with limited union presence (except in a few sectors) make employee compensation flexible, and this trend is reinforced by a greater use of performance-based pay, particularly in new business ventures, where employee stock options are often offered.

New and high growth ventures require skilled workers and up-skilling of existing workers. Despite the well-known weaknesses of the primary and secondary education system in the United States (OECD, 1994c), the diversified system of higher education does a good job in meeting these requirements. The US universities produce a large number of Ph.D.s and community colleges offer worker training that is often tailored to the needs of a particular business. And there appears to be much on-the-job training of workers occurring at the enterprise level.[17] Human capital gained at firms, however, tends to be general or industry-specific and, hence, is less likely to be lost with job changes.

The dynamic nature of the US labour markets is further enhanced by immigrant workers. Immigrants are important sources of entrepreneurship, skilled workers and unskilled ones. Notwithstanding some well-known anecdotes (*e.g.*, the CEO of Intel is foreign-born), there are few official statistics on immigrant entrepreneurs. In several countries where immigration is a significant phenomenon, self-employment rates are generally higher for immigrants. But there is no significant difference in self-employment rates between natives and foreign-born persons in the United States. This could be an indication of the prevalence of entrepreneurship among the Americans or an indication of a flexible US labour market which allows immigrants to find jobs rather than create their own. A significant number of skilled immigrant workers are found in high-tech ventures.

They are typically foreign graduate students who finished their advanced degrees and stay on in the United States. Finally, unskilled immigrant workers are found in many low-tech ventures.

A wide range of public programmes

The US government has introduced several programmes aimed at facilitating enterprise start-ups and development. These include programmes administered by the *Departments of Agriculture, Commerce, Defence, Energy, Transportation* and independent agencies such as *Export-Import Bank*, the *National Institutes of Health* and the *Small Business Administration*. The goals of these various bodies tend to differ because the target groups are different. For example, the *Department of Commerce* focuses on helping established enterprises become more competitive by providing assistance to raise productivity, develop new products or markets and expand R&D. The *Department of Agriculture* concentrates on developing businesses in rural areas and the SBA focuses on new and small businesses. The CATO *Institute* estimates that the federal government spends roughly US$65 billion each year (close to 1 per cent of GDP) on more than 125 programmes that provide direct assistance to US firms (Moore, 1997). Little is known about the overall economic impact of these programmes. As in many OECD countries, few of these programmes have been evaluated, in part because of the methodological difficulties involved. It is also difficult to establish how many existing firms or new firms would have emerged and grown anyway, in the absence of such programmes, given the overall favourable climate for entrepreneurial activity. Furthermore, it is difficult to measure the overall effectiveness of these programmes against alternative policies such as reducing corporate taxes by the same amount. (Such a reduction would be significant, since corporate taxes currently raise about US$200 billion.)

Among the programmes which have been evaluated are the *Advanced Technology Program* (ATP) and the *Manufacturing Extension Partnership* (MEP). ATP provides funding to assist US businesses to apply or commercialise new scientific discoveries. Evaluating ATP was difficult because while funded projects are intended to have a commercial impact, several years can elapse between the end of technical work and commercial results. A *Department of Commerce* evaluation found that the ATP increased high-risk research implying that stronger links were being forged between the research community and enterprise. However, this finding was disputed by the GAO (*General Accounting Office*) (1995a), because the claim was not adequately supported by survey data.

MEP is a nation-wide network of locally managed manufacturing extension centres dedicated to helping smaller manufacturers improve their competitiveness by adopting modern technologies. The programme was initially designed to transfer advanced technologies developed at the government's *Advanced Manufacturing Research Facility* in Maryland and at other government research institutes. However, once established, the centres quickly realised that most small US firms did not need advanced technologies and that most firms would be better served by off-the-shelf technologies (Shapira, Roessner & Barke, 1995). One survey showed that 73 per cent of the manufacturers who used the service believed that MEP assistance had positively affected their overall business performance (GAO, 1995*b*). However, the survey also asked companies that could have used a MEP why they had made limited or no use of the services. About 82 per cent reported that they had not used the services because they were unaware of these programmes. A further 10 per cent said that although they knew about MEP, they had not used the services because they believed the assistance would not be necessary.

Local and regional governments in the United States also offer a wide array of enterprise development programmes with a variety of objectives and target groups. These range from developing depressed inner city areas to diversifying rural economies. Beneficiaries include large corporations receiving government subsidies to train their workforce or to relocate to a disadvantaged region. Other beneficiaries are smaller firms participating in government programmes aimed at improving exports or encouraging networking among firms. Other programmes provide start-up assistance to individuals creating their own business. Sub-national programmes, much like their national counterparts, have not been rigorously evaluated and little is known of their impact (see Box 12.1 for an example). There is increasing concern that efforts by sub-national governments to attract existing firms from other regions may amount to a costly poaching exercise with little or no economy-wide impact. For example, the State of Alabama, caught in a bidding war with other states, offered tax breaks and other subsidies amounting to US$300 million in order to win a Mercedes car plant, resulting in a cost of US$200 000 per job created (*New York Times*, 1996). Also, New York City awarded more than US$30 million each to two large financial corporations threatening to relocate to other cities. In an attempt to counter this trend, legislation is being introduced in some states to curtail the bidding war and "claw-back" public funds when companies fail to deliver on their job creation promises or move out of the State.

Concluding remarks

This brief review of entrepreneurship in the United States has identified a range of institutional arrangements that work together to harness entrepreneurial zeal. These arrangements provide for low-cost entry to and exit from the entrepreneurial activity, multi-layered supply of risk capital to finance innovative ventures of varying size and nature at different stages in the life cycle, an abundant availability of managerial and technical advice, a flexible work force with varying skill levels, and relatively low levels of taxation of the rewards to entrepreneurial success. To be sure, there are also factors which tend to discourage entrepreneurship, such as high compliance costs of taxation and prohibitive costs of patent litigation; and the net impact of government programmes aimed at helping firms is ambiguous.

A remarkable feature of entrepreneurship in the United States is that constituents of the institutional set-ups are themselves also entrepreneurial. Venture

---

Box 12.1.   **United States policies supporting science parks**

During the 1980s, many sub-national governments, facing decreasing revenues and increasing unemployment, looked to technological development to revive their local economies and create jobs. One of the ways they attempted to promote this high-tech strategy was through the creation of science parks. Science parks differ in size and structure across the United States but share several characteristics. Science parks are a type of business park where the primary activity of the majority of the establishments is industry-driven R&D. As such, basic research and mass production are usually not undertaken. Science parks are also expected to generate new high-tech firms through spin-off or other forms of new investments. Most science parks also feature links with a research facility (a university or institute, for example). State and local authorities support science parks through the provision of infrastructure and land, tax breaks and tax holidays, promotion – primarily through marketing campaigns and lobbying – and other fiscal and physical incentives.

The impact of policies to support science parks is difficult to ascertain because few parks have been evaluated. Failure rates appear to be high with about a half of all parks closing down. In addition, a number of science parks have been criticised because the parks' growth has occurred largely through attracting new firms from outside the region rather than through new-firm formation or spin-offs. However, when successful, science parks can generate economic development and high job creation which spill over the borders of the park. The secrets of success are not known but it is argued that location and government assistance are critical. Successful parks have been located close to metropolitan areas which offer high-quality infrastructure such as good transportation linkages and a reputable university, suggesting that science parks are not viable in remote and sparsely populated regions. Government assistance is also required during the start-up phase and often for several years afterwards. For example, the Research Triangle Park, one of the largest science parks in the United States, took more than a decade to become viable at a significant cost to the state. Therefore, the promise offered by policies to establish or promote science parks must be viewed cautiously in view of their costs.

Source: Amirahmadi & Saff, 1993.

---

capitalists are highly entrepreneurial, and the NASDAQ is a result of an entrepreneurial endeavour. Universities are striving to expand their research capability and their capacity to commercialise the results, while community colleges offer custom-designed courses to meet the specific training needs of companies. And examples of municipalities taking initiatives to streamline regulations affecting emerging companies are not rare. The entrepreneurial nature of the whole system has allowed it to evolve in ways which further facilitate the creation and growth of innovative ventures, for example through a greater use of networking such as a syndication of venture capital to reach promising projects in remote States and even abroad. Given these trends and the way all the elements of the institutional framework fit together, the rest of the United States may well benefit from a "virtuous circle" effect as already illustrated by the much-publicised success of Silicon Valley as a high-tech, entrepreneurial cluster. Yet other countries striving to promote entrepreneurship should be aware that any attempt to replicate only a part of the US system is likely to be inefficient and ineffective. The key lesson from the US experience is that a recipe for success in stimulating entrepreneurial activity comprises a systemic approach to reforming the institutional set-ups in a wide range of areas.

OECD

Notes

1. Measuring the effects of new and small firms on job creation is difficult. A number of statistical biases tend to overstate the contribution of small firms in generating jobs. And in any case, the interpretation of differences in net job growth by firm or establishment size is questionable (see OECD, 1994a).

2. The average gazelle is neither young nor small; more than half are over 15 years of age, compared with 12 years for US companies as a whole, and most gazelles have over 100 employees. According to one study (Birch et al., 1997), fast-growing firms account for only 3 per cent of all firms but are responsible for nearly 80 per cent of gross job growth. A similar picture holds true in the United Kingdom and Australia, where it is estimated that about 5 to 20 per cent of firms are responsible for as much as 70 to 80 per cent of gross job creation (Hall, 1995).

3. The Reynolds study surveyed households to estimate the number of nascent entrepreneurs, defined as individuals who were identified as taking steps to found a new business but who had not yet succeeded in making the transition to new business ownership.

4. Legislation exists in all OECD countries to regulate business start-ups. The laws detail the necessary information and documents required by a firm before it can register, the various authorities with whom it must register, and can also define the internal structure of an enterprise, how it is taxed and, in some cases, special qualifications needed to enter certain activities.

5. These include commercial loans from banks and financing companies (both with and without collateral), trade credit and leasing, home equity loans and credit card loans.

6. For example Stiglitz and Weiss, 1981.

7. The private equity market comprises professionally managed private equity, angel capital, the informal market and the Rule 144A market. The informal and Rule 144A markets operate more like the public equities market where investors do not generally have controlling interests in the issuing firms. See Fenn et al. (1995) for a comprehensive study of the private equity market.

8. Venture capital firms average about US$90 million in size, compared with US$25-30 million in the early 1980s. Venture capital firms which specialise in early-stage investments tend to be smaller than those that are mainly involved in later-stage investments which carry lower risks.

9. This comparison is approximate due to definitional differences, particularly the inclusion of buy-outs in the European Venture Capital statistics. See EVCA (1997) and Fenn et al. (1995).

10. Venture capitalists typically receive an initiation fee of 1 per cent of investment, a 2 per cent annual management fee and 15 to 20 per cent of realised capital gains upon liquidation of a given project.

11. A survey carried out within the purview of Stanford University's project on emerging companies shows that 45 per cent of the companies are headed by a CEO who did not found the company.

12. The often-cited rule of thumb is that they do not invest in companies which are further than two hours drive or one hour plane ride.

13. A trade sale is the sale of a venture capital-backed company to another company. Private placement is the purchase of a venture capitalist's interest by another investor also acting as a venture capitalist.

14. IPOs of venture-backed companies amounted to US$11.8 billion in 1996, more than ten times the size in Europe. See Venture One (1997) and European Venture Capital Association (1997).

15. Tighter supervision followed the shocking revelation in June 1966 by the deputy administrator of the SBA that 232 of the nation's 700 SBICs were problem companies because of dubious practices and self-dealing and that the SBA was likely to lose US$18 million as the result. By 1977 the number of SBICs declined to 276 (Fenn *et al.*, 1995).

16. These figures are estimates for 1992 based on many assumptions, including those about the business share of total regulatory costs, the industry sector shares of the business costs and employee wages. These assumptions were needed in the absence of hard information and the resulting estimates are subject to considerable uncertainty.

17. Even so, employers may underinvest in on-the-job training because of a high job turnover, which is in turn partly due to inefficiency in the recruitment process (Bishop, 1996).

References

AMIRAHMADI, H. and SAFF, G. (1993),
"Science Parks: A Critical Assessment", *Journal of Planning Literature*, 8, 2, November.

BIRCH, D., HAGGERRY, A. and PARSONS, W. (1996),
Entrepreneurial Hot Spots: The Best Places in America to Start and Grow a Company, Cognetics Inc., Massachusetts.

BIRCH, D., HAGGERRY, A. and PARSONS, W. (1997),
Corporate Almanac 1994, Cognetics Inc., Massachusetts.

CENTER FOR THE STUDY OF ENTREPRENEURSHIP (1993),
"Wisconsin's Entrepreneurial Climate Study", Marquette University, mimeograph.

COOPER, A.C., DUNKELBERG, W.C, WOO, C.Y. and DENNIS, W.J. JR. (1990),
New Business in America: The Firms and their Owners, NFIB Foundation, Washington, D.C.

COOPERS & LYBRAND (eds.) (1996),
Money Tree Report, 1996 Results, New York.

DENNIS, W.J. Jr. (1995),
A Small Business Primer, NFIB Foundation, Washington, D.C.

DENNIS, W.J. Jr.(1996a),
Small Business Problems and Priorities, NFIB Education Foundation, Washington, D.C.

DENNIS, W.J. Jr.(1996b),
"Small Business Access to Capital: Impediments and Options", Testimony before the Committee on Small Business, House of Representatives, 28 February, Serial No. 104-62, US Government Printing Office, Washington, D.C.

EUROPEAN OBSERVATORY (1995),
Annual Report, EIM Small Business Research and Consultancy, the Netherlands.

EUROPEAN VENTURE CAPITAL ASSOCIATION (EVCA) (1997),
A Survey of Venture Capital and Private Equity in Europe, 1997 Yearbook, Zaventen, Belgium.

FENN, G.W., LIANG, N. and PROWSE, S. (1995),
The Economics of the Private Equity Market, Board of Governors of the Federal Revenue System, Washington, D.C.

GENERAL ACCOUNTING OFFICE (GAO) (1995a),
Efforts to Evaluate the Advanced Technology Program, Report GAO/RCED-95-68, Washington, D.C.

GENERAL ACCOUNTING OFFICE (GAO) (1995b),
Manufacturing Extension Programs: Manufacturers Views of Services, Report GAO/GGD-95-216BR, Washington, D.C.

GENERAL ACCOUNTING OFFICE (GAO) (1996),
Regulatory Burden: Measurement Challenges and Concerns Raised by Selected Companies, Report GAO/GGD-97-2, Washington, D.C.

HALL, C. (1995),
"Entrepreneurial Engine", paper presented at the OECD "High-Level Workshop on SMEs: Employment, Innovation and Growth", held in Washington, D.C., 16-17 June, mimeograph.

JACKSON, J.E. (1986),
The American Entrepreneurial and Small Business Culture, Institute for Enterprise Advancement, Washington, D.C.

JORGENSON, D.W. and LANDAU, R. (eds.) (1993),
Tax Reform and the Cost of Capital: An International Comparison, The Brookings Institution, Washington, D.C.

KRUGMAN, P. (1991),
Geography and Trade, MIT Press, Cambridge, Massachusetts.

MEAGER, N. (1993),
Self-Employment and Labour Market Policy in the European Community, WZB Discussion Paper FS I 93-201, Berlin.

MOORE, S. (1997),
"The Advanced Technology Program and Other Corporate Subsidies", Testimony before the Senate Committee on Governmental Affairs, Subcommittee on Government Management, Restructuring and the District of Columbia, Washington, D.C., 3 June.

MYERSON, A.R. (1996),
"O Governor, Won't You Buy Me a Mercedes-Benz?", New York Times 1 September.

OECD (1991),
Taxing Profits in a Global Economy, OECD Publications, Paris.

OECD (1994a),
The OECD Jobs Study: Facts, Analysis, and Strategies, OECD Publications, Paris.

OECD (1994b),
Taxation and Small Businesses, OECD Publications, Paris.

OECD (1994c),
OECD Economic Surveys – United States, OECD Publications, Paris, November.

OECD (1994d),
Employment Outlook, OECD Publications, Paris.

OECD (1996a),
"SMES: Employment, Innovation and Growth, The Washington Workshop", Paris.

OECD (1996b),
"Venture Capital in OECD Countries", Financial Market Trends, No. 63, OECD Publications, Paris, February.

OECD (1997),
Employment Outlook, OECD Publications, Paris.

REYNOLDS, P. (1995),
"Explaining Regional Variation in Business Births and Deaths: US 1976-88", in Small Business Economics, 7, 5, October.

REYNOLDS, P. (1997),
"Who Starts New Firms? – Preliminary Explorations of Firms-in-Gestation", *Small Business Economics*, Vol. 9.

REYNOLDS, P. and STOREY, D. (1993),
"Regional Characteristics Affecting Small Business Formation", ILE *Notebooks* No. 18, OECD, Paris.

SAXENIAN, A. (1994),
Regional Advantage: Culture and Competition in Silicon Valley and Route 128, Harvard University Press, Cambridge, Massachusetts.

SHAPIRA, P., ROESSNER, D. and BARKE, R. (1995),
"New Public Infrastructures for Small Firm Industrial Modernization in the USA", *Entrepreneurship and Regional Development*, 7, 4, October-December.

SMALL BUSINESS ADMINISTRATION (1996),
The State of Small Business 1995, Washington, D.C.

STIGLITZ, J.E. and WEISS, A. (1981),
"Credit Rationing in Markets with Imperfect Information", *American Economic Review*, 71, 3, June.

VENTURE ONE (1997),
National Venture Capital Association: 1996 Annual Report, San Francisco.

Chapter XIII

Entrepreneurship in Eastern Europe

Since 1989, the countries of central and eastern Europe have undertaken a process of dramatic transformation of their political and economic systems. In a matter of seven years, systems of central planning based on huge industrial complexes have been dismantled, state owned enterprises have been largely privatised, prices and trade have been liberalised, and the legal and institutional frameworks appropriate to a market economy have, in large part, been constructed. The four countries known as the *"Visegrad Group"* (Poland, Hungary, Czech Republic, and Slovak Republic) have made the most rapid progress, and all but the Slovak Republic are now Members of the OECD. However, the process has been slower in the other transition countries of the region. This chapter will focus on three countries considered by the EBRD (*European Bank for Reconstruction and Development*) to be at an intermediate stage of transition: the Russian Federation, Bulgaria and Romania. The intention is to indicate to policy makers in OECD countries the work left to be accomplished.

There is no precedent for a process of structural change and economic and political reform of this scale in recent history. For example, according to the *World Bank*, about one thousand enterprises were privatised world-wide between 1974 and 1989, of which more than half were in Chile alone. In contrast, Poland, Hungary and the Czech Republic sought to privatise several thousand large enterprises, and tens of thousands of small firms, in a much shorter time (Savoye, 1997). Moreover, privatisation was but one element of the transition. It is well recognised that the process of entrepreneurship is a critical facet of a market economy since it affects innovation, job creation, and economic growth. In the countries of eastern Europe, "free" markets have only recently been introduced to varying degrees. In addition to fulfilling the economic functions referred to above, entrepreneurship may contribute to the creation and evolution of a nascent market and accompanying institutions as well as to public understanding of what constitutes a market economy. Enterprise creation on the part of individuals represents a significant change from past patterns of behaviour under centrally planned economies in which private initiative was illegal and the state, in theory, saw to each and every need. Self-employment and individual firm ownership are two elements of entrepreneurship which have particular significance in the context of transition economies.

Framework conditions in the context of transition. This study has described the way in which positive framework conditions can remove impediments to entrepreneurship and business creation in OECD countries. In the context of transition from a centrally planned economy, the concept of "framework conditions" is more critical and much broader. It is linked to the creation of initial legislation and regulation *allowing* private economic activity, to the establishment of property rights, market-based institutions, a commercial banking system, competition and commercial law and business ethics. It extends to bankruptcy law and procedures, establishment of liberal trade regimes and market-based pricing for inputs, goods and services. Elements of framework conditions more specific to entrepreneurship include simple and inexpensive procedures for licensing and registration, a non-prohibitive and transparent system of taxation, as well as stable legislation and regulations. Access to capital is another more obvious element of framework conditions of primary importance to entrepreneurship.

There is little disagreement that positive framework conditions are a necessary element for the emergence of dynamic entrepreneurship and firm creation, however, there is controversy over whether they are a *sufficient* condition. Some lines of thought suggest that in transition countries, the long experience under a planned economic system (70 years in the case of Russia) has shaped the norms and values of the citizens to such an extent that there is no longer an *entrepreneurial spirit*. Research conducted more recently refutes this claim, and underlines the fact that entrepreneurial ability exists in many different types of societies, and that framework conditions are a principal determining factor (OECD, 1996a).

Evidence from more advanced transition countries like Hungary and Poland supports the pre-eminent role of framework conditions. In both of these countries, early policy experiments which allowed certain types of private enterprise lead to an outburst of new private economic activity. In Poland, the number of small firms doubled between 1981 and 1988, contributing up to 22 per cent of GDP (OECD, 1996a). In Bulgaria, a similar process occurred in 1989 when the still highly-centralised Zhivkov regime implemented "*Decree* 56" which allowed private firms to hire labour for the first time. The effects were impressive: 14 000 new private firms registered by February 1990 (Bartlett & Rangelova, 1997). This evidence illustrates that improvement of framework conditions can enable the emergence of entrepreneurship in many difficult circumstances. However, a more complete analysis of these trends would have to include an assessment of the real contribution of these new firms to the economy in terms of value added, employment, and whether they actually survived for any length of time.

An expanding private sector

One of the most obvious roles of entrepreneurship in the transition process is the direct creation of private firms offering new products and services demanded by the public. In Bulgaria, evidence points to the emergence of new private firms as one of the primary sources of GDP growth in 1994-95. The process of privatisation, or transfer of state-owned property into private hands, has also played a critical role in the growth of the private sector. In some cases, Bulgaria in particular, the process of restitution has also contributed to both the emergence of the private sector, as well as to the growth in the number of SMEs. The following section presents a brief overview of the emerging private sector in the three transition countries analysed, the results of privatisation programmes as they pertain to SMEs, followed by a synopsis of broad trends in the number of small firms.

In the Russian Federation, the contribution of the private sector to 1996 GDP was officially over 70 per cent, however, this includes enterprises with state-held shares. In Bulgaria, the private sector share of GDP was estimated at 45 per cent in 1996, and its share in employment at 41 per cent. In Romania, the private sector's share in GDP rose from 35 per cent in 1994 to 52 per cent in 1996, and its share in employment is 38.5 per cent of the labour force (OECD, 1998a). Private sector share in output and employment may not be the best proxy for entrepreneurial activity, but it provides a useful indicator, other things being the same. Table 13.1 compares these levels with those of more advanced transition economies, as well as against the number of registered small firms.

Privatisation. The Russian Federation, Bulgaria and Romania have moved gradually towards liberalising foreign trade to strengthen product market competition, and are reducing government subsidies and access to soft credit by enterprises. Enterprise restructuring is less advanced than in other transition countries, and varies between the three. In the Russian Federation, the mass privatisation programme through vouchers in 1993-1994 transferred more than 15 000 medium and large scale enterprises to private hands, representing more than 80 per cent of the industrial labour force. Since the completion of this phase of privatisation, Federal, regional and municipal governments have focused on the sale or transfer of remaining blocks of shares to the private sector. By mid-1996, the programme of small scale privatisation had transferred 100 000 state-owned small firms (with less than 200 employees) primarily through employee buy-outs and public auctions. These are in retail trade, public catering, and consumer services. Early on in the process, most shops and some smaller firms were transferred to local governments which would benefit from the revenues, as a concession to win their support for the programme (Boycko & Shleifer, 1996). A second phase of privatisation using cash-based sales resulted in partial privatisation of 2 770 medium and

Table 13.1. **Private sector share in selected transition countries**

% in 1996

	GDP	Employment	Number of SMEs
Russian Federation	60	81.8	894 000
Bulgaria	45	41.0	600 000[1]
Romania	50	62.0	439 627[2]
Poland	60		1 057 102
Hungary	73		519 502
Czech Republic	75		700 000

1.   Only half of these are active.
2.   1994 data.
Source: EBRD, compilation of OECD data, 1997.

large size firms. The primary goal in this second wave of privatisation at the Federal level has been to procure revenue for state budgets.

In Romania, 3 000 of 7 000 small units put up for sale had been privatised by mid-1996. These employ 13 500 workers. The privatisation process has suffered various delays since its inception. However, it is clear that small firms (with capital below Lei 2.5 billion) make up the largest proportion of the completed transactions. For example, in 1996, 41 large enterprises were privatised as compared to 1 068 small firms (OECD, 1998a). As a general trend in countries in transition, privatisation of small units typically precedes large privatisation for several important reasons: it is hoped that new small firms may partly absorb the labour which will be freed from restructuring of large firms, and that the more widespread ownership of small firms will help to raise popular support for privatisation in general.

For example, the impact of the privatisation process on the development of entrepreneurship has been significant in Bulgaria. The first successful privatisation programme was the small scale restitution, started in 1991, which had handed over some 22 000 small shops in urban areas to private individuals by mid-1995. In many cases, these "SMEs" were left to new entrepreneurs by state service companies that could no longer afford market rents. This process has had an enormous impact on the Bulgarian economy as it has contributed to the growth in importance of the services sector (OECD, 1997 a). Land restitution in agricultural areas has been more controversial and is still in progress. The mass privatisation programme, which has suffered delays since 1993, was completed in 1997, and involved 750 enterprises privatised for vouchers.

Small firm numbers and contribution to the economy. Small firm creation in the countries in transition has been in large part fuelled by the economic necessity of individuals. However, it can also be interpreted as more than simply an economic phenomenon. The growth in number of registered new firms in the earlier stages of transition can be seen partly as a social and political reaction to the past regime, and a recognition of the new. (The necessity to create wealth for oneself and perhaps a family, in a context of hard budget constraints and other market conditions, has an enormous social and economic impact.) However, data on small firms should be treated with caution as estimates for all three countries indicate that from 40 to 50 per cent of newly registered firms may never have actually started their activities.

In the Russian Federation, the emergence of new small firms began after promulgation of the *Law on Co-operation in the* USSR of 1988, which permitted the creation of private activity in co-operatives for the first time. Following this legislation, the number of co-operatives increased threefold by 1990. These co-operatives did not resemble the traditional Soviet co-operatives, and were more likely SMEs benefiting from the only possible legal status at the time. These grew in number from 15 900 in 1988, to 45 800 in 1990. The majority of SMEs emerged between 1991 and 1993 after the dissolution of the Soviet Union and the beginning of the transition to market structures. Many of the co-operatives of the earlier period changed legal status, or simply disappeared, and small firms increased from 268 000 in 1991 to approximately 870 000 in 1994. Since 1994, the growth in number of small firms has slowed substantially (Figure 13.1) and reached 842 000 by 1997.

Some experts link the rapid growth in the number of small firms in the early years to the existence of opportunities to siphon state resources through, for example, complex contractual agreements between co-operatives and large firms. In addition, fiscal incentives in the form of tax breaks and other advantages may have lured individuals to register a small business although their intentions were unrealistic. These possibilities may have been reduced due to market reform and privatisation. In addition, tight fiscal and monetary policies and the reduction of subsidies since 1994 have contributed to the decrease in firm births (OECD, 1997*b*).

In Bulgaria, in contrast to the Russian Federation, entrepreneurship was widespread prior to the nationalisation of the economy in 1948 when the private sector accounted for 58 per cent of GDP. The extent of suppression of private economic activity was quite severe, and by 1970, private business accounted for under 4.9 per cent of GDP. There was some private production in agriculture limited to personal consumption in rural households. After the political transformation in 1989, limited entrepreneurial activity began to emerge in the agricultural sector, and by 1990, 30 per cent of output was produced privately. Starting in 1991, key legislation was enacted in the areas of commercial law, competition, private property rights, accounting and auditing, as well as other reform measures which marked the start of the new private sector. By the close of 1996 there were

Figure 13.1.   **Growth in number of small firms in the Russian Federation**

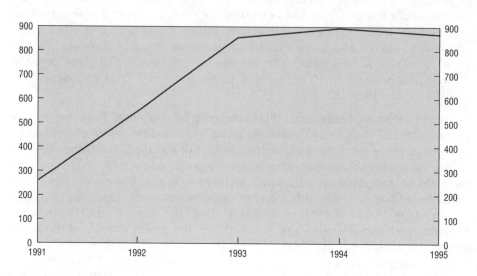

Source: OECD, 1998c.

321 000 registered private firms in Bulgaria, of which the majority were small enterprises with up to five employees (OECD, 1998*b*). More than half of these enterprises was in the start-up phase (in business for less than one year), compared to 12 per cent in Romania, and 27 per cent in Hungary. In Romania, after a smaller surge in the number of registered small business since 1990, there were about 546 500 registered SMEs (with less than 500 employees) by the end of 1996.

Employment in the private sector. Although the job creation potential of existing start-ups is unclear, it seems obvious that there is enormous potential for future employment creation through entrepreneurship in transition economies. In the Russian Federation, an estimated 9 million workers are employed in small and medium size enterprises on a full time basis, 1.3 million on a part time basis, and 3.6 million as contract workers. This represents 14 per cent of the active labour force. According to the *Russian Federation State Committee for Support and Development of Small Enterprise* (SCSME), smaller firms created over one million new jobs in 1995-1996, although the method for this calculation is not clear. In Bulgaria, data on levels of employment in small firms is scarce, however, estimates indicate that 30 per cent of the enterprise work force is employed in firms with up to fifty employees. In Romania, up to 75 per cent of enterprise employment is concentrated in firms of this size (Eurostat, 1996). Small firms are providing a substantial level of employment in central and eastern Europe after just seven years of transition.

Links between entrepreneurship and job creation are perhaps even more difficult to establish in the context of transition economies than in OECD countries. A distinction needs to be made between newly created firms which expand and create employment, and the creation of one job by a self-employed person. A 1996 *Eurostat* survey of enterprises in eleven countries in central and eastern Europe revealed the existence of approximately 2.5 million single-owner businesses throughout the region, implying that one active worker in twenty has tried to become self-employed in recent years. To this must be added the hundreds-of-thousands, or perhaps even millions, of non-registered individual activities. The survey revealed that the majority of newly created businesses has no salaried employees: over 80 per cent of firms in Bulgaria, and 60 per cent in Romania.

Self-employment is not always associated with innovative entrepreneurship, however, in the highly immobile labour markets characteristic of transition countries with their large pools of long-term unemployed, the prospect of self-employment presents a positive alternative (OECD, 1996*b*). Employment expansion in small firms is another possible source of job creation. One survey undertaken by the EBRD noted that in the Russian Federation, the job creation potential of newly created small firms seems to be quite high as compared to that of privatised existing firms. Start-ups experienced 30 per cent growth in employment over 1994 and 20 per cent declared the need for more workers. Privatised firms, in contrast, actually shed labour during that time, and only 9 per cent stated intentions of hiring more workers.

A survey conducted by the *Phare Programme* in Bulgaria revealed interesting employment creation trends in different size categories of small firms. In firms employing up to five people, the tendency has been to shed labour after the start-up phase, while firms with 6-10 employees substantially expanded employment. Motivations for starting a business stem more from the urgent need to have an income and avoid unemployment, rather than hopes of becoming wealthy, improving self-esteem, or innovating (Stoyanovska & Krastenova, 1996). Evidence from another survey (Bartlett & Rangelova, 1997) indicated that a small portion of high growth firms (one tenth of the sample) was responsible for 47 per cent of job creation over the previous year. These "growth" entrepreneurs had university degrees, employed professional managers to run their firms, were more likely to attribute success to good management and labour relations, and reinvested a larger portion of profits in their business.

The impact of entrepreneurship on employment in transition countries cannot be fully appreciated without taking into consideration the substantial unregistered activity in the so called "black market", which may be providing employment for millions of individuals. Quantitative data of unregistered activity is nonexistent for obvious reasons. However, there are estimates. According to the government of the Russian Federation, unregistered activities may make up 25 per cent of GDP, while Vladimir Ispravnikov head of an independent think tank, claims that 50 per cent of GDP is produced in the shadow economy, which employs 30 million workers (Ling, 1997). Removing disincentives to conduct business through legal channels is a fundamental policy issue in the economies in transition, one which merits further study and consideration by governments. The solution is partly found through establishing appropriate framework conditions. Russian officials are presently designing a programme to collect accurate data on the informal economy and to devise ways in which the state can draw illegal entrepreneurship back into the formal system.*

A persistent unfavourable environment

Despite the progress made in the transition to a market economy in central and eastern Europe, the persistence of an unfavourable environment for business and inadequate framework conditions still poses the greatest impediment to the development of a large and vibrant class of entrepreneurs. Many experts now recognise that one of the principal policy errors of the first six years of the transition was the assumption that the creation of market-oriented laws and institutions, the liberalisation of trade and prices, coupled with demand management through credit mechanisms, would bring about economic growth and reform. In 1996, the OECD noted that macroeconomic discipline had not been sufficient to induce the necessary depth of structural change, and stated that it was a general policy flaw not to have supported both private entrepreneurship and the general expansion of the private enterprise sector with greater determination. Evidence indicated that on the supply side of the economy, the revival of economic growth originated in the private enterprise sector and in export-oriented firms, rather than in the industrial giants created by the old regime. In order to favour overall economic revival, it was recognised that attention must be devoted to creating better conditions for entrepreneurship (OECD, 1997c).

This section presents an overview of the principal impediments to entrepreneurship in transition economies. Some are related to the overall macroeconomic environment, while others are specifically linked to insufficient legislative and regulatory frameworks, which are distinguishing features of the transition process. Although diverse in nature, these impediments are presented here as a group due to their combined negative impact on the development of entrepreneurship.

---

* Speech of Russian Deputy Minister of Finance to *OECD Economic Development Review Committee*, September 1997.

The order of presentation reflects the relative importance attached to them by entrepreneurs, based on survey data from Russia and Bulgaria.

Macroeconomic Instability. One of the difficulties identified frequently by entrepreneurs in all three countries, and confirmed by empirical data, is the unstable macroeconomic environment. The macroeconomic factors that have the most direct impact on small firms and entrepreneurs are high inflation, high nominal and real interest rates and exchange rate instability. The Russian Federation has come the furthest in controlling inflation and establishing a stable currency. However, in Bulgaria and Romania, high inflation, interest rates and exchange rate volatility continue to have a negative impact on private sector development. In an environment of scarce credit opportunities for entrepreneurial activities, high and unstable interest rates further decrease the possibilities of debt financing from banks. Moreover, medium-term financial planning for a business is difficult in an environment of double digit monthly inflation.

In terms of economic growth, GDP continued to contract in the Russian Federation by 5 per cent in 1996, while in Romania, positive growth has occurred since 1993, reaching a peak of 7.1 per cent in 1995. Growth has since declined to 4.1 in 1996. In Bulgaria, following a period of modest GDP growth in 1994-1995, a contraction of 10 per cent occurred in 1996 linked to a major financial sector crisis.

In the Russian Federation, after monthly inflation of 245 per cent in 1992 immediately following price liberalisation, stabilisation of prices in 1995 was a substantial accomplishment. The monthly CPI decreased from double-digit range to 3 per cent, and by 1997, the monthly inflation rate had reached 2 per cent (OECD, 1997b). It is interesting to note that in the Russian Federation from 1992-94 the number of registered small firms increased from 560 000 to 897 000 despite extremely tight credit constraints and high interest rates resulting from the economic reform policies of the *Gaidar Team* (OECD, 1997a). Inflation has plagued the Bulgarian economy since the onset of the restructuring process: from a monthly rate of under 3 per cent in 1995-96, it quickly accelerated to over 20 per cent in June 1996 and continued in the double-digit range for the rest of the year. Table 13.2 presents annual consumer price inflation rates for selected transition countries from 1990 to 1996. In Romania, inflation has been successfully reduced from 300 per cent annually at the end of 1993, to a rate of 25 per cent in October 1995. However, after a peak of 30.7 per cent in March 1997, monthly inflation slowed to 0.7 per cent in July, only to surge once again to 6.5 per cent in October. This took the annual rate to 169 per cent (OECD, 1998a).

At the early stages of transition in the Russian Federation, high interest rates contributed to the difficult environment for entrepreneurs, however, recently the annual real interest rate has declined steadily from a peak of 160 per cent in 1996, to below 20 per cent in 1997. In Bulgaria the basic (Central) rate of interest

Table 13.2. **Consumer price inflation in selected transition countries**

December-on-December percentage increase

	1990	1991	1992	1993	1994	1995	1996
Bulgaria		473.7	79.5	63.9	121.9	32.9	311
Czech Republic			12.5	20.8	10.0	9.1	9
Hungary	33.4	32.2	25.0	21.1	21.2	28.3	20
Poland		60.3	44.4	37.7	29.5	21.6	19
Romania		222.8	199.2	295.0	62.0	28.0	45
Slovakia		58.3	9.1	25.1	11.7	7.2	5
Slovenia	100.2	241.1	94.5	22.8	19.5	9.0	10

Source: NSI; OECD, 1997*a.*

decreased from 98 per cent in March 1995, to 39 per cent in August as a policy of the *Central Bank* authorities, only to rise again to over 150 per cent in the first half of 1996. This fluctuation reflected the efforts of the *National Bank* to counteract unexpected dips in demand for Leva, contributing to the severe financial crisis of 1996 and collapse of the banking system (OECD, 1997*a*). In Romania, 1997 witnessed extremely volatile interest and exchange rates: average lending rates of commercial banks have fallen from over 100 per cent in April to 47 per cent in August. The Leu depreciated from its *official* rate of 4 000 to the US$ at the beginning of 1997 to a low of 9 000 in mid-February. This nominal depreciation has hidden a large real appreciation which has implications for the competitiveness of Romanian SMEs dependent on exports. The consequences of an unstable currency run deeper than this, and in fact, are linked to confidence in the overall economic stabilisation programmes.

Taxation. Under the socialist planned economies, the tax system had the primary task of redistributing surplus between companies. The income tax regime was prohibitive and confiscatory, especially where some degree of private economic activity was permitted. The complete reorganisation of the tax system has therefore been necessary in the transition to a market economy (OECD, 1996*a*). Bulgaria, Romania and the Russian Federation have established new taxation laws and tax administrations. However, there has been a general trend of decreasing government revenues throughout the transition process due to an emerging culture of tax evasion, inability to enforce tax collection, and inefficiencies in tax administrations. Recent OECD data from the Russian Federation states that revenue as a share of GDP fell by almost 4 percentage points between 1994 and 1996, and arrears on taxes and social security contributions increased dramatically during 1995-1996 to 10 per cent of GDP (OECD, 1997*b*).

Although there is no empirical evidence proving that this difficult environment is directly dissuading entrepreneurship, strong anecdotal evidence suggests that the revenue crisis may be contributing to distorted incentives of tax authorities who choose to penalise those businesses that do register tax returns through blatant harassment, imposition of discretionary charges, and extremely high penalties for non-payment. Penalty rates on arrears were as high as 0.7 per cent per day through mid-1996. It is hence, not surprising, that of over 2.5 million enterprises registered with the state tax authorities at the end 1996, 788 000 were not paying taxes, nor submitting any records. An imbalanced government revenue structure may also be contributing to this problem. In the Russian Federation a mere one tenth of total revenue is drawn on personal income tax, 40 per cent from indirect taxes, and 17 per cent from profit taxes. Personal income tax share in total revenues for Poland and the Czech Republic are 22.7 and 11.2 per cent respectively.

Entrepreneurs in most transition countries commonly identify the heavy tax burden on enterprises as one of the most important impediments to their success. In Bulgaria, 77 per cent of enterprises recently surveyed identified taxation as the second most important obstacle, and similar results emerged from surveys in the Russian Federation (Stoyanovska & Krastenova, 1996). As shown in Table 13.3, statutory rates are close to those in more advanced transition countries like Poland and Hungary. However, effective tax rates are extremely difficult to calculate due to the existence of numerous exemptions and discretionary application of additional charges by lower levels of government. In the Russian Federation, regional and sectoral exemptions are so common and numerous that no single comprehensive list exists, and it is estimated that these may be equal to up to 8 per cent of GDP. Tax exemptions also exist for small firms in Romania and Bulgaria.

Entrepreneurs in Russia must submit complicated quarterly tax reports. It appears that the tax burden on small firms stems from several sources other than the tax burden: frequently changing and highly complex tax systems, corruption of

Table 13.3. **Key tax rates in selected transition countries**

	Income tax %	Corporate tax %
Bulgaria		30 to 50
Russian Federation	12 to 35	35 to 43
Romania		38
Poland	21, 33, 35	40
Hungary	Up to 44	36
Czech Republic	20-44	42

Source: OECD, 1996a.

local and regional authorities who take advantage of their discretion and apply exceptional charges and often target small firms who have submitted a tax return. Moreover, accounting practices for tax purposes sometimes follow irrational or antiquated procedures for calculation of exemptions which penalise the entrepreneurs. While the overall benefits of tax holidays in transition economies are difficult to assess, their application in highly disorganised tax systems like that of the Russian Federation may increase complexity. Perhaps a more appropriate strategy would be to concentrate on reform of the overall tax system, a process which will have positive spillover effects on the entire economy, not just on small firms. Establishment of stable and more equitable tax regimes in all transition countries may also reduce the disincentives for "informal" entrepreneurs to enter the system and create additional revenue for the state.

Barriers to entry. Registration procedures for newly created firms are notoriously bureaucratic and lengthy in the countries of central and eastern Europe. It appears that Poland, Hungary and the Czech Republic, have all made efforts to reduce the burden of registration procedures while in Bulgaria, Romania, and the Russian Federation, much progress has yet to be made. Bureaucratic delays and interference have been classified as one of the top five problems by Bulgarian entrepreneurs, and similar results emerge from the Russian Federation. Since 1990, registration procedures in the Russian Federation have been clearly defined and were backed by a *presidential decree in* 1994. In practice, the process lasts over three months and involves reporting to more than seven different government offices. The fee for registration of a business can vary from US$750 to US$2 500 plus additional charges which vary depending on the region. For example, in the Tomsk Oblast, Western Siberia, the estimated registration and other costs to start a typical kiosk add up to US$10 000, including the license to sell tobacco and spirits. Licensing procedures in the Russian Federation involve reporting to several state authorities, payment of between US$750 to US$5 000, depending on the type of activity, and can take up to thirty days. Only recently the period of validity of licences was increased from four months to one year.

Insufficient legislation and implementation. Although laws for the establishment of a private sector, starting with privatisation, bankruptcy laws and anti-monopoly legislation, exist in all three countries, the weakness of implementation and enforcement is a critical impediment to the emergence of new private sector actors, as well as a strong disincentive to potential investors. In the Russian Federation, the situation is even more complex due to the federal system in which regional authorities in some cases have the ability to impose additional regulations, taxation, and even monopoly protection of local industries and providers on a discretionary basis. Enforcement of bankruptcies is extremely difficult since the court system is overloaded. In Bulgaria, the law on private ownership and the use of farm land has been amended over ten times in six years and bankruptcies are equally difficult to enforce. In Romania the lack of a clear definition of property rights in urban areas is hampering the reform of housing and also efficient use of vacated sites by new private investors. Due to a highly legalistic tradition in Romania, hundreds of laws and regulations have been drafted since the start of the transition. However, their implementation is not complete. Anecdotal evidence is abundant on the difficulties of finding the actual owners of property in order to invest and purchase sites in these countries.

Finance Issues. Entrepreneurs in transition economies often identify the lack of capital, both start-up credit and equity, as one of the principal difficulties they face. In the uncertain macro-economic environment described above, high nominal and real interest rates and short-term loan maturities (usually three months) have been the norm. These difficult conditions are having a negative impact on the availability of both start-up capital, as well as capital for expansion of existing enterprises. Other types of domestic finance for entrepreneurs more common in OECD countries, such as venture capital, primary and secondary equity markets, institutional investors and others, are either very underdeveloped, or are simply not an important source of financing for entrepreneurial projects at this time. The legislative and institutional frameworks regulating securities exchange and stock markets exist in all three countries, however, these markets do not presently have a significant role in financing new enterprises.

An analysis of finance for small firms in transition economies must include recognition of the extremely fragile state of the financial sector in those countries at an intermediate stage of transition like Russia, Bulgaria, and Romania. The banking systems face severe liquidity constraints due to several complex factors: a high percentage of non-performing loans in their portfolios, frequent "runs" on foreign exchange reserves due to macro-economic uncertainty, insufficient reserve requirements and lack of prudential regulation, and many others. Many of the largest banks are still state-owned, although new private banks play an important role (EBRD, 1996). Moreover, a proliferation of new small private banks emerged in both Bulgaria and the Russian Federation due partly to the lack of regulation and low start-up capital requirements. The number of private banks increased in Bulgaria from 6 in 1991 to 34 in 1995, and in the Russian Federation, the number of operating commercial banks reached well above 2 000 by the mid-1990s (OECD, 1997a and 1997b). Many of these new banks extended credit to non-performing enterprises and embarked on heavy lending at the beginning of the transition in a context of inadequate regulation on capital requirements and limited supervision by the state. Some of these banks may also have been created as "pocket banks" to serve specific enterprises, and hence, disbursed credit based on criteria unrelated to market forces.

On the demand side, newly created private firms have constituted a substantial portion of bad debtors. In Bulgaria, for example, close to 50 per cent of new commercial credit has been disbursed to start-ups, of which a large share has defaulted. The excessive expansion of aggregate commercial credit to the insolvent borrowers in the non-financial sector in Bulgaria from 1994-1995 attested to the distorted incentives in the banking sector, and was also one of the contributing factors to the financial crisis of 1996 which resulted in the collapse of numerous banks. The *Bulgarian National Bank* has embarked on reform of the banking system. Efforts to reform the banking sector have intensified in the Russian Federation as well since a serious interbank loan crisis in 1995 caused the *Central Bank* to reduce its assistance to failing banks and to increase scrutiny and regulation of banking licenses. Over 700 banking licenses were revoked between mid-1995 and mid-1997 (OECD, 1997*b*).

Entrepreneurs use other sources of funding, as in OECD economies. For example, in the Russian Federation, it is common that entrepreneurs cover up to 20 per cent of start-up costs from personal savings, while less than half are able to access loans. In Bulgaria, personal savings were the principal source of start-up capital for 59 per cent of small firms in 1996, while family savings and loans from friends were used by 38 per cent and 26 per cent of entrepreneurs respectively. Only 30 per cent of entrepreneurs reported having received credit from a bank (Stoyanovska and Krastenova, 1996). Although bank credits to the private sector in Romania grew twenty-one times between 1991 and 1992, by 1994 the private sector accounted for only 20 per cent of total bank borrowing (OECD, 1996*c*).

Many new policies for entrepreneurship

The countries in Central and Eastern Europe now recognise the need to promote the development of new small firms, and have assigned public institutions the task of designing policies targeted specifically at entrepreneurs. As part of their reform strategies, Poland, Hungary and the Czech Republic all created national bodies or ministerial departments for promotion of small and medium size enterprises. The Russian Federation has created the *State Committee for Support and Development of Small Enterprise* (SCSME), Romania has assigned responsibility for SME promotion to the *National Privatisation Agency* (NAP), and Bulgaria has just recently created the *Agency for SME Development* under the responsibility of the *Ministry of Industry*.

Policies to promote entrepreneurship have fallen into several broad categories. First, there has been direct financial assistance such as grants and subsidies, loans at subsidised rates provided from the state budget, and credit guarantee schemes. Second, governments have increasingly begun to encourage the development of business infrastructure, both hard and soft, through provision of premises at preferential rents for the creation of business incubators and technology parks, and provision of business advisory services. Another type of public promotion of entrepreneurship is the creation of regional and local development agencies or other so-called "intermediaries" which often combine advice and financial assistance to entrepreneurs in the context of a larger development strategy based on local conditions. Many of these approaches have been largely modelled after experiences in OECD countries, and have been implemented in transition countries through various donor assistance programmes. In the complex context of transition to a market economy, it is not clear which types of programmes are appropriate and extensive evaluation will be necessary to determine the most efficient use of scarce public funds.

For example, the Romanian government, with the assistance of the EU *Phare Programme*, established a network of SME support agencies dedicated to collecting data on small business in different regions, and in supplying hands-on technical and financial assistance to enterprise start-ups. This network co-exists with others supported by other donors such as UNDP (*United Nations Development Programme*) and USAID (*United States Agency for International Development*). One of the policy challenges for the Romanian government will be to assess the results of these networks, and to co-ordinate them into coherent policies for entrepreneurs. The funding offered by foreign donors is limited and hence, the governments of all of the transition countries will have to evaluate these programmes in order to determine their value and set priorities.

In the Russian Federation, the Federal government has created its own SME support programmes since 1995 which are drafted by the *State Committee for Support and Development of Small Enterprise* (SCSME) in co-operation with the *Ministry of Economy*. This programme sets priority areas for action over a two year period, and allocates state budget resources. The programme is submitted to the *State Duma* and *Chamber of Deputies* for approval. One of the tasks of the SME programmes is to monitor and evaluate the hundreds of on-going initiatives taking place throughout the 89 regional entities within the Russian Federation, to provide support for infrastructure projects and limited finance for regionally-based lending schemes.

Regional and Local Approaches. Evidence from OECD countries demonstrates that local and regional economic, social and institutional characteristics can contribute to, or dissuade, the emergence of entrepreneurial activity. As a result, policies to support entrepreneurship need to take into account diverse regional and local conditions, and can be more effective when they do. These issues have been presented in Chapter 6 of this *Review*. The countries of central and eastern Europe have also begun to recognise the need to analyse issues at sub-national level in order to understand the impact of extreme structural change on their economies. As a result, policies for entrepreneurship now have an important regional and local dimension. These localised policies have been the result of a combination of factors. First, many donor-supported programmes for entrepreneurship were designed based on decentralised delivery models from OECD countries. Second, some of these initiatives have been bottom-up, based on the actions of local and regional authorities, associations of municipalities, local business consortia, and others. Through more decentralised design and implementation, policies to promote entrepreneurship may unleash significant energy and potential for innovation from local and regional actors and may have a more broad impact on the economic development of the regions. Public/private partnerships are a critical ingredient in many of these programmes, and funding is combined from many different sources to complement limited public funds.

In the Russian Federation, the SCSME has explicitly stated since 1995 the goal of decentralising delivery and funding of support to SMEs, and the *Federal programme* stipulated that 20 per cent of the overall budget in this area must be passed to the regions. The *Federal Foundation for Enterprise Support*, initially created in 1993 as the body to channel funding to SME policies, began its focus on the regions in 1995-96 when 16 pilot programmes were funded in localities from Murmansk to St. Petersburg. Although some regions actually created a *"Foundation for Enterprise Support"* as early as 1990, the number of regional foundations expanded from 14 in 1993 to over 60 in 1996. These bodies have varying legal statuses, and combine diverse sources of funding. In addition, there are networks of business support agencies throughout the Russian Federation supported be OECD donors, offering business plan advice, counselling, technical assistance, and sometimes limited start-up capital. The issue of co-ordination of Federal, regional and international efforts to support entrepreneurs will be critical for the next few years.

In Romania the regional network of business support agencies mentioned above has been largely donor sponsored, and it is not clear the extent to which the NAP will assume responsibility in terms of both funding and co-ordination. In some cases, support for entrepreneurs has been combined with more general local development projects with job creation as a main goal. The *Phare Programme* of the European Union supported the creation of 60 local "consortia" or partnerships throughout the country as part of the *Programme for Active Employment Measures* (PAEM). These aim to assist labour market adjustment through job clubs, support for active labour market policies linked to private sectors, organisation of training and other means. Some of the PAEM consortia have broader development goals, and have incorporated SME support services into their menu of options. EU funding for this project has come to an end, and hence the local partnerships will have to seek varied sources of funding. It is not clear the extent to which the Romanian government will actively adopt these experiences in national policy. However, the experience has spread awareness of the possibility of using local partnerships to attack the most basic development problems.

In Bulgaria has emerged a combination of agencies for SME support and *Regional Development Agencies* with a more broadly defined mandate. Once again, these have been primarily the result of foreign donor support. Three regional development agencies, located in Bourgas, Plovdiv, and Smolian, combine information and support for local SMEs with marketing services for the region and search for potential investors. The *Business Support Centres* located in several localities offer more technical industry-specific training and support for small business, combined with general issues such as taxation and financial analysis, etc. A recent innovation, which echoes the experience of Poland, has been the creation of the *Bulgarian Association of Regional Development Agencies and Business Centres* (BARDA), an umbrella organisation for the independent regional and local economic development agencies and business support centres throughout the country. Representatives of both the public and private sectors are members of BARDA whose principal goal is to promote regional economic and enterprise development. This may prove to be a powerful tool for co-ordination of the various support policies for entrepreneurs. However, the challenge of combining government policy goals with those of public/private partnerships in the difficult environment of transition remains. The experience of more advanced transition countries, Poland for example, has illustrated that the creation of local and regional agencies is a useful tool.

References

BARTLETT, W. and RANGELOVA, R., (1997),
   "Nature and Role of Small Firms in Bulgaria", in *The Bulgarian Economy: Lessons from Reform During Early Transition*, Ashgate Publishing, Aldershot.

EBRD (1996),
   Transition Report 1996, London.

EUROSTAT (1996),
   Enterprises in Central and Eastern Europe, Vol. 4D, Luxemburg.

LING, C. (1997),
   "Russian Shadow Economy Half Size of Real Says One Expert", *Reuters* Report 8 October, Moscow.

OECD (1996a),
   "Small Business in Transition Economies", LEED, document OECD/GD(96)20, Paris.

OECD (1996b),
   Lessons from Labour Market Policies in Transition Economies, OECD Publications, Paris.

OECD (1996c),
   Systems for Financing Newly Emerging Enterprises in Transition Economies, OECD Publications, Paris.

OECD (1997a),
   OECD *Economic Surveys – Bulgaria*, OECD Publications, Paris.

OECD (1997b),
   OECD *Economic Surveys – Russian Federation*, OECD Publication, Paris.

OECD (1997c),
   Lessons from The Economic Transition, OECD Publications, Paris.

OECD (1998a),
   OECD *Economic Surveys – Romania*, OECD Publications, Paris.

OECD (1998b),
   "Entrepreneurship and Private Sector Development in Bulgaria", Unclassified General Distribution Document CCNM/DT(98)45, Paris.

OECD (1998c),
   "Entrepreneurship and Small Business in the Russian Federation", General Distribution Document CCET/DT(90)11, Paris.

SAVOYE, B. (1997),
   "L'essor des micro-entreprises dans les pays d'Europe centrale et orientale", in *Le Courrier des Pays de l'Est*, No. 413, October.

STOYANOVSKA, A. and KRASTENOVA, E. (1996),
   "Development of SMEs in Bulgaria", paper delivered at SME Development Policy in Transition Economies, University of Bristol, October.

OECD PUBLICATIONS, 2, rue André-Pascal, 75775 PARIS CEDEX 16
PRINTED IN FRANCE
(04 98 04 1 P) ISBN 92-64-16139-2 – No. 50305 1998

Photo credit: **Thierry Parant**